Open With Love
A NOVEL OF DISCOVERY

By Roberta Raye

Copyright © 2011 Roberta Raye
All rights reserved.

ISBN:1-4537-3366-3
ISBN-13:978-1-4537-3366-0

Prologue

Her letters came without warning, but always just when I needed them most. Notice I said "needed," not "wanted." I didn't want them, at least not at first. See, I thought I was okay—not very good, maybe, but at least okay. I was surviving. But I felt as flat and lifeless as the statistic I was, a casualty of the 70 percent divorce rate in Los Angeles County. Just another single mom getting by. My kids made it to school; I made it to work; dinner made it to the table. Barely, but every night. If you'd seen me in line at the grocery store, you wouldn't have looked twice. No one would have. And no one did. Until Bea.

She was everything I was not: passionate, vivacious, alive. She was also old—really old. She never told me her exact age, and of course, I didn't ask. I never told her how I envied her or how she unnerved me. It seemed somehow inappropriate to be so energetic at her age, especially when I dragged myself through each day like a zombie. But she must have seen something in me—a longing, some flame that had not quite gone out—because she sent me the letters.

The postmarks came from all over the world, and the pages inside were just as exotic. Some were scented; some were embellished with drawings or collages—one letter even contained a rock—but the instructions and encouragement she wrote were the real magic. They enticed me onto a path I never imagined I would walk, a journey I might not have had the courage to make without her guidance. It was a trip to the core of myself—the last place on earth I wanted to visit. So, of course, I did what any normal woman would have. I resisted. I whined. I bitched.

But there was no arguing with the patient letters that just kept coming, kept beckoning me deeper into the forest of myself. Little by little, I found myself opening doors long sealed; cleaning out closets, both literal and metaphorical; and beginning to breathe fresh air into the angry stalemate of my life. And when the housecleaning was done, there was room for joy. My life became something to celebrate, not just endure. And even now, years later, it keeps getting better and bigger and more wonderful.

These days, I keep her letters tied with a purple ribbon in a special box under my bed. It is the box where I keep the first locks of my children's hair, where I keep my parents' wedding photo and the one photo of my own wedding that I didn't cut up in a rage when he left, where I keep the best of the baby pictures and the pressed flowers from my prom—the scraps of my life. The box I would run back for if there was a fire. Every so often, when I feel lost on a dark night or a miserable rainy day, I open the box, untie the ribbon, and search for the words that will help me. Though I think I know each letter by heart, there is always something I've missed or forgotten. There is always comfort.

I never saw her again. I doubt I will, though I imagine her traveling still, drinking life from a cup that is always more than half full. My cup was nearly empty the day I followed her into that café, and I hate to think how dry it would be now if I had not met her.

But I am no one special. It could have been you. That's why I've chosen to share the letters here. I know she would want me to; when I read them over, it seems they were written for all of us.

So here they are, along with the messy journey they led me on. I am curious where they will lead you. I hope you will open them with care, with excitement, with courage. Open with love.

CHAPTER ONE

Are You Willing?

Dear Grace,

Come with me into the dark forest. Inside the black and forbidden cave, guarded by sharp thorns and terrible demons, lives the source of your power, your nourishment, your freedom. She is waiting for your visit.

She has been longing for you and will not be satisfied until you come home to her, bringing your small offerings. Though I say "Come with me," you and I both know that I can only point the way. This journey will be yours alone. You must be the one to undertake it and persevere. You must face the demons and the gnats (far worse, the gnats) and the clinging vines that grow fast and cover the trail. This is your journey, your mystery, and finally—your power.

Are you willing? First and foremost, I ask you this. Are you willing to know yourself as you are? Are you willing to be completely free? Maybe you are not. Perhaps you worry about the cost. Perhaps you should. Do not force it. Only you know.

But notice this: I do not ask if you feel ready or if you think yourself capable. These things come from the journey itself. I only ask if you are willing to enter the forest.

"But wait," you may say, "there is no time, not today. There is much to do in my very important life." Of course. There is always too much to do—the children, the laundry, the bills. You might think, I have to watch that show tonight...or you might say, if you are more direct, "What are you talking about, you crazy old lady?" And if pushed, you may even offer the truth: "I don't want to. I am afraid." And then, then I would say to you—yes. You are afraid, and this is good. I do not ask if you are not afraid or if you have nothing else to do. I ask only, and again and again....Are you willing?

Come, I say to you. Come do the thing you think you cannot do. You will find yourself moving in monumental tiny steps. Each one may seem more than you can manage, until you look back and see it clearly, dwarfed as it is by the next one looming. Each will move you closer to the full expression of yourself, closer, in fact, to who you always were. What more terrifying journey than inward? Bring your courage. Bring your heart, which is larger than the heavens. You have all you need.

I ask again: Are you willing?

—B

* * *

What? What the heck? I turned the letter over. Twice. I looked at the envelope. Addressed to me, all right. From "B." *B. who?* Some tiny bell of recognition chimed in the cluttered back alleys of my mind, but it was dim and distant, and I couldn't be bothered to sort it out. It was just too early in the morning. Probably some kind of mistake. I didn't have time to worry about it. That's what I got for stopping at the mailbox when I was already late. Megan and Justin were in the car. I had to get them to school; get myself to work on time. I shoved the letter into my scuffed leather purse with the rest of the junk I hauled around.

It stayed in my purse for days. On the drive to work, I remembered the old lady from the beach. But I had too much on my plate to think about her right then. That night was the spring open house at school, and seeing Rick holding hands with his stewardess in our children's classrooms, watching that woman touch my children and talk to their teachers as if she had any business being there at all—made me want to puke. It was all I could do to get the kids home and into bed before I cried myself sick over a rerun of *Friends* and calmed down by stuffing chocolate chips in my mouth straight from the bag. I wasn't going to worry about it that night. I was going to be miserable. I let the letter sift to the bottom of my bag, past the wadded tissues, the broken crayons, the crumpled ATM receipts, and the half-eaten power bar that didn't give me energy but did give me the runs until it came to rest next to the turquoise business card with the address in New Mexico and the single initial: B.

Finally, a few nights later, after I'd gotten the kids to bed and while the ten o'clock news droned in the background, I dug both the letter and the card out of my purse and considered them.

I'd met her at the beach, Venice Beach, on the boardwalk, and it must have been two months earlier—so, February. Yes, because it was just after Valentine's Day and I was a wreck. The first anniversary of the end of my marriage. It was Sunday afternoon, and the Santa Anas, those hot winds from the east that made the valley a hell and the beach warm for a change, were blowing. My sister had taken the kids to a movie, and I found myself wandering around the boardwalk.

Trying to remember that people came here from all over the world to have *fun*, I dodged the skateboarders and the stroller pushers. Fun seemed a distant memory as I avoided the eyes of the palm readers, ignored the people selling their art, and steered clear of the street performers who were doing their best to gather a crowd for the next show. They all wanted something from me—money or attention or both. It didn't matter; I didn't have either to give. That's when I noticed her.

Walking toward me, she created a ripple as she went. Where I did my best to be invisible, she claimed attention. She engaged every person she saw. She looked right at them and smiled. They smiled back, and then they turned to watch her pass, as if unwilling to let her go. She left a wake of people immobilized and staring. But she came straight on. She didn't seem attached to their attention at all. She went on to the next moment, the next person. The closer she got, the more astonishing this woman became. Though I could clearly see the blaze of white hair, it wasn't until she got close enough for me to see her face that I realized how old she really was. She must have been seventy, maybe even eighty—heck, maybe more than that. Though she had the high cheekbones and wide forehead of a queen, her face was soft and crinkled, eyes deep and hollowed, and the folds of her neck could have been satellite pictures of the Grand Canyon. Her face looked lived in and well loved. Had she been standing still, she might have seemed like any old lady, except that it was unheard of to see an old lady in Los Angeles who still had her own face.

But she didn't stand still. She was moving. Moving so surely and fluidly that something deep inside me stirred, wanting to join her in her dance. Her body, set off by the brilliantly blue African tunic she wore, seemed to delight in itself. It was as if each time her foot hit the ground, she gathered some kind of energy and pulled it into her, fueling the next step. I know that sounds weird. It was weird. I had never seen anything like her. And then she smiled at *me*.

Suddenly, I knew why those people had stopped in their tracks. Her eyes, as bright blue as her outfit, looked right into mine. She seemed to see every part of me, and inexplicably, I felt she loved me. Her smile came from somewhere deep inside her, powerful and yet with a twinkle of mischief. I would have followed her anywhere. And so I did. After she passed, I found myself staring after her exactly as had the rest of the people she'd passed. But I could no longer content myself with aimless wandering. One after the other, clumsily, like a marionette's, my feet stepped in the direction she had gone. By the time I realized what I was doing and told myself to knock it off and stop acting like a stalker, I was following her into a doorway.

After the bright sunshine and heat of the boardwalk, the tiny café was a cave. I'd never been inside it before, and I couldn't see much except the squares of light that marked the open windows facing the ocean. I was trying to get my bearings and walk out of there without looking like too much of an idiot when she whirled round and grabbed my hand.

"You will have tea with me, yes?" Her voice was soft but certain.

My eyes were adjusting to the light. There were small tables covered with red and white plastic cloths, each with a little vase of dusty fake carnations. Most were occupied: tourists babbling about their adventures. They seemed happy to be so far from Iowa or Nebraska or wherever they had come from for their spring break. I felt dizzy. It might have been the sun or the heat. Or maybe the way she was looking at me—eagerly, as if I was an unexpected gift she couldn't wait to open. I probably imagined that. More likely, I was dehydrated. Some iced tea would be great. At least some water.

I nodded, and she led the way to an empty table next to the open window. She settled herself easily into the chair and placed a small beaded handbag on the table. It was lovely, the sort of thing you'd carry to a black-tie dinner. Odd, like everything about her so far. But perfect.

"They have chai here. It's not as good as the real thing, but it will do. You'll share a pot with me?"

I found myself nodding again, though I had no idea what I was agreeing to. I didn't care much, as long as it was nice and cold. I settled in to the chair, relieved to drop my ugly old purse to the floor. I carried it everywhere, and it weighed a ton. In addition to my personal cargo, I was carrying at least two battered Barbies and the components for a Lego robot. I hadn't thought to leave the kids' toys in the car. I hadn't been thinking very clearly in months.

The tattooed kid in the grimy white apron brought water and seemed to know what chai was when she asked for it. I was relieved about that. I guess I was a little afraid she was some kind of kook, that I might have to spend the afternoon trying to find out where she'd escaped from. With a twinkling smile for both me and the waiter, she also ordered us a chocolate chip muffin, cut in half. I watched him fall under her spell, nearly tripping over himself to make her happy. Was no one immune?

I'd vowed to cut out sweets, but I hadn't been very good at cutting out anything since Rick left, a fact that was becoming more and more apparent across my butt and thighs. I should have refused the muffin, but I didn't want to insult her. Well, that's half of it. I love chocolate. I didn't need convincing. I took a big drink of my water while we waited. She was watching me intently. It made me uncomfortable. I didn't even know her name.

"I'm Bea," she said, as if she'd read my mind. "B, like the letter, or Be like the verb, or short for Beatrice, however you like. Only not Sister Beatrice, unless you feel like tormenting me. Though it's no longer of any consequence. Just B." She paused and turned to me, one eyebrow raised.

"Grace," I mumbled, reaching out my hand to shake hers across the table, feeling like a child who'd forgotten her manners. "Grace, like—" and just then I managed to knock over my water glass. Face burning, I tried to mop up the mess with my napkin. The waiter was right there with a towel and a fresh glass for me. He was very careful to make sure no water got on Bea. He didn't seem too worried about water on me, though. I'd been upstaged by an eighty-year-old woman. I tried to convince myself it was just concern for the elderly on his part. He finally left the table, glancing back at least once. I looked at her and shrugged helplessly. "Grace, like that."

Always like that, I thought. Ever since I was a kid. It had been the family joke, the playground joke. I was definitely misnamed. I never felt like I fit properly into my body; I didn't quite know where I was in space. I was always knocking things over, bumping into people, always coloring outside the lines, no matter how hard I tried. Always messing things up. Like my life. I felt myself slipping into the familiar cesspool and looked up, hoping for a lifeline. I found her eyes, waiting to lock on mine, not in pity or sympathy or distaste or mockery—not any of the usual things I saw in people's eyes these days—but in a kind of quiet amusement. I felt she found me delightful, and it was disorienting enough to stop my thoughts entirely. I just sat there, looking into her eyes, not thinking a thing. Except finally to wonder how I could stare into anyone's eyes like that without being rude. I looked away.

"Hello, Grace-like-that," she said into the space where our eyes had met. "Exactly like that. Grace. You are, you know. You are Grace in the world. Maybe you just don't realize it."

I felt my eyes burn. I blinked them back into control, keeping the moisture just around the edges. It would hardly do to go blubbering in front of this stranger, this old lady I didn't even know, just because the way she said my name sounded so kind. Thank goodness the chai and chocolate muffin came just then.

Chai wasn't at all the cold drink I thought I needed. It was hot tea, and it came in a pot. Spicy Indian black tea, prepared with milk. I liked it. It was sweet and rich. But this chai, as good as it tasted to me (and an eternity better than Starbucks' later premixed version), was still, apparently, not quite the real thing.

She told me then about the chai she'd tasted one sweltering afternoon in India, on the banks of the river Ganges; the pepper and other spices ground between two rocks by a tiny gnarled woman, the tea and milk cooked together in an iron pot over a small wood fire and then served to her in a miniature plastic cup, the sort of cup we might use for medical specimens or for candy samples at Costco. Her brilliant blue eyes sparkled as she drew me into the story. Looking past her wild mane of shockingly white hair, past her pale, crinkled skin and into those eyes, I could almost smell the wood smoke, practically see the flowers and discarded minicups bobbing on the steel-gray water of the Ganges, which she called the Great Mother. She never took her eyes off me as she told the story.

I nibbled at my half of the muffin and sipped the chai, carefully, having burnt my tongue on the first taste. I felt the chocolate and caffeine work their magic on my mood, and for a few moments, I forgot to be miserable about my stupid life. She told me another story, about Carnival in Brazil, and then said she was planning to go to Africa sometime next year. But that was really too much.

"Africa! Come on, Bea, you can't go to Africa, not by yourself."

She stared at me, her eyebrow delicately raised. I realized I had stepped over my bounds, way over. But seriously, Africa?

How could she, at her age? "Well, it's not like you're…" I couldn't make myself say it. "Bea, look at you, I mean you seem to be in great shape and everything, but you're, well, you know, you're…"

"Old?" She didn't seem offended, more amused than anything. "It's all right, Grace; you can say it. It's not lost on me. I am, inescapably, old."

She had the damnedest twinkle in her eye, as if being old was actually great news, some marvelous secret she was keeping, just for herself. And maybe it was for her. Who was I to say, anyhow? What was I doing, trying to tell this woman what she could and couldn't do? She looked like she could climb Machu Picchu. Probably had. I was the one who could barely climb a flight of stairs anymore. What did this woman have that I didn't have? And why did I suddenly feel hopeless and clumsy and angry?

I looked at my watch. It was well after five. The movie must be long over, and Susan would be wondering where I was. I couldn't afford to antagonize her, not if I ever hoped to get another afternoon to myself. But the price would be Sunday dinner, family style. My sister Susan was the only family I had left, really, and when she and her husband invited me and the kids, it was mandatory—and horrible. While Phil grilled the burgers, Susan grilled me. In the months since my divorce, Susan had never once missed a chance to corner me and interrogate me as to whether or not I was dating. When I told her I wasn't, which of course she knew full well, she'd berate me for not "getting back into the game" and point out that I wasn't getting any younger (or any thinner), as if finding a new man was the only thing that mattered about me at all. Yuck. That was my real life, and it was time to get back to it. I looked at Bea.

"I'm sorry, I didn't mean...of course you should go if you want to. You could send me a postcard. That's probably as close as I'll ever get to Africa." I tried to smile, but I felt my eyes water up again. It was so terribly true.

"If you say so, dear. But I think Africa is not so far away as you imagine. Most things aren't."

I didn't know what to make of that, and I really did have to go. "What do I owe you for the chai?" I asked her, fumbling for the couple of bucks that were usually somewhere near the bottom of my purse. I always paid my own way.

She waved my offer away and leaned in closer. "Is it a postcard you want, Grace? Or is it Africa herself you need?" She grabbed hold of my arm. "What's missing, Grace? What do you long for?"

I laughed it off and tried politely to remove my arm. It unnerved me, all of it: her look, her touch, the way she had called Africa "her."

"Well, I don't know about Africa, but I always wanted to see Paris," I said and smiled at my little diversion. She did not. She waited. Finally, I went on, "You want to know what I want? What's missing?" She nodded silently. That lump was back in my throat. I was blinking back tears yet again. I wanted to flee, but she still held my arm. Her eyes bored into mine, though not unkindly.

I couldn't think how to tell her the truth. I wanted whatever it was she had. That magic. I wanted to be the kind of person that waiters actually wanted to wait on, the kind of woman who could smile at everyone, and they would smile back. I wanted to be fearless. I wanted to be alive. As alive as this very old woman. I'd have traded places with her in an instant and felt I'd gotten the better end of the stick. I didn't know how to say it, and I was afraid I'd burst into big helpless sobs in another moment. She smiled kindly and kept waiting. I took a breath. Maybe I could say it after all.

"To be…like you. To be really…" I paused, trying to find the right words. "Really alive. Not like I am, I mean…not like…" I shrugged helplessly. It was all I could get out, all I could do to say that much without losing it. Somehow, she seemed to understand. Or maybe she took pity on me at last. Possibly she didn't want to have a grown woman dissolve into a puddle before her eyes.

The sun was setting. I could see the pink edges of clouds out the window. I had to get out of there. My kids were waiting for me. At last, she took her hand from my arm.

"And you really want this?"

I nodded silently. I didn't know what else to do. It was true, though I hadn't known it until just then. Probably the truest thing I'd said in a long time. Maybe ever. She reached into her tiny evening bag and pulled out a small turquoise business card. "Send me your address," she said simply. "Paris is closer than you think, but further than you can imagine. I might be able to point you in the right direction."

Still looking in her eyes, I took the card and stood up, knocking the wooden chair down behind me. Yeah, that's me, Grace, all right. While I set it on its four feet and tried to push it into place without making any more noise, she slowly and precisely folded her napkin and stared out the window at the changing sky. She seemed to have forgotten I was there. There was nothing more to say, and frankly, I couldn't wait to escape. All the air seemed to have been sucked out of the dark room and into the wide open sky beyond the window. The tourists had departed, and it was quiet except for distant clanking from the kitchen. I had to go. I walked quickly to the doorway of the café, then turned back to say good-bye. She was gone. I had the strangest sense that she had simply lifted herself up and flown out of the window into the sunset. That it had never happened at all. But there was a neat pile of dollar bills stacked next to the teapot, and I had the brightly colored card in my hand. I turned and hurried to the car. It was getting dark. Susan was going to kill me.

I never told Susan why I was late. I never told anyone about my afternoon with the mysterious old woman. A few days later, I dropped her a postcard, thanking her for the tea and the wonderful stories and wished her well in Africa. But frankly, I didn't expect anything back. I lived in Los Angeles, after all. I was used to people saying they'd do something or get together sometime or whatever, and it wouldn't happen. I wasn't going to get my hopes up. It was just the way things went in the City of Angels. I'd lived there most of my life, so even though I never quite felt like one, I was pretty much a native. Weeks went past, and then a month, and another, and I have to admit I forgot about it, and her. Between work and the kids, there was plenty else to think about. Until that crazy letter appeared in my mailbox. *"Come with me into the dark forest…"* Please. It was too weird. Who did she think she was, Yoda? I threw it away and went to bed.

Then I got up and fished it out of the trash. Taped it to the fridge. The next day, I took it down. Then I lost it in a pile of bills. Panicked until I found it. I considered asking my friends at work what they thought, then chickened out. I knew I'd ignore every word they said anyway. Strange dreams haunted me, full of lions and drums. I fingered the turquoise card until it was soft and creased. In gold letters, it said simply: "B," and listed a PO box in Albuquerque, New Mexico. No phone number, nothing more. A week passed. Another began.

Finally, one morning, early—and quickly, so I wouldn't change my mind—I replied. Three words on a plain white postcard: "I am willing." I had no idea what I was agreeing to, so I convinced myself I was just humoring a lonely old woman. Funny about that. I was. But the old and lonely woman wasn't her at all. It was me.

CHAPTER TWO

Get Ready

Dear Grace,

You are willing. Good. Where is this willingness? Where does it live? It is in your body. Start there. Return there. Anchor yourself there. You are a being incarnate. You are in the flesh—the very flesh you reject and even despise. This body will take you on your journey, so begin there now. Breathe in till it hurts. Notice. Where must you force breath in, push it out? Become aware of what is happening in you. Is some part screaming out "Don't do this!"? Are you thinking, "This is stupid, and what about the laundry?" Find where those voices dwell in your body. Find the timid ones, which are quivering with the tiniest flame of hope. Breathe right into the core of each of them, and allow them their say. They've always been there and always will be. These are the beasts you'll encounter. You know them already; they *are not strangers. Can you begin to make friends with them? These guardians? This walk we are starting will be filled with messy contradictions and not-so-civil wars. We are going deep into the mountain to find the cave, which is your home. Through the chatter, can you hear the call of the one who waits there to feed you with her soul-warming soup? Is at least one of the voices saying, "Yes"?*

Then come, let us gather the things we will need for the journey.

—B

* * *

Just like that, the letter ended. What things? What journey? What was this all about? Who did she think she was? It made me angry, irritated, a little frightened even. I'd read the whole letter standing in front of the mailbox. In the courtyard, where anyone could have been watching. And I was muttering to myself. Out loud. Because she was nothing but a crazy old woman, that's why. And I was encouraging her. I'd probably go to hell for it. Not that I believed in hell. Not that I believed in anything. There was too much to do each day. Too many hassles. I seriously did not have time to play witchy games with a nutty old lady.

Open With Love

I crumpled the letter and shoved it into my purse with the rest of the mail—the phone bill, the Visa bill, a catalogue from Pottery Barn, a couple of "pre-approved" credit card offers, and (surprise!) another coupon for a 20 percent discount at Bed, Bath and Beyond. I already had a dozen of them. I kept meaning to use them, but I could never quite commit to spending money on things like sheets and towels. We just made do with what we had. Too bad you couldn't combine them: 20 percent off of 20 percent off made…You see? I already had many very important things on my mind, without getting weird letters from a crazy woman.

Justin and Megan were playing tag around the planters, using my butt as "home safe." They were running around squealing like any normal third and first grade kids would after a long day at school. But I knew that the bitch from the condo association would be posting another "general notice" about quiet in the common areas any day now. She hated me. I was the only one there with young kids. Dogs weren't allowed; cats were barely tolerated, and they had to stay indoors. I think she saw kids as some variation of big, loud dogs, invented to torture her. I had to get the kids inside and feed them before they had a total meltdown. I didn't have time to breathe—let alone to listen to voices in my head or body or whatever. Crazy old bat. I'd have to figure out what to do about her later. Or not.

CHAPTER THREE
Basic Cartography

Saturday morning. The kids were watching cartoons, squabbling as usual. Justin always took control of the remote, and his little sister just couldn't stand it. I took it away from both of them. I was too tired to deal with it. The one day we could actually sleep in, and they were always up at dawn. What I wouldn't have given just to lie in bed all day. Hah. No chance when you were the mom. Breakfast was cornflakes and a box of powdered-sugar minidonuts. I skipped the cornflakes.

Mostly to get away from the kids, who'd decided to play dog and were lapping the cereal milk out of their bowls on the floor, I went to check the mail. I figured they were acting out some deep, repressed anxiety caused by living under the thumb of the Condo Nazi, and it was probably best if I just left them to it.

The envelope was lumpy, too heavy. This time, I didn't open it right away. I didn't want to be caught muttering at the mailbox. So I took it, along with the usual bills and the morning paper, and went back inside. Then I pulled the last letter out of the bottom of my purse and smoothed it out. I told the kids I was going to sit on the lanai in the sun, and they were not to bother me. They barked their agreement, mostly relieved, I think, that I hadn't yelled at them about the puddles of milk on the kitchen floor. I had to keep things in perspective. Milk puddles were okay; other puddles, not so much.

Carrying both letters and the *Los Angeles Times* as backup, I went out and wrestled the door closed behind me. The cheap metal frame had been no match for the weight of the glass pane and the torque of Southern California earthquakes. Buying a condo had seemed like such a good idea after the divorce. My sister—everyone—had said so. But no landlord, no husband, and very little money meant we just lived with a lot of things broken.

Lanai is a fancy Hawaiian word for "tiny deck where most of your junk accumulates." It was one of the main reasons I'd bought the place, though. It got morning sun, more in the winter. Mostly, I was too busy in the mornings, and it was always such a mess, but sometimes I did go out and sit on the plastic chair. The one that wasn't broken—yet.

I closed my eyes and let the sun hit my face. My brain started in. *You should put on sunscreen. You should get a hat.*

You're going to get wrinkles or skin cancer or both. How much damage are the kids doing in there? What if they stay dogs? Will they need therapy? How much is that going to cost? Is there such a thing as a dog therapist? Maybe that would be cheaper...Don't forget to change the oil. How long until my transmission gives out? God. It never let up. Yak, yak, yak, worry, worry, worry...I reread the letter I'd taken from my purse. Those voices? That mess in my head, I was supposed to make friends with that? I just wanted it to stop. But, of course, it only got louder. *This is stupid. I don't have time for this. Maybe I should sign up for that tae bo class...What is tae bo anyway? Is it hard? I shouldn't have eaten those donuts...*

Suddenly, I laughed out loud. It was exactly what she'd written in her last letter. I was doing it already. So I took that deep breath. It hurt across my shoulders, down the right side of my back. I took another breath and opened the lumpy envelope.

The lump was a small, flat rock wrapped in tissue paper and tucked between the pages. It was sandstone, vaguely heart-shaped, but with a dark line, almost a crack, running diagonally through it. It slipped comfortably into the palm of my hand, and though it was cold at first, it warmed quickly to my touch. I held it while I read the new letter.

Dear Grace,

The willingness you have found, if only in that one quivering butterfly of a yes in your stomach, is the greatest tool of all. The one you must remember to pick up again and again, starting over with the most powerful question: Are you willing to begin, and begin again, now, in this moment? Are you willing to be exactly here? Be willing to be willing, if that is all you can find. It is enough. You will call on this tool as you enter each battle. You will use it in each celebration. Each new wonder is possible only with willingness. Children differ from us only in that they are still willing to trust and play and learn and be amazed. The great masters say, "Be as little children." This gift is your own to give yourself. Use it well and often.

I looked up from the letter and listened for the kids. Apparently, they were still dogs because there was a muffled woofing coming from the direction of the sofa. They'd probably torn the cushions off to use as a dog bed. Oh well, at least they weren't fighting. Thank God for small favors.

The second tool you have also begun to find. It is the body. Your body. It is here that truth is found. You have not always honored this wise and faithful shell you travel in, but know that it will forgive you and stay with you as long as you continue the journey in this realm. Your body is wise beyond measure and will guide you along the way. Your body speaks a sacred language, one you can learn. When you do, you will be overcome with respect and admiration, and even, yes, love.

Your willingness and your wise and faithful body give you the rest of what you'll need: Honesty. Courage. Will you be honest where it counts most? Within yourself? Can you find enough honesty to say, "I'm afraid," to say "I don't know"? Honesty enough to say "I was wrong"? And the most courageous honesty of all, which says, "This, exactly this, only this, all of this, this is who I am in this moment."

Yes, you will need courage for these. Courage is a gift of the heart. Your heart, broken perhaps—battered, certainly—trembling there in your breast. Are you afraid? That is good. Know that courage is not a lack of fear. It takes no courage to do that which you do not fear. You find courage only in the face of fear.

Honesty and courage together make wholeness possible. This inner wholeness is what you will be awakening, remembering. The time may come when you will curse me for taking you home to yourself. When you find you are no longer able to cheat yourself or lie to yourself or let yourself down without feeling it. This journey comes with a cost. There is a price for power. This is potent magic, which will take away all illusion and return you to your rightful place. You will no longer be enslaved, addicted, ignorant. You will be free and full and as alive as you choose to be.

Are you nervous? You should be. Take a moment right now to breathe it in. Who will you be when you hide nothing from yourself, when the games fall away? What will you do—what will you no longer do? Perhaps nothing will change on the outside. It's possible no one else will see it. But you will be different. More spacious. There will be more room inside of you. So much space is freed when there is nothing left to keep hidden, no fear to blind you to what is so.

Yikes. Of course I was nervous, although I thought "enslaved, addicted, ignorant," sounded a bit harsh. Certainly,

I was none of those things. What exactly had I gotten myself into? What gave her the right? I tried to remember the woman I'd seen all those months ago, the magnetic power she possessed that had so impressed me I couldn't take my eyes off her. Watching her on the boardwalk, it seemed she walked in her own personal ray of sunlight, her dazzling white hair making a halo around her. So often lately I felt the opposite, as if the sun specifically and precisely avoided me, like I was surrounded by my own personal dark cloud or the swirl of dirt and flies that always went with Pig-Pen, the cartoon kid from *Peanuts*. But I could feel the sun as I read; the kids were fine, and I was safe on my porch, so I guessed I could be willing. Willing to keep reading what she had to say, at least.

I can almost see you there, excited but nervous, steeling yourself for this battle, this struggle, this ordeal. Yes, perhaps it will be all of those things, those huge and terrible things, on certain overcast days, certain dark nights, but you must be sure to bring along playfulness and curiosity. Without these, the travel will be only hardship, the vine thorny and fruitless. This journey is, after all, imaginary. It is a mythic adventure into a world you made up. The monsters and demons have the forms and faces you assigned to them. What could be more interesting? What could be more fun?

Yes, you will go deep into the shadowy darkness of yourself, but do you think that is all there is in you? Do you think you have no green meadows, no flowers? You think, perhaps, that you are only tragedy and sorrow inside, so dark you must keep parts of yourself buried, hidden, locked away. You will be turning the key, blasting through the armor of yourself until you get to the tender core. Do you think it is a grim and terrible place in there? Yes, it is everything you fear, every dark thing you have felt. In fact, it is everything that you are capable of, which is far more than you suspect. It is all that is dark, but it is also all that is light. As your eyes become accustomed, you will be able to take in more and more. You'll play more, laugh more, dance more, even as you cry more, yearn more, ache more. It is a wondrous and terrible life, and you have all you need to enter it. You are ready.

I had never felt less ready for anything in my life.

The sun was shining; the kids were happily barking away in there. I sat in the middle of my mess, among the broken bits and pieces of my life, holding her letter in one hand and the stone in the other. I felt tired, like always. Tired, sick of myself, of my life, and utterly trapped. Resentful. Helpless, hopeless, and fat.

I didn't understand what she had written, but what I had said to her that day was true. I did want more life than I had. So I was willing to follow her lead if it meant my life could be different. What did I have to lose? I turned my face to the sun and breathed in and out. To heck with wrinkles, it felt really good. I remembered the soft creases of her face. Well loved, it had seemed to me at the time.

Something in me was quivering. The running commentary in my head didn't stop exactly, but it slowed down a little as I just sat there breathing into the quivery feeling. I wasn't sure if it was excitement, fear, or the donuts. I'm not sure it mattered. What mattered was I sat. I breathed. Something in me began to be curious about what this old woman was asking of me.

This moment, we begin. Take a paper and pen. Any paper and pen will do. Later, we will be more specific. I am asking you to begin where you are, at this moment. This will never change. Each time we will begin from this place, this particular moment, which is all you have and which can never be the same. Let go of any expectations about it. It is. It is all that is. And when I am gone, this still remains. This now. And this one. And the next. Here is the only place you will ever be, now is the only instant you will ever have.

Many journeys have never begun because the travelers were waiting for the "right" time or trying to get to the "best" place to start from. Do not cheat yourself in this way. Take paper and pen and write simply that you are willing to begin right now. Use those very words. It is important to put your willingness where you can see it. Add your name— any of your names, all of them. I am willing to begin right now. I am willing to be exactly in this moment, in this place where I am.

So where are you? Breathe deeply and notice. How does it feel to breathe today? To be in this body of yours? This mind? Does something distract you? Write it down and continue to be willing. You are simply locating yourself, noticing where you are, becoming familiar with the terrain. Do you think you are doing it wrong? That it should be different than it is? Write that, and notice that you made it up. You do not know how it is supposed to be. You do not know what is wrong or right. Can you accept not *knowing how to do this? Can you write even that and continue to be willing?*

Writing? By hand? A pen and paper? I was going to have to write something? This crazy old biddy was giving me homework already? Was I going to have to send her my assignments and get them back all marked up in red? No way. Not only did I have lousy penmanship, I sucked at spelling and grammar, and, well, all of it. The only writing I ever did by hand was the occasional thank-you note or a message to one of the kids' teachers ("Please excuse so-and-so," you know the kind.) Maybe a grocery list, although I usually forgot to bring it, even if I did manage to write it. I was deeply skeptical. Deeply. The morning *Times* was looking more appealing by the minute.

But that glimmer of hope was still there. I decided I could just read the rest of the long letter and then not do what she said. She couldn't make me do anything if I didn't want to. It wasn't like she had any power over me. I wasn't in school anymore. I knew I was pouting like a little kid. But it was too late. I was hooked. I read on.

Do you know this is not art, this is not for posterity, this is not a precious piece of parchment? This is any old scrap of paper and yourself showing up. Just begin. See if you can fill a page with your willingness and your resistance, all of your reactions. Do not write what you think you should, only what is there. "But I don't have time." "But this is so stupid." "But this will never work." "But I have to take care of the crying baby." Sometimes the buts are important. Take care of the crying baby if there is one. That is a true commitment you have made. But do not let it stop you. Pick up the baby and cuddle her and continue to write. "I am willing to begin right now with this crying baby on my lap." This is the truth of your life. It is already full. You do not have an empty life with unlimited time. No one does. It is only your willingness that creates the space. With willingness, you notice time where there was none. This is the magic. Today it is hard, but you are willing to begin. Today the crying baby on your lap may be your own smallest self. Write why, exactly, it is hard for you, why you know you can't do this. Whine all you like. And return to the willingness, gently.

Did you get distracted there, just for a moment? I did. It happens. I thought, "Yes, but I just remembered those bulbs. They've been sitting there a month. If I don't get them in the ground this minute they will *be ruined!" Is there something urgent calling you? Something you suddenly must do now? Be honest about it. Bring your honesty and your courage to this moment and write it down. Write it down and sit with it. Most likely you can let it be. Those bulbs have been there for a month. In this moment, we are beginning the journey. Keep writing. The bulbs will wait.*

Your mind has evolved exactly as it has to keep you safe. Change equals danger, do you see? Even doing this simple thing might lead to change. Your clever and wonderful mind loves you so much, it will do whatever it takes to keep you from danger. Anything, even washing the dishes, is safer than change. So of course you suddenly remember the overdue bills, the bulbs, that phone call. Just write it down. Maybe keep an extra scrap page to write a list of all the urgent things you must do the second you are finished. Don't worry; you probably still won't get to them for another week or two.

Today and for the rest of our time, you will be strengthening the muscle of attention, but not by force. There is no forcing attention. It rebels. There is far too much to notice, and your mind must notice everything. How dare you say to your unruly and wonderful mind, "Sit still, and don't notice anything." It will not. It should not. Its mission is to sense dangers and delights and point them both out. Would you want it to stop? Your mind is not the enemy. Sometimes it is offering a valuable warning or a clue in disguise. Do not do violence to your wonderful, observant mind by attempting to force it to ignore all but what you demand. Attention becomes a matter of respect, not force. With practice, and respect, your mind will become willing to stay with you for longer and longer, slowly relaxing its grip. When it rebels, telling you why you absolutely must stop writing and do something else, you simply listen, notice, and gently return to your willingness, your exploration.

Above all, do not berate yourself or your mind for becoming distracted. This is part of the process. Your task is to befriend your mind, to learn its subtle language. By your willingness to begin, and begin again, you are demonstrating to your mind that you are serious about this inner path.

By noticing and allowing whatever shows up, yet not giving in to the distractions, you are inviting your busy mind to become your ally. Very soon, you will find you are becoming friends, you are learning its mysterious, private logic. You will begin to sort the chatter from the valuable gifts. But do not be certain immediately which is which. Sometimes it is worth attending to the noise. What looks like a weed may, with attention and tenderness, offer the most exotic blossom. Your mind has many gifts and treasures hidden in strange disguises. What you are writing will become the field guide to your own mind, the key. I am not sending you in without a map. You are making the map. This is basic cartography, the little arrow on the big diagram: You are here.

So I did it. Right then. Before I'd even finished reading her letter. I thought, *What the heck? I might as well give the old lady a run for her money.* I could always tear it up afterward. So I found some paper, an old yellow pad, and a pen. At the top, I wrote, "I, Grace Jane Nash, am willing to begin. I am willing to be where I am." And I felt as awkward and stupid and distracted as she said I would. But really, so what? It was Saturday morning in the sun. There were a million things I probably should have been doing instead. But the kids were entertaining themselves for once, so I just sat and wrote it down. All the reasons I didn't have time to do this, all the important things that were waiting, and I noticed that many of them had been waiting a very long time. So maybe they could wait a while longer. And as I wrote that I was willing to get to know myself, I also wrote all the reasons why it wouldn't work and how I already knew everything anyway. I was pretty convincing, if I do say so myself. But the important thing was—I did it. I began. After I'd written a short page, I went back to the letter.

So you take in your distractions, your red herrings, your blind alleys, and you write them down. Yes, the bulbs, yes the bills. This is where your mind gets itself to. Follow a few leads, if you like. What is it about the bulbs? Why have they been sitting so long? Ah, yes, I haven't been taking care of my garden at all, have I? Too busy having adventures. And I "should." Really? Says who? Just questions. Perhaps they will demand an answer. So answer. This is exactly where your mind is at this moment. There is no place else to be, you know. What if we simply let the bulbs be and return to the willingness? Can you stay with it for a whole page? Two? Three pages of willingness? Will you do it?

Maybe you say, "But I'm just repeating myself," and the litany begins again. Yes. Stay with it for three pages. Don't cheat. This is a very important step. Maybe after two and a half pages, something begins to happen. Maybe you find you've written,

"I'm willing to do this, but I'm afraid it's too selfish, and I'm afraid I have nothing to say..." or even "I can't." Yes. This is good. This is what we've been mining for. This is solid ground to begin with, when the excuses have used themselves up. This is what the chatter wants to keep you away from, what it doesn't want to see on the page. This is where the work and the play begin. Not at the top of the page. Not unless you are very courageous, and probably not even then. What is important will not come at the top of the page. The tops of the pages, the first pages, the first weeks perhaps (and don't worry about it) are smoke screen. Today, you begin to teach yourself about your commitment. You are willing, and the journey has already begun.

Can you finish three pages of willingness? More? Write fast, write sloppy, repeat yourself, and don't begin to bother about spelling. Don't worry about capturing them all. You can return tomorrow. When you have used up today's words, when you are spent, put them someplace safe. Do not, do not, show them to anyone. Do not even reread them. This is not the time to expose your tender willingness to a critical eye—yours or anyone's. This is private. If you were to share them or judge them now, you *would be telling your words that they must be "good enough" for someone else to see. This is violence, akin to murder. It can kill any trust that is beginning to develop between your inner and outer selves. You are creating a safe place to be, a haven where what is wretched and vulnerable and what is delicate and tentative and new—where all the parts of you can be whole and be healed. This time is tender and raw. Awkward and messy. Let it be that. Respect it. Keep it messy and raw. Beginnings are like that. Birth is.*

Happy birthday.

—B

* * *

Yuck. I had to keep going. Two more pages. Okay, she asked for it. I finished three scrawling, awkward pages. Bea needn't have worried, though, because I would *never* have shown them to anyone. I put the pages into a drawer in the kitchen. No one would find them there. I couldn't even find anything there. I stepped over the barking children and went straight to the shower.

I couldn't believe how vulnerable I felt, just allowing all the garbage that floats around in my mind to escape onto a page where I could see it, and how hard it was to write the simple, "I am willing" that she asked of me. But as the water ran off my skin, it seemed to be taking something away with it, some kind of invisible heaviness that was all over me. When I got in the shower, I felt sort of drained by all that writing, but by the time I stepped out, I felt more energetic than I had in ages. I took the kids to the park and even ran around with them. Barking.

The first couple of letters had come close together. It took a while for another letter to arrive. A couple of weeks. I didn't know whether she was waiting for a reply or what. But I couldn't figure out what I'd say, and she didn't seem to be asking for anything, so I just waited—and wrote. Not every day, like I suspect she wanted me to, but every couple of days.

Some days, the whole thing pissed me off and I avoided it entirely. Occasionally, it was a relief to get that swirling garbage out of my brain and just let it drain onto a piece of paper that I knew no one would ever see. And once in a while, I found it almost fun. I could see a glimmer of why I'd do this regularly, how it might make me calmer, more in control. This surprised me. Maybe I liked it because I kept it private, just for me. Writing had always been for someone else to judge, for grades and penmanship and careful politeness (those horrible thank-you letters to relatives for ugly sweaters and other gifts I didn't really like, stuff like that). This was completely different. And I really liked taking time for myself, for my own thoughts and ideas, instead of always rushing to take care of the things I had to.

But it didn't seem like enough. Writing a few pages hardly seemed like a trip into some deep, dark forest and all that voodoo nonsense. I wondered what came next. I have to admit I hoped something did. That the old lady hadn't abandoned me already. I kept waiting. It was like the endless days before Christmas. Or my birthday, back when those days seemed to come slowly. Now they ambush me. Anymore, it's always Christmas or my birthday. I had another birthday coming up in October. Ugh. But the mysterious letters brought up an eager hoping, the anxious question of an earlier time. What would Santa bring in his pouch? I waited.

At last, another letter arrived. I managed to hold off opening it until the kids were asleep. The house was a mess. The letter sat there, on the coffee table where I had left it with the rest of the mail. I wanted to rip it open, but I was suddenly anxious. I didn't even know why. I made myself a cup of tea, pushed the toys off the couch, took a deep breath, and sat down.

CHAPTER FOUR

The Sun in the Shadow

Dear Grace,

It always begins the same way. With willingness, and sometimes very little more. You have been writing. When you have found yourself on the page for the first time, the fifth, or the five-hundredth, you have made a good beginning. Stretch and breathe and today begin to notice what surrounds you. Become aware of your world and the pleasures of it. Notice things to love. I will do it with you. I notice the sun coming through the window, the lazy fly buzzing through the glimmering dust motes. Where you are, do you see these? Or is there a darkness outside and the sweet smell of rain coming?

Find five things and name what you love about them. Then notice this: each of these things contains the seeds of something else entirely, and you are the one who chooses. The sun is lovely, but damaging, too hot, too bright for the artwork, the carpet, your lovely face. The fly with his mysterious right-angle turns, the dust motes themselves, you can love them or wish them gone forever. The moist darkness, you call it cozy or oppressive. There is nothing that does not contain a shadow. Then notice five things which trouble you. Even in these, these things you "hate," can you see the sun peeking past the shadow?

Huh? I looked around. All I saw was the messy room, that ugly purple stain on the beige carpet. I'd been too tired (or too lazy) to fold the laundry; it lay in a heap on the chair, hopelessly wrinkled. Newspapers I meant to read were scattered among the toys, the whole room made me feel pathetic. I was such a loser in the housekeeping department. I sipped my tea. I had a feeling this might get rough. I couldn't find a single thing to love.

You must begin to see that the world around you is infinite. It is only you who locked it into a single form, imprisoning yourself and everyone around you. You think life just comes at you with its good and bad, never noticing your part in the naming. Can you see how little space this leaves? How little room for the infinite possibility that you are? By your habits and judgments you invent the world, and in your certainty, you find proof.

I say to you that everything and its opposite exist at once, and I challenge you to look for yourself. By doing so, you will be carving more space to play in. Try it; stretch yourself to see the shadow in the sun and the sun in the shadow.

I am merely asking you to notice where you always stand, to make the acquaintance of your mind's habits. And then, to gently look for other footholds. In time, you may find yourself becoming looser, more at ease. You will have more space, which you may or may not choose to step into. That remains up to you. I simply invite you to play this game with me.

Yes, a game of awareness, that's all any of this is. An old woman's indulgence, a young woman's initiation. Will you join me in a game of "I spy with my little eye" for a while? Play whenever you remember. Allow it to become part of the way you notice. Notice yourself noticing. Just for fun, see if you can discern the other side. The shadow or the light. Can you allow them to both exist at once, without choosing? Can you stretch what you perceive?

You will be able to do this only a little at first. You are building a new muscle. You are carving out permission for yourself to be the contradictory creature that you are. And space for everyone to share that freedom. You are stretching so that you can move into the larger space, discovering that it is safe to allow things to be less than clear. Then you can go deeper into the mystery, where hope and fear coexist, openness and contraction, love and pain, hate and tenderness. Baby steps, maybe, but you are inching this door open and oiling its hinges.

Challenge yourself. Look at a spider, if by chance you hate spiders. Can you see that it is beautiful? Can you look at someone who has hurt you and find a wisp of tenderness? Maybe not today. Maybe today you will forget even to try. You may put down this letter and forget completely. Your important life will keep you busy. This thing, like all things worth doing, seems simple enough. Not at all important. Perhaps even too easy; maybe you think you can understand this, so you needn't actually do it.

Boy, did she have my number or what? I always did that. All through school, I'd think I understood something, so I'd skip doing it. Or fake it. Even now, sometimes I pretended to understand something when I thought I should, just so I wouldn't look stupid. I was already thinking, as I read, *Yeah, yeah, okay, I get it…sounds easy enough,* and *Let's get on to the hard stuff; the real thing here.* I wondered if everyone did that, or if the old lady was really onto my tricks. Weird.

Try anyway. Then try again, each time you remember. Start with the easy things, and believe me, no matter how much you may hate spiders, a spider is an easy thing. There will come times in your life when it is not easy. But begin now, so you will be ready. Begin with the willingness. Begin today. It is the only day there is. There is nowhere to go, no place to get to; there is only this place from which to begin. And begin again, and again. It is practice, exercise, play. Children run for the joy of running. They explore for pure pleasure. It is your birthright, this playing.

Are you ready for more? Try this: name three people you love. Name yourself. Can you see that you love them, and yet they are weak in places? Cruel somewhere in their lives? Are they forgetful, sad, wounded, fearful, or somehow less than perfect? Be honest. Can you look clearly at their "faults" and still love them? Yours?

I thought about my kids, my sister. I certainly loved them, especially my kids, and of course I loved them when they weren't perfect. They were just kids; they weren't supposed to be perfect. Not yet, anyway. I wondered when you crossed that line. When you stopped being perfect, just because you were a kid, and had to start measuring up? Was it puberty? Well, puberty made it worse, but when was I ever perfect in my mother's eyes? Was I ever not too fat, too clumsy, too wrong? Had she ever looked clearly at my faults and loved me anyway? Had I?

What about my sister? I mean, Susan was bossy and opinionated and couldn't stop sticking her nose in my business, but that was just the way she was. I wouldn't stop loving her for that. I saw her clearly and still loved her. But thinking about myself, that was a different matter. Funny, when I thought about my sister's faults, I thought about her personality, her actions. Those bugged me. I didn't think about her thighs or the bump in the middle of her nose. Those things didn't even matter to me about her.

But when I thought about myself, I didn't even make it to personality traits. I started with all the things that were wrong with the way I looked. My thick-waisted body that had always been a problem, my dishwater brown hair with cowlicks in the wrong places, my blotchy skin too, and I didn't even want to consider my thighs. I'd spent my whole life trying to "minimize my flaws," covering them up or hiding them away as best I could. Would I ever be able to look clearly at them and have them not matter—like I could see the bump on Susan's nose and know that I loved her, bump and all? Could I have my faults and love myself?

What did my kids see when they looked at me? What did they love? Did they even look at me at all? Was I just a collection of flawed body parts to them, as I seemed to be to myself, or did they see me as whole? In their drawings, I had the proper number of eyes and arms and such. And sometimes a huge smile. I liked those drawings. How would someone who truly loved me describe me? Right. Certainly not the way I'd describe myself. I was reasonably certain no one would love me if they saw me clearly. How could they? So I tried to protect them from seeing the really ugly parts. Yuck. She was right; spiders would be easier. I would definitely have to start with spiders. Sighing, I turned to the next page of the letter.

Name three people you hate or reject. Name yourself. Is there even one part of each person you can love and hold blameless? Some part that is pure and wounded? Some part that is laughing and free and beautiful? Can you love that part even a little bit? Can you see that everything exists in each of us? This is advanced play; it may require paper and pen.

Is it too much for today? Come back to it another day. Everything is simply process. You will find yourself returning to these basic things again and again. The task will be the same, but you will be different. Today, simply begin. Start with the spider. With the dirty dishes. With whatever it was that used to be inside that Tupperware in the back of your fridge. Can you look at it? Even if you only sneak a peek before tossing the whole thing in the trash, sneak that precious peek.

Yes, I am calling you to set aside your squeamishness. For there will be things to examine that will make you want to turn away. It is by stretching slowly that you open yourself wide enough to encompass this ugliness; only if you stay with it will you see the dazzling beauty shining through. The one does not exist without the other.

You have come this far because you already know this. It would not speak to you if you were not capable of it. You would not have this yearning to come home, truly home, if you did not have the courage and strength to get there. Take heart in this, and be kind. Do not rush yourself. Do not be in a hurry to force open this door. An inch at a time is all that is required, and that you oil it with your willingness.

—B

* * *

Okay. Be willing. Breathe. I'd give it a shot. I looked around the messy room again, figuring physical objects would be easier than people. Or even spiders. The stain on the carpet caught my eye again. It was from Justin's grape juice that he'd known better than to bring into the living room. I could have killed him. The carpet wasn't much, but it had been clean. I had so few nice things. Spilling it was bad enough, but then he lied to me about how it got there. And I'd punished him. Big-time. I was furious. I couldn't stand lying. I would not raise a child, a son, who lied to me. That mark wasn't just a stain to me, it was a symbol. It was my son, lying to me, just like his father did, anything to get out of trouble. I pounded my fist into the damned stain, proof that I was a failure as a mother, as a wife, as a breadwinner even, because I couldn't afford a new carpet, couldn't get the stain out, couldn't get or keep a good man, couldn't, couldn't, couldn't.

I stared at the purple stain, its edges blued and blurred from my endless scrubbing and, frankly, more than a few tears. I got down on my knees to look at it more closely. I saw the twisted fibers of each strand of plush, permanently dyed to a soft rose. It wouldn't have been a bad color, somewhere else. I touched it, spread the little yarns apart and studied it. In my mind's eye, I could see Justin's face, his blond hair falling over his glaring blue eyes, his juice-stained lower lip trembling even through the pout. Eight years old, frightened but defiant, looking so much like Rick it broke my heart, telling me he didn't do it. I heard myself yelling, furious, all out of proportion. He was just a kid, after all. He spilled some juice.

How had I become such an angry person? I'd totally lost it. I'd raged at him, this child I loved. Who loved me so much. My fury scared both the kids. Justin stood still as a stone, while Megan tried to hide behind the couch. I sent both of them to bed without supper. Poor Megan hadn't even done anything wrong. After they went to bed, I'd continued my rampage, slamming doors and throwing pillows until I'd finally sat down on the floor, right where I was sitting now, and cried until I fell asleep. It happened months ago, but the whole thing was somehow trapped right there in the stain. The whole scene came back in an instant. I sat there, stroking the carpet and sort of rocking back and forth. Could I possibly do what Bea was asking of me? Could I find some tenderness, something to love, in this stain and all it held for me? It was all of the assignments at once: a thing I hated, a boy I loved, a man I hated, and myself.

I wanted to stop, but she was right. I somehow knew the answer was in me, that I could find it if I looked. But I didn't know how. Something was there, some raw, bitter tenderness was rolling around inside of me, but I didn't know how to get to it. Maybe it was too much. Maybe I'd picked the wrong thing to start with. I'd thought it was just a stain on the carpet, but it was so much more. It would be simpler to keep it locked up, to stay angry or to just try to ignore it. But every time I looked at that stain, all those feelings were already sitting there. How much of my life was like that, I wondered. Maybe she was right, and I was carrying so much around inside me that there was no space to breathe.

I looked at the rest of the mess in the room. The toys and newspapers that seemed magically to reappear each time I thought I'd picked them up, the laundry past the time for folding, now so rumpled it needed ironing. I knew it wouldn't get ironed; it'd just get worn with wrinkles, and we would look like ragamuffins. I was such a lousy homemaker. There was the framed poster of the Eiffel Tower that Rick had bought for me when we were first dating. I loved the photo, in black and white with Parisians rushing by under their umbrellas. But every time I looked at it, I felt sad because we never went to Paris after all. Paris. What had Bea said about helping me get to Paris? The way to Paris was through this stain? I would have laughed out loud, but my throat had locked up tight.

I was still sitting on the floor, my fingers combing through the stain. She was right. I carried judgments about every single thing. How did she know? Had she seen something in me that day? Was I so obvious? So pathetic? Couldn't I ever just relax for even a minute? I stared at the stain until my eyes lost focus. Funny, it looked kind of like a flower. My little son's face was so purple when he was just born, exactly the color of this mark, this flower. Was it silly to try to think of this stain as a flower he'd painted just for me? Could I look at this stain and instead remember how much I loved him? God, what if he were gone tomorrow and nothing remained but this mark? I'd cut it from the carpet and carry it with me everywhere, wouldn't I? Why had I gotten so angry at him? He was so little. Could I forgive him? Forgive myself?

I hated that he was so much like his father. His stupid, asshole father, who'd run off with that…that stewardess or whatever you're supposed to call them now. I could not forgive him. I could never, ever…

"This is too much, Bea. I can't do it. I cannot let myself find compassion for that man. It's too late, and I don't want to, and

I can't. I'd fall apart. You said to be where I am; well, this is where I am. Maybe you were wrong, you know. I don't think I want this. Maybe I'm not so courageous after all."

How did she manage to do this to me? I was talking out loud again. To nobody. Nobody who could answer, at least. I felt like I might explode. I stood up and walked around the place, hating that I couldn't even go out for a drive, because I couldn't leave my sleeping children. I paced like a tiger. I picked up every one of the unread newspapers and threw them in the trash. It was all bad news anyway. I wrestled the sliding door open and went out on the lanai. I could hear the usual drone of police helicopters circling. Another thing I hadn't counted on when I bought the condo in Inglewood. It probably wouldn't have been a good idea to go out even if I hadn't had to stay with the kids. Talk about feeling trapped.

The three-quarter moon stared down at me, and I saw the stone Bea'd sent sitting in the moonlight. I picked it up and held it. Tight, in a fist. My whole body was a tight fist. My whole being was a tight fist. The moon just hung there, taunting me. It grew cold, and I brought the rock, my tight fist, my whole tight self, inside. Opening my numb fingers, I set the stone on the stain and went to bed.

That stone sat there for days, until the next letter came. And somehow, each time I passed it, the pain was less. Not gone exactly, just different. Sitting there, the stone became the center of the flower I had almost seen that night. It's not as if I suddenly forgave Rick or that I never got mad at Justin anymore. But occasionally, I would catch a glimpse of that stone on the angry purple mark and remember how much I loved my little boy instead of the other things.

CHAPTER FIVE

Dance with Fear

It was midweek, and the kids had gone to dinner and an early movie with my sister. I knew they'd come back all sugared up and wild, but it was nice to have a few hours alone. The letter had arrived in my mailbox the day before. A fat letter, with extra stamps. It was postmarked from Greenwich, Connecticut, and on the envelope, she'd painted turtles. Or tortoises, I never knew which was which. Anyway, it was pretty marvelous. Sometimes I thought I was the least creative person I'd ever met. I wanted to do artistic things, like paint turtles on an envelope. Every time the Learning Annex catalogue came or the community college extension schedule, I looked at all of the art classes. I really wanted to take one. But I didn't. I couldn't find a sitter or the money or whatever. Oh well. I settled in and opened the envelope carefully.

Dear Grace,

You are carrying a home on your back. A protective shell. Any journey is a matter of knowing where you are, taking one step, and then learning where you have gotten to. Your task is to discover where you are. The next step shines as clearly as a beacon, as soon as you have found yourself. And not until. I am asking you to examine your shell—not the shell you wish you had, but the one you're actually wearing. You are willing, and so you are able.

This shell, this battered, broken, held-together-with-duct-tape-and-chewing gum identity you created, this is your current home. It has served you well. Do you know that? You are intact. More than that, you long to expand. This is a marvelous safe home to allow you the courage to even consider stepping out of it. Can you honor that? This life, exactly as it is, has somehow been nourishing enough that you have outgrown this shell. You are strong and healthy. No matter your opinion of this life, this shell, it is yours. I am asking you to begin examining it with clear eyes. This is no time to pretend anything is any way other than it is. Only when you know your exact location will your next step become clear. Are you willing to look deeply? Good. Let's begin.

Well, that explained the turtles.

Every time I got a letter, I started out excited and then got irritated. I mean, I didn't have to do this. My life was just fine, thank you. Why dig around and upset myself? And just who did she think she was, sending me this stuff like some kind of guru or something? She was probably just an old crackpot. There were plenty of other ways I could be spending my free evening.

I stopped myself. Like what exactly—these other ways? Television? Surfing the Net? Eating? Folding the clothes? Right. The truth was, my life was boring. Since the divorce, I'd let go of almost everything I used to enjoy. I might as well keep reading.

Take pen and paper. Again, any paper will do, but soon it may be easier to keep a notebook, a journal, a sketchbook. You will spend much time with this book, so it must be easy to use, comfortable to the hand. Not too small, this book is a place for you to expand. Try blank pages. Can you write on a page with no lines? Try. Here, there are no rules, no penmanship, no walls. There will be times when the words scream across the page, diagonally, upside down even. Times when you will write tiny precise letters in neat rows.

This is not a paved road you're taking, but a walk in wild and changeable territory.

Start with a plain book. You are finding yourself, not fitting into something. Fancy books intimidate their owners into writing fancy words or none at all. Save the fancy books for later, if you like. Start now with an empty blank page and your willingness. There is nothing else you need.

If you are thinking, Yes, there is a store in town where I can get just the thing. I'll go there Saturday. I'll wait until then to begin, please do yourself the favor of beginning now, since now is the moment you are in. Saturday may be a lifetime away. Begin now on an old napkin, if that's what you have at hand. Later, staple the napkin, the legal sheet, whatever scrap you start with, into the book. Perhaps it is best to begin like this. The first page will be written, and you won't have to face it. So take your pen and whatever you find and begin again with your willingness.

You are writing yourself home. Writing yourself to exactly where you are. You will always begin with willingness, until it becomes so natural you don't need to affirm it. Except on those times when you do.

Because I promise you there will be times when even the willingness seems too much. So you simply start there. Start here. "I am willing to tell the truth. I am willing to expose myself on this page. It is safe."

Yes. Write next, "It is safe." This is the simple truth. You alone hold the safety you need in this work. You make it safe for yourself by protecting yourself from ridicule, even your own. You make it safe by affirming that it is so. You make it safe because you can choose, at last, to do yourself no harm. It is safe because you control the speed and depth of your own growth. There is no schedule to this journey, no timetable. Your contract is not with me; it is with yourself. You may do what I ask in a short time, or over months or years. Or never at all. I only point out your path, merely clear away some of the brush. You walk it. Do not force the tender bud of yourself to open before it is ready.

You will return many times to this same place, this beginning. Make each beginning simple; make each tender opening safe for yourself. Bring your willingness. The beginnings, the first words are fumbling, messy, awkward. This book is just a tool. It is not precious, though it is holy.

Paper with no lines? Holy, but not precious? Right. Okay. Funny thing, there really was a little store I knew that had journals. In Santa Monica. I could get one on Saturday. How did she know these things? But she had said to begin now. I thought a journal sounded like a good idea, though, because I was getting quite a pile of loose pages in my desk drawer. I found some blank paper in the kid's school stuff and sat down again. Was I ready? I didn't think so. Was I willing? I still wasn't quite sure what I was being asked to be willing to do. But I wrote it down at the top of the paper, "I am willing." And somehow, I found that I was.

Here you are at the blank page. Taking your temperature, finding where you are this moment. Can we start with something big? Will you dive right in? Good. Prepare to get muddy; you're going into the swamp. The deep, dark, rich, stinky swamp you hide away from view, as if that would make it disappear. All that is festering and rotten, locked up inside of you, that's your destination. Today, your route is fear. Your fear. Other paths include anger, resentment, regret, envy, pettiness, sorrow...There are many roads in. But today, start with fear.

"Wait a minute," you may say. "Why would I ever want to do that?" Hah. Want to? Of course you don't want to. Not until you're very familiar with the swamp would you want to, and sometimes not even then. That's why I'm here. It's less frightening at first with a guide. And it's no use pretending you don't have a swampy core. It is home to the richest soil of human growth. Death and decay are always the food for new growth. But compost must be mixed, the soil tilled, weeds and overgrowth cleared away. Sun and air and clean water must be allowed to find their way to the ground.

That's why you're going in. To build a garden in the swamp. As you get more familiar with it, you will come to know when it is time to return and tend to it. You will begin to cherish the time you spend there, tenderly caring for yourself, turning the raw messiness of yourself into rich, fertile soil for your exuberant life, growing the food for your own nourishment. When you feed yourself from the inside, you need not depend so much on outside sources, outside distractions. When nothing inside you is secretly buried away, shameful, hidden, then you are free to dance with whatever life offers.

Disappointment and loss, or joy and freedom, and the most magical of all, everything at once.

Today, begin the dance with fear. Are you safe? Look around you right now. Touch something solid, your chair perhaps, or your own skin. See that you are safe. In this moment, you are a child trying something new; resolve to be a good mother to yourself. Know that you will not abandon yourself in the swamp, that you will not throw yourself on the sword of judgment and criticism, yours or any others', and that you will not turn back simply because the ground is rough. Be gentle and curious. And willing to start over. Be willing to fail, and know that whatever you call failure is just another place to begin.

Whew. Okay, Bea, whatever. The whole thing was freaking me out. I did reach out and touch the couch, and the solidness of it reassured me. So I rubbed my hands together and then massaged my face for a second. Scratched my nails across my scalp. Took a breath. I don't know why, but it helped. I got calmer, more willing to start. But I still wasn't sure exactly what I was going to be starting. So I decided to get a glass of water. And then to close the curtains and put on some comfy sweats. I lit a candle. Finally, I picked up the letter again.

So begin. From where you are. Write it down. What are you afraid of? Every single thing. Spiders. Sharks. Death. Pimples. Getting laid off. Taxes. Cellulite. Old age. Write all the generic ones first. Try to get all of them. Are you afraid of death? Of life? How about fear itself? Of looking stupid? Of blowing it? How? Be very, very specific. No one is looking. What do you hide even from yourself? Keep going long past when you think you're through. Explore a little. This is your swamp. What are you afraid someone will find out about you? What are you afraid you'll never do or be? What are you afraid you'll always do or be? Include the stupid things, the ugly things, and look especially for the random things that don't seem to make any sense. This is your map.

Who was she kidding? I was supposed to write down every single thing I was afraid of? All of it? I couldn't think where to begin, and I didn't think there was enough paper in the house…maybe not even in the whole city. What I was afraid was that this was going to take all night.

Fear sometimes hides in anger, embarrassment, and boredom. Does this irritate you? Good. Keep writing.

Are you ashamed? Write faster. If you think this is boring or stupid or you really don't have time for it; if you think you'll just do this later, that this isn't the right time to begin; if you suspect you'll probably never bother, I beg you, do it now. Write three pages, five, more. Write in big, sloppy letters even if all you write is about how stupid this is and you're not afraid of anything anyhow...just keep writing. Write ten times: "What I'm afraid of is:...." and fill it out. Then write, "What I'm really afraid of is:...." and do it ten more times. And then, just when you think you're off the hook, write "I'm scared that:...." and finish the sentence another ten times. For dessert, write: "If anyone really knew me, I'm afraid they'd:...." and see what happens.

Do not cheat yourself. If you are ever to know how brave you are, you must begin here. Courage is not the absence of fear; it is free choice in the face of fear. You are so very courageous. Fear is the only access to bravery. You must know where you are standing. Fear hides itself, disguises itself, eats into the heart of you and consumes your vitality. When you become more familiar with the typical landscape of your fears, you will have freedom. You will recognize the disguised fear for what it is and be able to make real choices. But while it hides, while you allow it to burrow through your soul, whispering unchecked its doomsday warnings, fear is in charge.

I am calling on you now to begin to know this wise friend. Yes, friend. Fear can be a terrific ally. It calls you back from cliff edges and tells you whom not to trust. Beware the stranger, no matter how close, who encourages you to ignore your fear. Instead, begin to distinguish your favorite flavors of fear, and notice where they take you. You are making friends with fear, so its voice will speak more clearly to you. When you honor fear by allowing yourself to know what's swirling around inside, you'll find the chaos eases, and you can distill what is valuable in this moment.

Do you think I will ask you to deny or throw away your fear? Or worse, surrender to its howling voice and spend your life cowering in your room? Not at all. I am simply asking you to name it, to know it. I invite you to cultivate the rich, dark soil of yourself with your bare hands. Asking you to find compassion for yourself, to allow yourself to exist exactly as you are. Inviting you to bring out all that you have hidden away and embrace it.

Do this today, and do it again later. When you can, how you can. Tell the story of your fear. Keep telling it. Trace it back; stretch it forward. Do it until you are bored with some of the usual refrains, and they begin to drop away. Do it until the individual voices become distinct, rather than one giant tangle. Do it until you can clearly hear the ones that must be answered.

Just—and this is important—don't bother asking "why" questions. "Why" is an invitation for your very clever mind to start spinning out useless explanations. You can become so caught in your own cleverness that you'll never escape. Worse still, you may start offering excuses, reasons, blame, justifications. Smoke and mirrors. None of that matters at all, and I suggest you do not indulge. Stick with statements. "I am afraid that..." "What I'm afraid is..." Do not get bogged down in the seductive, psychological whys. Simply begin. Right now.

So I did. But it was hard not to get into the whys. For example, I was scared to death (ha-ha) of getting cancer. So scared of it I just refused to think about it. But I had a right to be scared of that. Didn't I? I had a very big why. I mean, just look what happened to my mother. And I was afraid of little things too, like being teased, and well, I knew all of the reasons for that too. It was hard not to get defensive about my fears, even just on a piece of paper no one would ever see. But I stuck to the instructions. I started with a list. "I'm afraid of…" "I'm afraid that…" I won't bore you with the details; I mean, I guess we're all afraid of a lot of things. But I did it. I just sat there and did it. I began with being willing to do it, and then just did it.

I felt like I was going to have to write forever. Every time I thought I'd finished, some other fear would tap me on the shoulder, demanding to be included. What a pathetic bundle of neuroses I turned out to be. And don't think it was easy, either. I swung from tears to rage to irritation…I fidgeted, got cold, got a sweater, got hot, moved to a chair. Moved back to the couch. Decided not to do it, decided to throw out the whole letter—you know, all my usual stuff. I got very distracted at one point and wrote a whole page about my daughter's teacher at school. I wrote petty fears, outlandish fears, physical safety fears, parenting fears…and finally, there weren't any more. Anything else I wrote, I was just making up.

And I caught myself making it up. Maybe I was trying to do it "right" and keep going, or maybe I'm just weird, but I actually started putting things down that I'd never really bothered to be afraid of, although other people thought I should be, like terrorist attacks. I caught myself convincing myself that I was afraid of them. Really convincing myself. I had to laugh out loud at one point, it was so absurd. Actually, it made me start to wonder about the rest of the stuff on the page. How much of *that* was stuff I'd made up and convinced myself of? And it occurred to me that just maybe all of it was made up. I mean, none of it had actually happened yet, right? It was all some kind of story about what might happen. It made me feel really weird and a little light-headed. I mean, it was all pretty crazy, if you thought about it. At last, I put my writing down and turned Bea's letter to the final page.

When you have finished, you can see it there, splayed out before you on the paper. Everything you never wanted to know, all those worst possible things. What must you do with it? Can you simply allow it to be? Can you find your next breath and the one after it without abandoning yourself? Can you welcome yourself home covered in this mud? Will you look with tender compassion at the mind that made all this up? Can you admire your cleverness and notice, perhaps, that you are not so different from anyone else? You're not, I promise.

You carry all of this around and somehow still manage to get through your day. Take a look at it. Did you catch them all? Probably not. But it is enough for today. Is anything so horrible it has burned straight through the page? I suspect not. Still, you have gone very deep.

As deep as you can today. Tomorrow, there will be something new, something else to get out. It is one of the blessings of life that it keeps offering new chances for fear as well as openings for love. They are the same, you know. There is tomorrow and tomorrow as long as you keep waking up. Don't feel you must have completed this. I promise you haven't. But you have begun.

Now close your book or put away the pages and look around you with soft eyes, knowing you have done something very brave and worthwhile. You have. Stand up and shake yourself all over. Get a glass of water and drink it. You have flushed some things up to the surface, and you want to allow them to flow all the way out. Water is good. Breathing is very good. A walk around the block is good. Notice how your skin feels on your body. How the air is touching you and your opinions about it.

You have mapped your fears, now the only thing left is to allow them to be. Cease to resist them, and you will cease to hold them so tightly. There is nothing more to be done today. You have traveled far, all the way around the inside of your shell.

—B

* * *

I stood up and shook myself all over. It felt good to move after sitting for so long. The pages were spread across the coffee table. I gathered them up and put them in my drawer with the rest. I didn't know I could write so much. I was definitely going to have to get that journal, if only to keep from making too much of a mess. God knows I didn't need one more mess around the place.

I shook myself again and realized a shower would feel really good. It was true, a lot of stuff was rising to the surface, and I wanted to get it off of me and down the drain. So I took one, even though the kids might be back any minute. Even though I was afraid I wouldn't hear the door buzzer afraid they'd have to wait outside until I was done. Afraid of what my sister would say about that. So what? Just fears. I had a million of them. A billion. Wet and soapy, I had the strangest urge to laugh out loud at myself. So I did. Weird.

CHAPTER SIX
Life Goes On

It was almost a month before another letter came. So I kept doing what she said. I kept trying to notice things and my opinions about them. I kept writing, pages of nothing but getting to know where I stood at any moment, what anxieties raced around in my head, what I was afraid of, what this thing called fear was. I didn't write every day, but a lot of them.

I'd like to be able to tell you that all my fears magically went away. They didn't. Bea would probably have laughed at my even wanting to say that. She never told me to make them go away. She just wanted me to get to know them. Without doing anything about them. But that was the funny thing. When I didn't keep trying to push them away, when I stopped denying them and just let them have their say, they did seem to ease up. Quite a bit. And it became easier to catch myself making them up. It was kind of funny sometimes, how easily I'd slip into that.

Meanwhile, my life continued pretty much the same. The alarm went off at six thirty, but somehow, I never managed to get up until seven, so I always raced through breakfast and dressing, left the dishes in the sink, and pretended to listen as Justin and Megan told me why the other one was so mean to them. We had to be out the door by 7:50. I dropped them off at school by 8:25 and did my makeup in the car as I drove downtown to work. That wasn't as dangerous as it sounds. I never bothered with much makeup, for one thing, maybe just blush and mascara, and for another, remember, this was LA traffic. We weren't exactly speeding along. LA drivers have a reputation for speeding, and it's true. We go as fast as we can, but normally, that's about fifteen miles an hour. So if we can go faster, you'd better believe we do.

Anyway, like I said, my appearance wasn't something I spent much effort on. I'd pull my hair up in a ponytail to keep it out of my face. No one saw me except the other women in the office anyway. Who cared? I was in customer service for the DWP, the Department of Water and Power. I answered phones all day long, took service orders, and got yelled at by people who'd had their electricity cut off. Not fun, not by a long shot, but it was steady, had good benefits, blah-blah-blah. I knew I was lucky to still have it after all the layoffs. Especially now that I was on my own.

Open With Love

Someone at work was always having a birthday, or a baby, or an anniversary, or an operation, so there was usually cake or donuts or fudge floating around the office. For a long time, I could stick to my diet, but the ladies were always teasing me, and finally, I gave up. So I was getting a butt to match the rest of them. Which I sat on till 5:15 then I'd fight my way through traffic to get the kids out of after-school day care by 6:00, 'cause it was a dollar a minute if I was late picking them up.

If I had food in the house, I'd cook dinner, but Justin didn't like tomato sauce and Megan wouldn't eat vegetables except carrots. Neither one of them would touch fish, and I was so worried about mad cow disease and hormones in the chicken (fears, I know, but come on, that stuff is gross) that unless it was from the health-food store, we wouldn't have meat. And we were all sick of tofu, so it was a real struggle to figure out what to feed us. A lot of the time, we'd have Chinese or Thai takeout or burritos. I just tried not to think about the chicken. Then we had homework and baths and maybe a game of Chutes and Ladders, until I wrestled them into bed by 8:30. Then I'd wander around the house picking things up or talking on the phone to my one best friend who'd moved away to Sacramento the year before Rick left. But there wasn't much to say anymore. We'd grown apart. So maybe I'd watch a little TV or surf the Net. Yee-haa.

I'd been looking a lot at Match.com. I mean, I was curious about it. This lady in the checkout line at Albertson's told me her friend had just married a guy she met on Match. So I guess it worked for some people. Sometimes, my kids caught me doing it. They'd tease me. "Mommy's man-shopping," they'd say. Yeah, real cute. But they had a point. It felt sleazy. So I waited until they'd gone to bed. I know, it was like hiding cigarettes from your parents, but I was bored and lonely. Once I even tried to write a profile, just, you know. But I couldn't think of anything interesting or funny, and I didn't have a picture I'd want anyone to see, so I gave it up. I wasn't really date material anyway. When would I have time? It's not like I had a lot of free evenings. So it was man *window shopping*, I guess. With no intention even to try one on. I know, pathetic.

When Rick was in town—which wasn't often these days (I guess the stewardess was getting him free flights. He always seemed to be going somewhere exotic at the last minute. He'd say it was for work, of course, but it had to be her. I mean, how many sporting equipment conventions do they hold in Bali anyway?)—he was supposed to take the kids every other weekend. It was almost better if he didn't, though. He wasn't good with them. They wouldn't eat right or they'd get hurt or he'd just leave them with a babysitter the whole time. So I didn't make too much of a fuss if he didn't do it.

He paid the child support on time. That was something. I was luckier than a lot of divorced moms. It was hard on the kids, though. They didn't understand. They missed their dad—Justin, especially. He was starting to act out. When Rick would call on Thursday to say he couldn't take the kids on Friday, Justin would yell and throw things, or worse, sit and stare at the wall. I think he blamed me for keeping him away from his dad. I didn't know what to tell him. I thought it was almost better for him to think I was keeping him away from his dad. I mean, how would he take knowing that his own father didn't want to see him? This way, at least he wouldn't feel unwanted. I knew what that felt like, and it sucked. Sometimes, I didn't say anything and just let him be angry at me. Yeah, right. Fun. This single-parent thing was so tricky. I tried never to criticize Rick in front of the kids, but it was not easy. I was really mad at him. Everyone said it would get better with time. So far, it was getting worse.

Me, I guess I'd have liked to have a little more free time, but it wasn't worth fighting Rick for. If I brought it up, he just told me to talk to his lawyer. He knew I wouldn't. His lawyer was C. Richard Harcourt III, Esquire. With the penthouse office in Century City. Somehow, C. Richard always managed to cost me money. Rick knew I was afraid of lawyers. Anyway, it wasn't as if I had anything important to do. My sister helped out when she could. She said it was good practice, since she and

Phil claimed to want kids. Seemed like a good idea, but I was pretty sure they reconsidered the whole kid thing every time she babysat. My kids could destroy her Martha Stewart home in a matter of minutes. I knew I probably shouldn't let her take them. I did want to be an auntie someday. And they weren't getting any younger either. I felt guilty. But I was so grateful. I was pretty sure I'd go mad without a break now and then, as much as I loved my kids. To tell you the truth, I'd have liked to have a whole week to myself. Even if all I did was sleep. But that was way too much to ask of Susan and Phil. Especially since I'd probably just mope around. So why bother? But I did think about it.

And that was pretty much my life. Normal, boring, except for those letters from the weird old lady and the "path" she claimed to have set me on. I never mentioned her to anyone. I was sure they'd tell me to throw the letters away and forget about her. I guess it was pretty wacko, really. But there was something to what she wrote, something more I wanted from my life, though I wasn't even quite sure what it was. I thought she might just know how to get it. Somehow, I was willing to do what she asked.

So I thought about fear. I tried to notice that everything had light and dark sides. That love and hate weren't really so far apart. I did go buy myself a journal. I got it at an art store. It was the only place I could find one without lines. It was big, eleven by fourteen inches, and had a nice black cover. It was a sketchbook, really, but like I said, I am not artistic. So I wrote, and I looked, and I listened, and I noticed the steady stream of opinions I held about everything. It was kind of exhausting, all that chatter. I couldn't seem to just let anything be, including myself. Especially myself. From morning to night, it was the *What's Wrong with Grace?* show.

So many of my fears—not the big ones, the cancer or earthquake ones, but the daily, constant fears—centered around "doing it wrong" or "being found out" or "never measuring up; never being good enough" to get the right man, the right job, the right life, the one I was supposed to have, the one that would prove once and for all that I was valuable, that I was good enough, that I deserved to be alive—yes, even that, really. If I could just be good enough or successful enough or have a good enough man, then my life would be worth living. Somehow, I suspected it wasn't and might never be—unless I could just nag myself enough or worry enough. Then maybe I could somehow force myself into becoming a meaningful person.

I noticed that most days, it was only fear that ran me, driving me to get out of bed in the morning, to make sure the kids had decent clothes and full stomachs, getting me to work on time so I wouldn't get in trouble. It was my fear of being found out, of being exposed as less than perfect. Fear, all of it. Me trying to do everything right just to keep the fear at bay.

It made me angry once I let myself notice it. I felt like a robot. I hated the idea that pretty much every single move I made was based on some kind of fear. Where was the fun in that? I really wanted to just quit all of it, right then, just take off and run away from my whole life.

And it made me angrier still that the first thoughts in my mind after I imagined myself running away with the kids to some funky town in Mexico and wearing lots of brightly colored dresses and enormous jewelry and living in an orange adobe hut with flowers everywhere and lots of cats and dogs wandering around and the kids laughing in the sunshine and never having to come back to Los Angeles…were all just fears about what might happen and what people would think; we'd probably get murdered on the way or kidnapped or dysentery, and I'd lose my job and never find another one. For crying out loud, those endless fears wouldn't even let me have two minutes of a silly fantasy. That pissed me off.

But her voice was there in my head, gently reminding me about finding something to love inside what I hated. Finding some piece of beauty there. So I took a deep breath and looked right at it. Well, I guess the fears did serve a certain purpose. They kept me doing what I needed to do; they kept me safe and the kids safe. They kept me bringing home a paycheck and kept us off the street. I guess I could appreciate that. It did seem as if there had to be a better way to live, though.

CHAPTER SEVEN

Measuring Up

Dear Grace,

Are we having fun yet?

The letter was waiting when I got home from work on Friday. It was a rare weekend when Rick actually had both kids, and I was looking at forty-eight hours to myself. I was already making lists of all the things I needed to take care of, the endless chores that never quite got done when I had the kids on the weekend. I was already tired just thinking about it. What I really wanted was to get into bed and pull the covers over my head. But there it was, with the junk mail, peeking out. It was postmarked Kansas City, Missouri. I didn't even take off my coat before I opened it.

Can you find a spark of fun in the discovery of your secret demons? Is there any part of you that can laugh at the drama you create to force your life to have meaning?

Do you notice, as I have, that we battle all our lives trying to prove ourselves worthy? Is there a core of you that is so hungry for meaning, so hungry for proof of your value, that it can never be filled? How many of your fears fight to keep this emptiness at bay? How many of your fears try to force you to measure up?

Here is the good news: you will not measure up. You will never be loved enough, be beautiful enough, thin enough, rich enough, or successful enough to satisfy this hungry demon. Nothing you do will make you safe. Of course, you know this.

We all know this, but still the fears circle. Knowing it, you can do one thing only, and this you must do often—daily, hourly, even every minute when it is very difficult—you must breathe in and out, and thank the fear that unites you with every other human being. Do you think there is anyone not afflicted? Some saint, some movie star, some billionaire who has somehow found a way to calm the fears by being "perfect"? Do you think if only you could be like them, do what they do, you would be safe?

I told you that it was good news, the fact that you will never, ever measure up—never be perfect enough to calm your fears. It is, indeed, the best news of all. Someday, when you can fully embrace that fact, you will find that you are free. When you no longer expect, or even hope, to be able to fix yourself enough to be safe, then finally you will be free to choose. The choice to act or not act will come from a place of power, a place of love. If there was even the slightest hope of making yourself good enough to quiet the fears, you would be doomed to a lifetime of trying. Your choices would never be your own. But once you see that the fears will simply find something else to harp on, no matter what you do or what you fix, then you can relax. Then you can play like a child in the garden of your life. This is simple to see, difficult to remember. Do not think you will learn this only once.

Okay. Fear again. Oh joy. Not. I dropped my jacket on the back of the couch, kicked off my shoes, heated up some leftover pad Thai in the microwave, decided to skip messing up a plate, brought the whole box to the living room with a fork, and settled in. I looked at the envelope. What the heck was she doing in Kansas City? How did she do it? Was she one of those old people who just traveled around in an RV? I tried to imagine it, but it didn't seem right. Maybe she was running drugs. I giggled to myself at the thought. What about the witness protection program? That might be it. Or didn't she sort of say she used to be a nun? Sister Beatrice? Maybe she turned evidence on the Mafia and now had to keep moving. Or…I realized I was making up stories about her life to avoid dealing with the letter. That was probably why she never wrote anything about herself. Maybe she knew how distractible I was.

I was having kind of a hard time with her statement that I would never measure up. I mean, on the one hand, there was part of me that had always suspected this was true. I was almost thirty-five years old, after all; the clock was ticking. Not the baby clock, but the have-a-great-life clock. I knew I'd better hurry if I was going to make a huge success of myself, become a famous actress or a powerful lawyer or have men lined up around the block for a chance to go out with me or…I stopped to picture that one. I liked the idea, but it was absurd. I was no supermodel. I was a dumpy, drab, single mother of two. What had happened to me? I used to be pretty hot. Now I doubted I could buy a date. It didn't matter that I didn't really want one. It would be nice to be asked.

And it wasn't so much that I wanted to be an actress either; I didn't think I'd actually like it. Or a lawyer, that was way too much work. But I hated that it was starting to look like I was never going to have the fabulous, fairy-tale life I'd been hoping for when I married Rick. And of course, I believed if I had that life, I'd never have to worry about anything, that I'd never be afraid of anything. I'd be happy all the time. Somewhere inside me, I was holding tight to the hope that I still had a shot at it, if only…

Yeah. If only I tried harder, worked harder, stopped being a slob, worked out, lost weight, studied yoga…. If only I could cover up my failings so nobody would notice, if only I was different. But I had this sinking feeling that it wouldn't really work that way—that even if I managed to do everything right, even if I could force myself to be perfect, I might still not be happy. I didn't want to know that. I wanted to keep believing. What else did I have?

But she seemed to be hinting at something interesting: this idea that I could do things because I chose to, not because of the fear of what would happen if I didn't. I wasn't sure what that meant, though. Would that make me happier? Was the goal to be happier? I sure hoped so.

I finished the pad Thai and set the box down. I wasn't sure where all of this was leading, but then, with Bea, I never was.

I wiped my fingers and mouth on a paper towel and picked up her letter again. Breathe. Be willing. Okay.

Do you notice your fears grow stronger when you try to talk yourself out of them? When you bully yourself through them or ignore them? Mine do. Oh, I may be able to shut them up during the day, ignore them or distract them or outshout them...but after dark, when I'm alone or not sleeping when I need to, when the phone rings, or doesn't, the fears have their way with me. Their merciless claws rip through my guts, tearing away my carefully constructed fortress of identity, laying me bare for the soft-bellied helpless weakling I am. This is the price of resistance.

After countless long and ugly battles, I now choose instead to allow my fears when they present themselves, to welcome them and ask what they really have to say to me. This being human, it is no small matter. We have survived without tough hides, without claws or terrible sharp teeth—we got by on brains. These brains are wired for fear, and fear is there for a reason. Always. It is your friend, one of your allies on the path.

Once you have come to know your particular fear habits, when you allow yourself to notice and recognize the fear under anger, under apathy, under resistance, then you will be able to be a wise steward of this powerful force. Then you become the general, the commander, and fear simply the messenger, bringing information. When the messenger is attended to respectfully, it ceases throwing tantrums to make itself heard. Knowing its message has been delivered and action will be chosen wisely, it will cease crying wolf at every twig that snaps. Who are you to decide millions of years of evolution are better ignored? Fear is not the enemy.

Hear me. Fear is not the enemy. It has just spent too long trying to get your attention. It no longer trusts you and thinks it needs to run the show. Fear must be escorted to its rightful place and, yes, should even be thanked for trying so hard to protect you. Fear is essential in the physical world. The lions and tigers and bears on two or four legs—fear can smell them out for you, advising flight or fight as needed. This is fear at its finest. Welcome it, reward it. Heed it.

But what about the fears warning you away from the emptiness? The fears that keep you fighting to prove your worthiness, fleeing from your very self? It is here that fear has overstepped its bounds. Fear heralds from an earlier time; it hasn't got the tools for certain modern forms of angst. It is here that we must thank the messenger and simply breathe through the message. Here that we must choose not to act on fear's counsel. Are you looking into an existential pit? Then fight or flight is useless at best. Fear alerts you to the nearness of the edge. Fear wants you to be safe. But safety is not where growth occurs. Safety is not where love shows up. Safety does not hold the key to joy. Do we disregard fear itself? Do we shoot the messenger? Do we give in to its doomsday tactics? No. We thank it for showing us our place on the map. Thank it for pointing out the edge of the pit. And then we choose love.

Continue, Grace, the challenging task of making friends with fear. Of listening wisely, knowing that you are the commander in chief. You must guide the troops, not fear. And yes, I use military terms, me, the old hippie peacenik. Fear is a warrior. Fear counsels action from a place and time in our history when we didn't have so many genteel options, when our survival was not assured.

When fear strikes, know that he intends a bloody military campaign or hasty retreat, and sometimes it is necessary to reassure him that you speak the language. Once he knows you are not asleep at the wheel and is satisfied that you are up to the task, fear will be more respectful of you as well. Listen to his warnings and his advice, but learn to discern the real location of the danger. Is this a tiger or a despair pit? This is cumbersome at first. But thank your messenger and remind him you are running the show.

And like everything else, this is only a game you are playing. You will make mistakes; you will forget; you will have to start again and again. How fortunate that you have your whole life to practice. Can you laugh at yourself? At this power-mad messenger trying to stir up trouble? Can you take him in and offer your appreciation for all his hard work without being trapped in his complaint? Can you stop feeding him stories to stir him up? Where do you think he gets these crazy notions anyway?

Try to recognize that we are all engaged in the same skirmishes. Breathe in and out for me, my battle, for your children's battles, your neighbor's.

You can create more space for all of us by simply breathing through it.

I am breathing with you.

—B

* * *

A power-hungry messenger? Yes, that about summed it up. And I liked the idea of being the commander in chief. That I could be the one who chose what to do with fear's warnings. It made me puff up, a little. I sat up straighter when I thought of myself as the general.

Rick always used to say to me, "That's just your fear talking," which was probably true, you know, but the way he said it was so dismissive, so disrespectful, that I felt my fears were somehow shameful and that I was bad for having them. But what were my fears telling me? That he was not to be trusted. Through all the nightmares and the anxious times when he wasn't where he said he'd be. The way he always made it my fault when I caught him in a lie. Of course it was "just my fear talking," it was my fear sounding a warning, one I should have heeded much earlier. He wasn't to be trusted. My perfect life was in danger.

I let him talk me into ignoring my fears. I had reasons. There was too much at stake: the kids, the house, our friends.

Well, they were his friends really. Somehow, I'd misplaced most of mine. Rick never liked my friends, so I just let them drop. They'd moved away or moved on. His business was getting more and more successful; the commissions were getting bigger; everything seemed golden. But it was an illusion. And as he grew more distant and critical, my fear did begin to throw tantrums. It got bigger and wilder and more irrational. It began to yell and scream and eat away at my stomach lining. Fear spread out and took over. I became afraid of everything, jealous and suspicious of everyone, until even I could see it wasn't rational. I was misbehaving. I was snooping. Rick's advice was Prozac. Well, really, he would have preferred I got Prozac and a boob job. I considered both.

But the fears wouldn't have it. They kept me on edge. I thought I was going crazy until the whole house of cards came down. Until his lies were so clear even he couldn't convince me it was just my neurosis. Until the truth was out.

After he left, after the horrible dividing of assets, after losing my home and everything I thought made up my life, things were harder for sure. And there were times, while the divorce and the custody battle (he didn't really want custody; he just wanted to look good and hurt me) dragged on and on, that I almost wanted my old life back, lies and all. But the nightmares had stopped. I woke up in the mornings and wasn't bathed in cold sweat. I guess I did owe my fears a thank-you.

If I had acted like a good general and heeded their warnings early on, they might not have needed to get so out of control. It would have still been messy and ugly, I guess, but maybe I could've stayed a little saner and kept some self-respect, some dignity. Maybe even kept a few of my friends.

But what did she mean by the "existential pit"? I knew I should have stayed awake in Philosophy 101. Maybe that's what kept me in the marriage for as long as I was. Or got me in there in the first place. Because honestly, my fears were already warning me about Rick long before we got married. I knew what he was like. I knew he was a playboy. And I knew how he bullied me out of my opinions, bullied me out of what I thought or wanted and into most everything he wanted. But he was a good catch; that's what we all thought—with his big brown eyes, his shiny black Jaguar, and his jet-set lifestyle. He was just a salesman, really, but he flew all over to his conventions and to meet with clients. He supplied top-of-the-line equipment to elite private gyms, celebrity trainers, that sort of thing. It seemed pretty glamorous to me. His clients loved him. He was charming, handsome, seemed to have money, and was in great shape. He was a catch.

And it was time to get married. All my friends from high school were either already married or chasing some fabulous career. I didn't have a fabulous career. I had a good job at the DWP. I'd never decided on a career; the job was just to pass the time until I got married. I wanted to have kids, and I knew that. It was a different kind of fear that was speaking in my ear then. It was the fear of getting old alone. The fear of missing my chance, that time was running out. The fear of never finding the right one. The belief that I had to have a perfect husband like my friends, like I was supposed to. That kind of fear—that might be the existential pit. And Bea was right, those fears weren't helpful. Not at all.

Those were the fears that let me ignore the other warnings: the way he'd insult me if he'd been drinking, the way he made me keep my job to support him through the lean times in the business and still always put me down about it, the fact that he called me white trash and told me I was "just a secretary." Oh, he was charming when he wanted something. But he was really nasty when he didn't get it. Or when he drank.

When we met, I could hardly believe that such a handsome, charming guy wanted me. I worked very hard to be what he wanted. I let him tell me what I should wear, how I should act. I wore the perfume he gave me (Chanel No. 5, because his mother wore it) even though I absolutely hated it. I was his pet project. He was grooming me, as if I was some kind of Eliza Doolittle or something. He seemed to get a kick out of it. I'd wished he liked me the way I was. But, truthfully, I didn't much like me the way I was, and I would have done anything to win him. I didn't want to be alone. My mother was the only one who tried to warn me. But she was already sick by then, and I was really angry at her for it. So I was determined to marry him, in spite of what she thought about him. Or maybe because of it.

I guess if I could have straightened out the fear warnings in my head back then, I could have saved myself a lot of trouble. Maybe there was a difference between voices—ones warning me about him and the ones screaming that I'd wind up old and alone and pathetic. With cats. But how could I say what might have been? I might have gone and married him anyway. Or maybe wound up with the cats. Ugh. How did I know this stuff even worked, huh, Bea? Besides, I had two wonderful children, no matter how I got them. That was something, wasn't it?

I was having a hard time sitting still by then. I got off the couch and started straightening the room. I just had to be doing something. Anyway, I really did prefer things to be tidy, but I was such a horrible slob...wait. Just stop. Was that fair? That's what Rick always called me. It wasn't nice. Did I need to abuse myself too? Couldn't I just stop at the first half of that sentence? I really did like for the room to be tidy, period. And then I could simply tidy it up. That was the choice, the one Bea was talking about. The second half was that bully in me that seemed to think if it called me names I'd become a better person. Was that what she meant about measuring up? The voice of the fear of never being good enough? I kept moving, putting away toys, straightening the room, as I thought about all of this. That bully was related to the fear that had told me I'd better marry Rick while I could. That I should be grateful. That if I didn't, someone else would.

I hung my coat in the closet. The room was clean. I preferred it that way. But without fear running the show, I guess it didn't mean anything about me whether it was clean or it wasn't. So maybe that was what this was all about: knowing my fears, actually listening and evaluating them, and not just reacting blindly. I could choose to tidy the room because I chose to and not to prove I was worthwhile. Maybe I could learn to separate the bully fear from the warning fear if I just gave them both a little space. If I simply *noticed*. What did she say? Breathe in and out and thank it for the message. Choose how to respond. If I'll never measure up, I guess I can start to look at what matters to me. I could try it, anyway. What did I have to lose? At least the living room was clean. That was something. A good way to start my free weekend.

CHAPTER EIGHT

Sadness

Dear Grace,

How are you feeling? In all this exploring, have you touched something tender, maybe some sadness? At any time, you may be visited by this ache, this dull or sharp twinge, and you will want to make it stop. "I cannot handle this," you think. "It will engulf me." There is no escape. But just once—today, perhaps—instead of running from this feeling, instead of rushing to fix it, bury it, or hide it, could you first simply touch it lightly with your awareness? Tenderly explore it, as with your tongue you'd test a sore spot in your mouth. How big is it exactly? How sore? Is it unbearable, really? There is a deep and tender sadness to being alive. It is simply there, and sometimes you will be more aware of it. If this is one of those times, I beg you to trust that nothing is wrong, that this is simply one of the many flavors of life itself. What flavor is your sadness? What color? Is it a dull grey, stealing passion, leaving a muffled quality to everything, or today is it a sharp red—bitter, burning?

Does it have a special home in your body at this moment? Can you find it? Look. Is it lodged in your chest? Maybe it is making your legs tremble, or it may have taken up residence behind your face—in that tight, clenched feeling that turns your features into a mask. Are you holding it in your jaw? Wherever you find it, go right there and breathe into it. But wait, has it shifted? Yes, it will move around. Keep gently finding it and breathing into it. Do not try to chase it away, simply be there and sit with it. For this is not a new sadness. It is not a problem to be solved. This is simply a friend who comes and goes. You know this sadness; it is your very own.

If you allowed this sadness to be, welcomed it even, do you think it would never let go of you? Would it suck you down until there was nothing left? Is this why you keep running and eating and talking and flipping channels? Is this why you'd give anything to drive it away for good? Try this for me. Just sit with it today. For as long as you can. You can do what you always do to escape it, whenever you must. But *just for a moment, be with your friend sadness. Can you do it?*

If not, if today, it is too much, don't worry. You will get another chance. This friend will come calling again, I promise. And maybe on that occasion you can give it one minute—or even ten simple seconds. Taste its particular essence. Know that this is an exquisite gift, this ability to be sad. It is human, and it is one of the sources of your power. Like fear, it is not the enemy, though you have treated it as such. I say to you it is an ally. It is a deep connection to the sadness of all life. It is not going away.

If you are able to sit with this sorrow, even for one minute, you may find it turns to you another face. The red may run down the edges, leaving a tender pink. It may offer you a memory, an image, a gift. Later, you may want to write it down, give it a home in the world. Now just sit quietly and hold it in your stretching heart. Perhaps when you allow your body to share its sadness with you, your breath will find itself slowing and becoming deeper, the muscles loosening a little. Maybe when you breathe into the tight mask of your face, the tears will come. Welcome them. They are carrying your sadness—and the sadness of all beings—out of your body and back into the world. Tears are your gift to all creation, a precious alchemy by which you have taken the sadness deep into you and returned it as pure, clean water. You are healing and bathing yourself and all of us.

This friend, this feeling, will stay as long as she chooses, and when she is ready, will simply slip away. Do not resist. Do not reach out to hold her as she turns to leave you. It is not for you to capture her and hold her imprisoned in your breast. Yes, when she goes, you will be emptied of this feeling, but you will not be empty. Do not attempt to magnify your sorrow, digging through your life story for morsels to add to its weight. Each sorrow visits as it is ready and departs when it will. This is not the time to force a cleansing. Today, you merely allow what arrives. Cease to cling to these feelings of sadness or any other visitor. Simply befriend them. Relax in their presence. Leave the doors of your heart open so they can come and go as they will.

You will become looser as you practice this. The subtle notes will become easier to discern, and the visitors will become more delicate and refined. Joy will come when she comes, and you will be able to set a place for her without trying to chain her to *your table. Love, pain, tenderness, envy, sorrow, joy, delight—all these and more are simply visitors. Open wide your door and sit with them; be curious about their visits. Allow them to join you as they will. Know that each will depart in its turn. They are come to stretch your heart that more may visit. Welcome them all.*

—B

* * *

How did she do it? I swear there was something supernatural about that woman's timing. After the last letter, I'd been doing really well. I even went out with some of my old friends. I was starting to feel good again, but then I'd started waking up sad, going through my day sad, going to bed sad, thinking, no, *promising* myself I'd get up early in the morning and do something productive and still lie there until the last possible minute. Nothing helped—not coffee, not chocolate, not TV. Exercise probably would've helped, but I was too tired and miserable to make myself do it.

I was really ashamed of feeling like that. Afraid if I didn't drive it away, I'd fall apart and never be able to function again. I didn't want the kids to know. It would frighten them. My job was to be "the happy mommy" all the time. But they must have been able to tell, because they were acting out—fighting, breaking things. Driving me crazy. It was all I could do to hold it together. I wanted to cry all the time. And it wasn't even PMS. Not for another week at least. I didn't know what to do.

But what would happen if I simply was sad and didn't try to make it all better? What if there was nothing wrong with being sad, or melancholy, if that's what I was that day? Would the world fall apart? My mother thought it would. She was uncomfortable with any feelings at all. It must have had something to do with the way she was raised. And the times. Or her personality. Whatever it was, she couldn't stand it if we were sad. She was a strategist, always coming up with a plan. It was awful. All I wanted was to just have my mommy make me feel better, and it seemed that all she ever did was tell me to wash my face, tell me that if I'd just lose weight I'd be happy. Then she'd map out the plan. Sometimes, I just wanted comfort, not a new diet.

That was just the way she was, my mother. She knew all the answers; she could tell everyone exactly what they should do. She was bossy. My sister is just like her. I guess it was because she loved us, and she probably couldn't bear to see us suffer. She had to make it better. Of course she did. I know what it's like when my kids are hurting. It's the worst thing on earth. I'd do anything to make it stop. I guess she must have felt the same. I'd never really thought about it in that way before. Funny.

There I was, lying in bed, another Saturday morning that summer, with this unusual woman telling me to make friends with sadness, when it suddenly dawned on me how much my mother had loved me. I always felt I wasn't measuring up to her standards, that I was blowing it because, on top of being fat, I couldn't be happy all the time; I couldn't keep myself under control. I thought it was about me not being good enough. What if it had really been just the opposite? She was as hard on herself as I ever was on myself. Maybe harder. Where else would I have learned it? I bet she thought if we were sad, it meant she wasn't a good mother. How she must have struggled to keep her happy face on, raising us after Dad left. Did she cry alone at night like I did? I would have gone to her had I known. How much of my mother's life did I miss out on? How much did she keep from me because she thought she needed to be strong and protect me? How much did we withhold from each other, trying to keep up appearances?

The tears that had been threatening all week were leaking out of my eyes. I didn't even try to stop them. My mother was dead. She was gone, and there was no way to fix it. I'd never know if she cried alone in her room at night, if her distance was really just her way of protecting me, or if I made that up. I wouldn't ever know how much we could have shared if we had welcomed sadness as an occasional visitor, instead of banishing it from our door. Had I been cheating my own children out of their full range of feelings because I couldn't bear their sadness, their fear, their anger? Because, like my mother, I somehow thought their feelings were a reflection on me. It seemed natural to want your children to be happy all the time, but was it? Maybe it was nothing but my own fears of looking bad. Perhaps it was selfishness, not love at all.

Selfishness? I hadn't thought of it that way, but I guess that was the word. I thought I was trying to protect them. But from what? From learning that sadness, fear, and anger would come and go in their lives and it wouldn't destroy them? Had I been setting them up for a fall? Even at that very moment, I was trying to cry quietly, not to let them hear it, because I didn't want to upset them. Who was I kidding to think I could protect them from sorrow? Wouldn't it be better if I prepared them for it? Showed them with my own life that it was not to be feared?

Of course, to do that, I'd somehow have to stop fearing it myself—and that was the tricky part. Easier said than done. I was afraid of it. And I never, ever wanted to see my kids sad. What mother does? But the cat was out of the bag, and I didn't think it'd go back in. I wondered if this was one of the times Bea had warned me about. How could I go back to the way I'd always done it knowing what I now knew? I wondered what my mother would have said about this whole idea. Would she have freaked out and told me not to even think of it? No, I bet she would have encouraged me to keep on hiding my sorrow, to protect the children.

I was always so sorry that she'd never gotten to see her grandchildren. I'd been pregnant with Justin when she died. She'd always wanted to be a grandma, though it was hard to imagine she would have been any better at that than she'd been at being a mother. Maybe it was just as well I couldn't ask her advice. I might have taken it. No, I was on my own now. But I held tight to this unexpected discovery that it just might have been her love for me, and not her disapproval, that made my sadness impossible for her to bear.

Still a little teary, I called the kids into my room for a good cuddle on the bed. I told them I'd been very sad lately, but that being sad was nothing to be ashamed of. I watched for any signs of surprise or alarm. But of course they already knew. It was as if they'd just been waiting to be invited into my world and were finally able to be there to offer support. Megan wanted to stroke my hair, and Justin punched me in the shoulder and told me to "get over it already." Typical boy. It made me laugh. Then I had these two squirmy teddy-bear kids wrapped around me. And as unexpectedly as it had come, the sadness slipped away. Funny about that. A massive tickle-fest erupted. I think I even started it. As we lay there panting, the kids asked me to make their favorite: French toast. Sounded pretty good to me. Now that was more like the Saturday morning I wanted to have with my kids.

CHAPTER NINE
If You Had a Friend in Your Head

Dear Grace,

We will soon be moving out of your mind and back into the "real" world, and you must begin choosing your companions. But pause first.

Before you can really know the people you meet out there, you must look and see who you are dragging along inside yourself. What friends and foes already peek out from behind your eyes, judging every little or big thing you think, do, feel, say, or don't say? Can you recognize that you fill your outer life with people who match the opinions of those you carry inside? There will never be room for anything different unless you carve space for it.

Can you begin to hear the voices you carry? If you are like me—like most women with these lovely, busy brains of ours—every single move you make is accompanied by a whole chorus of advice. Can you notice the smaller, softer voices, or are they drowned out by the loudest shouts? Whose voice, which warning memory is yelling loudest today? Is there a feeling or color to the voice? Angry red? Muddy brown? Is it a muttering donkey: "It'll never work"? Is it your worried mother, angry father, disdainful lover, jealous sister?

How much energy have you spent trying not to listen? Do you cram your fingers in your ears and try to outshout them? Or are you so cowed that you follow them blindly? How many moves have you made or not made because of their advice? Can you notice? Didn't you buy this sweater because that certain someone loved you in green? Not buy that one because your mother told you never to wear purple with your skin tone? These are tiny examples. What about the heartbreakers? The job you didn't go for, the trip you didn't take, the fascinating man you walked away from before he saw the real you?

Would you do it differently if you had a friend in your head?

Are you willing to listen deeply enough to distinguish the words, the voices? Can you write them down, capture them for a week or so? As ever, you can only start at the exact place you find yourself, and sometimes it takes real work to discover that place. Dis-cover. Yes, you must remove the covering, clean away the mess, in order to see exactly the place where you stand. Are you willing? Are you curious? There is a source of power here, right in the middle of all the noise. Are you ready to meet your inner committee? Would you like to make some new friends?

—B

* * *

That was inside the envelope. She was back home, I guess. The postmark, where I could make it out, was Albuquerque. The envelope itself was covered with a collage of faces, all kinds of faces. Shouting, angry-looking faces; docile, frightened faces; happy ones…she couldn't even write my address; it was totally covered…She'd used a sticker. Weird, but really cool. I was so utterly not creative. So just…not. My sister was the artistic one. I couldn't do that sort of thing at all.

I sat there, turning the envelope over and over, thinking about what she'd written, looking at all the faces she'd carefully cut out (from magazines, I guess) and glued on to an envelope to send to me. It must have taken her a long time. They weren't random faces either; they each seemed to be trying to communicate something. To me. I wondered if she'd had fun making it. I wondered again what had possessed her to put all of this energy and effort into me. Why she thought I was worth it.

Who else did anything special like this for me? My kids, I guess. They always brought home pictures they'd made for me. But did I notice? I mean really notice? Sometimes I'd put them on the wall for a while. But did I really think about the attention and love they put into them? Did I put attention and love into anything at all? I mean, look what she'd made here. For *me*. And she barely knew me.

I didn't know what to make of it at all. I was really uncomfortable all of a sudden. Did what I was thinking relate to what she wrote? All those faces on the envelope, were they supposed to be the voices in my head? I was pretty sure I didn't have any actual voices in my head. Just the usual thoughts. Did she think I was psycho or something? "Doctor, I hear voices." Right. Whatever.

Why did this always seem to happen? Her letters got me so agitated. It wasn't like she was asking me to do something really ridiculous or even very hard. Just listen to what went on in my head. It was the same as noticing my fears. A lot of those fears must have come from what someone said to me, right? I guessed those must be the voices. And to tell the truth, it had already started. I mean, wasn't it some voice in my head that was telling me I wasn't creative? That I could never do anything cool? That only my sister was allowed to do the creative things because I was the practical one? But why did I have to be the practical one? Somebody must have told me that once. I didn't think I just randomly made it up. And then it got stuck in my head, acting like it was the law or something.

What if I didn't want to be the practical one? What if I wanted to be the creative one? What did she say in the letter? I looked again: "Would you do it differently if you had a friend in your head?" Yeah, maybe. She also said that thing about having people in my life who matched the opinions I already had. That was probably true as well. Damn her, anyway. I hoped I would be as wise when I was her age. Maybe I'd even take on a pen pal of my own. I could make her cool collages and send cryptic, bossy letters. It made me smile to think about it. I could just see myself, old and wacky, freaking out some young woman. Hah. I liked the notion.

I got out my black sketchbook and began, still smiling at the image of myself being somebody's mentor. Maybe that's what she meant about having a friend in my head. Maybe that's what she was becoming for me. Maybe I did need to clear some space, to make room for someone new. Someone who liked me enough to think I was worth something. Someone like her, maybe. Anyway, if it was true, I guessed I'd better find out who was already taking up real estate in my brain. I would need to know who I was going to evict.

I wrote across the top of the page, "I am willing to pay attention to the voices in my head. I am willing to listen. I am willing to discover who is saying what, when. I am willing to know them, so I can choose who to listen to." I always felt a little stupid when I wrote that sort of thing, but it seemed to work. It kind of declared what I was up to. I had a feeling there'd be plenty to listen to over the next week or so. Of course, I wasn't about to mention it to anybody. I really was afraid they'd think I was crazy. Totally insane. I'm not positive I wasn't, to tell the truth. But so what? I mean, this whole thing was pretty crazy, wasn't it?

I tried to pay attention all week. It pretty quickly became clear who the major players were. My ex-husband, Rick the prick, for sure. Seemed like everything I did, I could almost hear him approving or not. Grocery shopping—I still avoided the foods he didn't approve of, or if I bought them, I felt defensive about it. His favorite insult, "white trash," followed me everywhere, so I tried to pick foods that were cool and trendy. But they were also expensive. And not necessarily tasty. I wound up throwing away a lot of food that I or the kids wouldn't eat. What a waste. Driving—yep, there he was, still looking over my shoulder, making me nervous. Even getting dressed in the morning, I couldn't escape his opinions. His and my mother's. How did Bea know about all of that? I used to think I was special, that my private thoughts, at least, were unique. Was it true what she'd said? Did all women have to deal with this? Was I ordinary, after all? I wasn't sure how I felt about that. You'd think it would be a relief, but it wasn't, not quite.

Then I noticed something else about Rick's voice in my mind. Something that really upset me. I caught myself looking at other women as if through his eyes. He spent a lot of time looking at women, judging them, checking them out. It was so obvious. He even commented on them as they walked by—right in front of me. Somewhere along the line, I started doing it too. I felt like I had to, so I could figure out where I stood with him. I was still trying to be exactly what he wanted, so I had to know what he wanted, right? So I learned to look at them the way he did and always with an eye to how well I measured up. Was that one better than me? Prettier? Sexier? Better body? After the kids, it was so painful. My body did change and not for the better, either. It was torture, for years. And then when I found out about her, the stewardess...okay, yes, she did have a name. When I found out about Tiffany (I know, do you think I could make this up?), it was almost unbearable. He had a naked picture of her in his wallet. I found it behind the picture of the kids with Santa. He didn't carry a picture of me at all. Yeah. Ouch.

Of course I'd always compared myself to other women, even before Rick. I mean, who didn't? But ever since I found out about her, Tiffany, it had been really bad. I mean, it got to the point where I almost couldn't stand to be around any beautiful, sexy women, because I was so sure that their very existence meant I was totally worthless. That these women would always get my man, every man, so why even bother? Who would ever want me? I'd look at these beautiful women (and in Los Angeles, believe me, there were a lot of beautiful women) and all I could see was myself not measuring up. Especially if they were the kind of perfect, manicured trophy women Rick liked. The diamond tennis bracelet kind. You know the ones. Yuck. I hated having to listen to what I was saying to myself. I really hated it. But it was going on all the time in there. There was no use pretending it wasn't.

With the kids, too, there was always some thought-voice who never quite approved of anything—my mother, my sister, Rick, Rick's mother, Dr. Spock. It was almost silly to notice how many people were in my head telling me what to do all the time. And I listened. That was the sad thing. Most of the time, I let them make my choices. Maybe this had something to do with why I felt as if so much of my life was just a matter of going through the motions.

Open With Love

After a while, I started to get mad about it. Becoming aware of how much of my energy went into all of this constant internal judging, how much effort I spent trying to prove them wrong about me, or how much time I spent feeling bad because they were right was driving me crazy. And if my strange pen pal was correct, my outer life was filled with this kind of garbage. I listened to the kids bickering. "You're so stupid," my son would yell at my daughter. Or at me. My co-workers, how they complained every single day about their husbands but still treated me like an object of pity because I didn't have one. My sister, always trying to change me, put me on a diet, trying to get me to try a new hairstyle, wanting to control everything about me. I couldn't stand it! Bea said I filled my outer world with people who matched my inner world, and these were the people around me. I felt completely trapped. Inside and out. After a week of this, just when I was starting to get really discouraged, another letter came.

Dear Grace,

Would you like me to tell you the secret for getting all these people out of your head? Will you be able to forgive me when I tell you that even if I knew such a secret I would keep it from you? For what good is it to take aim and attempt to kill off these mirrors? At best, they'd only splinter into a thousand fractured voices; at worst, you'd shoot yourself between the eyes. For truly there is no one but yourself in there, using the familiar words and voices you chose to attend to throughout your life. The ones you believed in, the ones you selected. That you have borrowed your self-reflection from those who've touched you is but proof of your large and flexible soul. When you are touched deeply, whether by someone you've loved or by someone you refused to love, you have actually stretched yourself and taken some part of them inside. I suggest this is not a bad thing, but a beautiful facet of being a woman. Our very molecules are affected by another.

Do you feel anxious at the notion? Are you exhausted from the discovery? Do you think you must protect yourself from invasion? Do you wish to sterilize yourself? Perhaps you can. Perhaps there is a formula somewhere for becoming self-contained, isolated from all others. Maybe there is some mountaintop hermitage where no one could reach you at all. And from there, you might be able to create such rigid boundaries that you would become truly separate. You could be utterly alone. But do not look to me for guidance on this. For I would never wish such aloneness on any woman.

Oh, I hated that. I almost ripped the damned letter to pieces and quit the whole freaking "journey" right there. To heck with the old biddy. I wanted the secret to getting those damned voices *out* of my head! Especially Rick's voice. How dare he keep following me around all the time? I was so angry at Bea for starting this whole thing and now telling me I was stuck with it. And how dare she tell me that I put them there and that I was the one keeping them there? I didn't choose for Rick to be mean to me, to say all those things to me. In or out of my head. No way! Why did I have to have anything to do with him anymore? I wanted to be through with him. It was bad enough that I was saddled with dealing with him about the kids until they were grown, and probably beyond; I sure didn't want him inside my mind too!

I threw the letter on the couch and went to wash my face. Thanks, Mom, for that. I scrubbed at it, as if I could get him off of me, out of my head through my skin. The kids were with him for the evening; he had deigned to take them to dinner to make up for the fact that he was going to miss yet another weekend. I had been holding it together through a week of noticing his voice in my head, tormenting me, just praying that Bea was going to send me something soon that would make it all better. And now she'd sent me this. Christ.

I stopped scrubbing my face when it started to hurt. Well, actually not until I couldn't stand it anymore. I looked in the mirror. I was all pink, but the anger was clear in my eyes. They were icy. Bluer than normal against the raw pink skin. It wasn't just anger, it was more like rage. I wanted to be free. Just free of all of it—him, this crazy old lady, this lousy condo, this stupid job, this whole city full of people who were better and happier than me. I hated my life. I just wanted to be one of the happy ones for once. To feel I was in control of something.

I wandered back into the living room, toying with the idea of turning on the TV and making popcorn dripping with butter and forgetting all about the letter. I glanced at it on the couch, almost against my will. There were more pages peeking out. She'd written each page on a different color of paper. Typical Bea weirdness. The next page was pink. Pale pink. I decided I would read the pink page, and if it wasn't any better news than the first page, the yellow one, I was tossing the whole project. So there, Bea. I might not have been able to get the voices out of my head, but I could certainly get your letters out of my house. Yeah. I took the pink page and stood by the so-called "sliding" door to get the last light of day.

We are made up of everyone we've ever loved or admired, just as they, in their turn, are made of us. And we are also made of everyone we've truly feared, despised, or rejected. They have all become part of the fabric of us. We are full of everything we've loved and everything we've hated. The dark and the light. But which is which? Just notice. And who's to say, really, whether any of it was ever outside of us at all? Can you say with absolute conviction that anything you know about yourself or anyone else is true? That you've ever seen anyone (including yourself) clearly exactly as they are? Which came first, the projection or the projector?

Whichever came first, you only chose to keep the ones that matched your opinion of yourself. You cemented the story with evidence. It is just your story of yourself. That is the only thing you need to know. Not whether what these voices say is true about you now or then or ever. Not how to get rid of them. But a simple recognition that, on your journey so far, you chose these warnings, these concerns, these companions to create yourself with. You heard something you believed needed attending to in yourself. And so you invited them in.

It is an unfortunate fact of human nature, and especially women's nature, that we seem best to remember the criticisms. The "don'ts" and the "can'ts" and the "shouldn'ts" speak loudest to us. If you are able to look deeply enough, gently enough, lovingly and patiently enough, you will find the other, softer voices, those quietly approving friends, the ones who are proud of your little steps. Even these use borrowed voices and phrases from those you've loved. That is, from those whose love you have allowed yourself to notice. Sometimes they are even the same voices that thwart you. Only when you lay down your weapons and remove your fingers from your ears can you hear the whole choir. Only then can you choose.

Okay, I had to admit the pink page was slightly better news. So if Rick's voice was inside my head, and I put it there because I already believed what he said, at least it meant he wasn't in charge of the story. I was. I don't know why it helped, but it did, a little. And I guess it made sense. He wasn't the first one who'd tried to change me. It's true I'd already believed I needed to be remodeled. And there were probably some better voices in my head if I could just get his to stop yelling at me all the time. Maybe I had been fighting him for so long that I kept it up inside of my head. Maybe I did have my fingers stuck in my ears. What did we do when we were kids? Stick our fingers in our ears and yell, "Blah blah blah, I'm not listening to you!" But no matter how loud we yelled it, we always knew what they were trying to say to us, didn't we?

When you realize that you created the entire thing, that you auditioned each and every member of the chorus, that you assigned their parts, when you realize that it is all but proof of your participation in this shared life journey, then whose counsel might you knowingly choose to follow? Some you may want always, right where they are; some may be moved forward to center stage. You may ask certain voices to try a new key. Some may be invited to move on. Can you thank them for where they have gotten you so far? Admit that you gained something by listening?

These are not random influences in your life. You chose them to make you exactly the person you are today. You are no one's victim, you have freely chosen those you associate with in your mind. And if by now they seem to be running the show, it's simply because they, like your fears, have been left too long unattended. Now that you have met them, will you continue to allow them their unchecked liberty? It becomes your choice.

As you become more powerful, you will find yourself choosing to whom you listen. But it will happen, as with all growth, as it happens. Maybe there will be some violent upheavals, some grand rebellions, but lasting transformation is not built by force. Simply begin to breathe fresh air into the stale chambers of your mind. You start, as always, from where you are. You may even find a new appreciation for what these friends have given you and want to thank them for their guidance. Thanking them always disarms them. All they ever wanted was to be heard. You begin to see where their concerns are valid and where they are unwarranted. You'll find you can transform them into allies, make them part of the team.

Perhaps before too long, when you have allowed these noisy voices their say, you will notice a different voice. A steady voice, singing deeper than the rest. Or perhaps not even a voice like the others, but a gentle tone below the fray, a patiently amused watcher who knows that you have been through all of this before and that you will go through it again. One whose counsel is never violent or rash, but quiet and simple and true. Never fighting to be loudest, it simply waits until the rest have had their say.

It is the sound of your own heart. As you learn to simply allow the other voices to sing their parts and notice them, without fighting them or fanning their flames, you will find that they run out of words and eventually become still while the heart-tone becomes easier to distinguish. This is the music that will lead you to the center of yourself, for it emanates from there. This voice, when invited, will guide you as you explore your world, inside and out. Attend to it. Practice listening for it. Strengthen it by honoring it. Draw the words you speak to yourself and others from it. Become the heart voice for yourself and those around you. "To give heart" is the simple meaning of the word encourage. From the French coeur, "heart." Listen carefully for the heart voice speaking in those around you, and when you hear it, cherish it. Soon, you may find it everywhere. Except, of course, when you don't. When you forget to listen. Then simply, quietly, and without drama, begin again. From the exact where and when and how you find yourself. Listen.

Love, B

* * *

I sure didn't like the idea that I chose these nagging, pesky voices. That I shouldn't just eliminate them. That I couldn't. But it was probably true. Hundreds of people had probably said thousands of things to me over the years, but what I heard in my head was pretty much the same things over and over. And it sure wasn't the good things, either. She was right on about that one. But I was getting sick of letting them have their say. Sick of listening to them, Bored even. Maybe that was good. I got out my old trusty pen and my by now slightly battered black journal and decided to give it a go. Do what she said, listen all the way through, and see if I could even hear that heart voice on the other side.

I wrote out everything I always heard rattling around in my brain and where it came from. All the stuff from Rick, all the advice from my mother, the warnings about eating the wrong foods. I wrote everything anyone had ever told me about how I should be thinner, prettier, happier, richer, nicer. I just let it rip. Pages and pages came out. Kind of like writing those fears. A lot of the stuff was the same. But it was really weird to notice what was going on; it was like transcribing the constant chatter and logging where it came from.

After about a dozen pages (I'm not kidding, it was a lot) this little voice said, "Are you through yet?" So I wrote that down, those words. And then I answered, "Yeah, I guess so." And then I found I was writing this dialogue with myself. Well, not my normal self. This sort of calm, amused self. The heart voice? Maybe. I wasn't sure. I guess it didn't matter. It's probably different for everybody. But for me, it was this really specific point of view that started reminding me of the good things about me, about my life. It started pointing out what I had learned from Rick, from a lot of the people in my life, what great kids

I had, how much love I had to give, and how much of myself I had been afraid to show. It was like talking to an old friend or a therapist even, but I knew everything I was writing was coming out of me. I know this sounds a little weird, and I'm not even sure I should be saying it here, but that's what happened. And it continued to happen when I wrote again later, if I just stayed put long enough to write all the way through all the negative crap, all the off-key lyrics. I learned to just write it all out and not to judge it or fight it. Once or twice, I even tried to sing it. It was a lot like Bea said: a chorus, where I could move around the different parts. But I never would have believed it until it happened.

I thought it would be way better if I could just skip the negative stuff and go straight to this place. And it did become easier to get to as I kept on doing it, but there was no way around making friends with whoever was yelling loudest. I had to always begin where I was. There was no way to ignore any nagging fear or worry or anger. It would just get louder and louder until I let it have its say and thanked it. I learned just to allow it to be there, fully, without fighting it either direction. I just let it pour out onto the page, and then it would sort of ease up, and I'd get to this clear place. And after being there a while, I'd be refreshed, energized, clear, and focused—until I forgot, like she said. And then when I would notice it was getting noisy in my head. Eventually I'd remember and start again. I wish I could say I didn't beat myself up for forgetting or that I mostly remembered. I didn't. But when I did, I was a little kinder to myself.

CHAPTER TEN

Be Beauty

I hadn't received a letter in quite a while. Over a month, almost half the summer. I probably should have been concerned, but I'd been busy. The kids and I had gone to Oregon for my vacation. I have cousins up there, so we went on a road trip to see them. It was pretty fun. We went to the sea lion caves and everything. My car started acting up on the way home, though, and I'd spent the last few days before I had to go back to work dealing with it. I figured Bea was traveling somewhere and didn't have time to write.

When I did the things she'd asked me to do, I felt a little more at ease in my life, more like myself. Of course, mostly I didn't do the things she suggested. But when I did, something definitely shifted. And it was she herself who had told me not to beat myself up for anything. Whenever I did remember, I took her advice and just began again. At least I hadn't completely forgotten.

So I was glad to see her familiar script on the envelope after work that day. I didn't want to wait till the kids went to bed, so I confess I popped *Shrek* in the VCR and stole a few moments to read it. It was postmarked Vancouver, British Columbia. The stamp had a picture of Queen Elizabeth on it. The first one, with the big collar and the hair.

Dear Grace,

It is time to consider Beauty.

Beauty is your birthright, your blessing, and the access to the highest and best there is in you. Do you know this? The world has stolen your precious and particular access to your personal glory, and it is time to restake your claim, to wrest it back, and never again let it out of your control. Beauty is yours to define, yours to express, yours to create, yours to be. You, my beloved, are Beauty.

I do not speak of transient physical beauty, as defined by the world for its commercial purposes. That is but a mimic of the thing itself, a watered-down facsimile of Beauty. I speak of its essence, Beauty, the divine birthright of every woman, the living energy which calls forth the very best in men and all beings, the grace and loveliness which keeps the world from spinning out of control.

The world is desperate for this and yet terrified of it. Even today, wars are being fought over this power I name Beauty and the control of it. Modern woman is numb to what has been taken from her, her divine glory, her power, and her gifts—your gifts, your power, your Grace.

Your Beauty has been denied, neglected. But even worn out as you are by the demands of your complicated, busy life, it is not gone from you. It is the sleeping essence, which I now ask you to tenderly kiss awake. Begin to revive her; begin to express her right there in your specific corner of the universe, in order that you may be part of the reawakening of all women. I charge you with living a life of Beauty.

I invite you to bring forth your own beautiful essence. I ask you to bring Beauty to everything you touch. Celebrate your own unique, specific, majestic, particular, essential, sensual, and delightfully precise Beauty.

Yes, yours. Your Beauty is what the world is craving right now, right where you live—in your body, in your home, in your actions, in your words, *in your thoughts, in your breath. Your Beauty, not your prettiness. We have had enough Disney princesses. The world needs your Beauty, your Grace, your essence made manifest. Mankind is starving for true beauty. Women are starving; indeed, they are carving themselves to bits, anything to be pretty enough in the world's eye. But this only keeps us from stepping into true ownership of the power and glory of our Beauty. Your true Beauty is the exact antidote to the craving that keeps you in chaos and exhaustion. The relentless quest for a polished outer beauty is nothing but a desperate cry for the buried essence of Beauty itself.*

You see, Beauty is not just outside decoration. It is the actual core of the thing. Of everything. It is the nature of our souls to hunger for it. It is part of the key to what we so clumsily call salvation. And it is the province of woman. Somewhere all of us know this. And it has been stolen from its rightful place and used to sell you what you don't need. The promise of Beauty for sale keeps you endlessly hungry, and even though you know better, you still slip under its seductive spell. No amount of consumption can fill the hole where your own Beauty belongs.

You have believed the lie that you are not Beauty-full, that your loveliness is just a matter of how well or poorly you measure up to some standard. You have hidden yourself behind a false face, a brittle life...a brittle lie...which keeps you docile and keeps you buying the promise, only to be disappointed again and again. You are so hungry for your own Beauty that sometimes you eat desperately to fill the void; sometimes you have other, subtler methods, but you are always trying desperately to replace something that is already, by divine right, yours.

This hunger is not a benign thing. It will eat you away until there is nothing left of your soul. When Beauty was stolen for commerce, a void was created in all of us. The unquenchable ache of the empty soul will buy anything that promises to ease the pain.

Perhaps you think I exaggerate. Perhaps I do. But I am speaking to your soul now, calling you to reclaim Beauty for yourself, to reignite the fire of Beauty, which is barely a flicker in you now. I am speaking to your soul's longing for its own Beauty. A Beauty that has been wrested from its only and true source: the pure essence of woman. Beauty is the truth of each and every woman, starting at this moment with you.

Yes, you. Did you forget you were the key to the salvation of the species? Did you think there was nothing at stake? That your life was a random accident? Women are the keepers of Beauty. Your awakening is the key for all women. Your essential Beauty calls forth all Beauty. You are the most important woman on earth at this moment, for you are the one waking up. You are now part of the chain. When your flame becomes strong and true, you will inspire others, as I have inspired you. Do not turn your back on the women who need to see your Beauty. Your Beauty will give them permission to find theirs. You can begin now. You must begin now. Much time has already been lost. Much damage has already been done.

Perhaps you think I am overstating the case. Your arguments are good ones. Why you? You are nothing but another exhausted, cranky, single mom, barely making ends meet. How can you be the key to anyone's salvation, let alone everyone's? But I say that you are. And therefore I implore you to be the Beauty that you and only you can be. Be Beauty everywhere. Begin now. In this instant, breathe out every lie you've ever told yourself: that you don't matter, that you're not pretty enough to count, that maybe when you lose that ten pounds or twenty; breathe out all the comparisons, all the if-onlys, all the stories about why you can't have, why you don't deserve, why you aren't enough.

Yes, those lies. All of them. Breathe them out. Yell them out. Write them down and tear them up; there are a hundred ways to release them, and you'll probably have to do all hundred of them twice, for these lies have a powerful hold on you. But I beg you—do not make your precious Beauty wait until the lies have all gone, for they may never go. In truth, they don't even matter once you know yourself as Beauty. Release them as they show up, and again and again, while you begin to discover your particular Beauty. Begin this minute! Be Beauty in your world now!

But wait, you say, hold on, what do you mean, "Be Beauty?" How does one "Be Beauty?" It's not even grammatical.

Of course it's not. Do you think something so large can be stated in proper English? Do you think English is large enough to hold the truth of you? Do you think there would be a proper way to say such a heretical thing? This thing is a mystery. You are claiming what has been buried, what has been lost or stolen or denied so long ago you forgot its nature.

No one else can ever know or say exactly what your Beauty is and does. Maybe you can't even say it, not yet. And that is fine. It is not a destination; it is a journey. It is an expedition into uncharted territory, an invitation to discover. Dis-cover what is in there, simply by attending to it.

I assert that your Beauty is and that it does, and that by your choosing to notice it, it will define itself. Notice what things are Beautiful to you. Notice how Beauty feels in your body. Notice what actions are Beautiful to you, which words and colors and sounds and tastes and touches are Beautiful to you—exactly, and perhaps only to you—in exactly the way you experience them. When you choose to notice these things, when you make room for them, when you invite them into your life, into your home, into your heart, into your body, and into your thoughts, they will take root and will begin to grow in you. Your preferences themselves will teach you surer and faster than anything specific I could tell you. Funny how something so radical can be so simple.

I leave you with this:

Only this:

Be Beauty.

—B

* * *

What? I mean, what the heck was that about? Be Beauty. She'd capitalized the word *Beauty* everywhere, like it was some kind of proper name. Like it was God. As usual, this letter completely unnerved me. No, this one was worse than usual. This one was completely off the deep end. Maybe she really was a nutcase. I wondered if I should try to call someone about her. Maybe she needed what they politely call "assistance."

I checked the kids. Shrek was off on his quest to find the Princess Fiona. Justin knows all of Donkey's lines. Megan likes to watch him act them out. They were fine. It was a full-length movie, so I had some time left to myself. I decided to give the letter another chance, maybe reread it. Try to make sense of it all.

But first I went to the bathroom and looked in the mirror. In the harsh overhead light reflecting off the green walls, I looked ill. What the heck made me buy a condo with a green bathroom, I'll never know. It had seemed pretty with the matching towels, shower curtain, the works, but the truth was I looked like shit in green light, and I was pretty sure I wasn't the only one. Mostly, I tried not to pay attention to this mirror, but now I looked more closely. At my hair, which I struggled to dry straight, but never quite got right. Instead of smooth and sleek, it was just flat and damaged, and the cowlicks on each side of my face were back by mid-afternoon. Maybe I should give up on sleek. I looked at the dark shadows under my eyes and scratched at the painful pimple trying to come to a head in my hairline. I glared at the crease forming between my eyebrows from squinting when I forgot my sunglasses or when I concentrated or when I yelled at the kids or worried or...well, okay, most of the time. I'd been considering Botox for it, but it was so expensive and it wore off in only a couple of months, and sometimes people look really weird after they have it...

I looked again and saw something else too. I don't know how to describe it exactly, except for what she had said in the letter: a brittleness. A hardness around my mouth, a guardedness around my eyes. Almost as if I was hiding in there and wasn't available to the world. To anyone or anything. Just protecting myself. What had happened to the face I used to have? Didn't I used to be fun? When did I become so stiff and hidden? Hardly beautiful. Was this how she'd seen me that day? Was this the face I hid behind? Yuck.

I went back to the letter and held it up to the light. She had written it on delicate lavender stationery, and it looked as if she'd painted the bottom of each page a watercolor blue, like the hint of a magical lake. Using colored pencils, she'd drawn butterflies flying up each page, in and around the words. They were very faint, and I hadn't really noticed them when I'd read through it before. It was scented as well, or maybe it had just been her own scent getting on the page as she wrote. Something earthy and natural, patchouli, maybe? Why, I wondered again, did she go to so much trouble for me? We'd met just once. I tried to remember her face. She must have been close to eighty. Maybe even more; when people were that old, I just couldn't tell.

She'd had this lion's mane of wild, wavy, silver-white hair and the most amazing eyes. They were the opposite of my eyes, even though they were more or less the same shade of blue. There was nothing guarded about her eyes. They came right out to meet you. When she smiled, you knew she was smiling to you, with you, for you. She just glowed with something, life itself, I guess. And her wrinkles seemed to be a perfect part of the package, not a distraction or a problem at all. She carried herself like a queen. I followed her into the little café. Before I could duck away, she'd turned and invited me for tea. What could I say?

Six months later, I was standing in front of the bathroom mirror pondering Beauty. She obviously was trying to give me a gift, a gift of something so wonderful (or horrible—sometimes it seemed that this whole thing could go either way) that I couldn't even get my mind around it. I thought maybe it was the gift of how to live. How to have eyes like hers? If eyes were the window to the soul, then maybe even how to have a soul so vibrant that you could turn heads at eighty. Or ninety, or whatever the heck she was.

So maybe this was the Beauty she was talking about. Sometimes I did wish the woman could just come right out and say things directly. Not this witchy…freaky…deep…spiritual…whatever it was. Beauty with a capital B? "Yeah, right," I said out loud. "Sure, Bea, whatever you say. Me, the key to reviving Beauty for all women. Who are you trying to kid?" I looked in the mirror again. She must have made a mistake. If I was the hope for women and beauty, we all might as well give up now.

I took the letter, walked into my bedroom, and flopped on my back on the bed. I stared at the cottage cheese ceiling and tried to get my mind around what she'd written. What exactly was she asking me to do? Was this crazy old woman trying to turn me into some kind of a "lady," the way my mother had tried? I shuddered because the whole idea made me think about Rick and his stewardess. I bet she never skipped any of the beauty stuff. I rubbed my eyes. I dropped the letter on the floor and flopped over onto my stomach, pressing my face into the pillow, trying to get the images out of my mind. Of her naked body, from that photo he kept and I'd found. Of her and Rick, laughing and kissing as they walked away together that day I ran into them at the movies. Laughing at me, I was sure, in my baggy sweats with popcorn grease on the front. Me, be Beauty? Hardly. I rolled back over and sat up.

Was that what Bea was up to? Trying to turn me into a Tiffany? Not possible, even if I wanted it. Okay, sure I wanted it. Who didn't want to look perfect? But I really didn't think that was Bea's intention. It just didn't seem to be in character. And she did say that thing about Disney princesses, so I guess it wasn't really about—what did she call it? "A watered-down facsimile of Beauty?" Something like that. I smiled. I liked to think of Tiffany like that. A facsimile. That was more like it. Maybe she was just pretend beautiful, not the real thing.

I shivered. I had no idea what Bea wanted from me, or where or how to begin. But I suspected that like everything else she'd been encouraging me to do, it would start small and then take on a life of its own. So maybe painting my toenails was a start. I couldn't remember the last time I'd painted them, let alone did any other "beauty" thing. At least it was something I could do, right in that moment. Just for me. Not to compete with Tiffany or anyone else. So what if no one would see them? I could have pretty toes just for myself. I could start there anyway and leave the bigger question of how the heck someone could "Be Beauty" for later. I decided it was worth a try.

First, I checked on the kids, who were still watching *Shrek*. Princess Fiona had just found out that "her true love's kiss" had actually turned her into a full-time ogre, not a perfect princess. And she still lived happily ever after. It seemed appropriate to the evening. Maybe there was hope for all of womankind after all. I rewound the tape. There was still half an hour before bedtime.

I went back to the bathroom and rummaged around under the sink until I found my box of nail polishes. Quite a few were so dried up they went straight into the trash, but I finally found the color I wanted. A particular shade of metallic copper that I loved and Rick hated. The bottle was practically full because I'd only been able to endure his criticism of it for two days before I'd changed back to the little-girl pinks he'd preferred. I got it out and decided maybe I'd just go ahead and do it right, the whole shebang. A pedicure. This was getting ridiculous. I hadn't done that since before the kids were born. But why not? If I was going to take on this "Be Beauty" business, I might as well go all out. So I ran some water in the tub and tried to remember what a pedicure consisted of.

"What are you doing, Mommy?" It was Megan in the doorway. "I just had a bath last night. Did you forget?"

"No, honey. It's a special bubble bath for my feet. Like a treat."

"I want a treat." She looked at me expectantly.

What the heck? Maybe we could do "Be Beauty" together. So we both stuck our feet in the tub and then proceeded to give ourselves matching copper-colored toenails. I enjoyed imagining the look on Rick's face when he saw that. Tough tootsies, Rick, she's my daughter too.

When we were done, Megan ran to my closet and dug out a pair of high-heeled sandals. She must have gone all the way to the back to find those. I couldn't remember the last time I'd worn them.

"Can I play dress-up, Mommy? Can I show off my pretty toes?" I couldn't think of a reason why not.

"Sure honey, just be careful. And don't forget it's almost bedtime."

"Justin! Look at my pretty toes!" she ran screeching to her brother. "Mommy and me have beautiful feet together!"

"That's stupid girl stuff. I don't care about that." Justin pushed his sister away and went off to crash his trucks into his Legos while I watched her parade, unfazed, around the place like she had invented the world. All because of some nail polish and an old pair of sandals?

Boys and girls were just different, I guess. What was it Bea'd written, "Women are the keepers of Beauty," and something about how it was in us, but sleeping. Well, Megan, in that moment, was no Sleeping Beauty. She was full-on Beauty and loving it. Loving herself, fearless, not needing her brother's approval or even mine. Just delighted with her own lovely toes. Too young to worry about all the things that kept me from enjoying being in my body. Too young for cellulite, for flab, for any of it. She just pranced around like she was perfect, like everything was perfect. It was so great to see. And who could say she wasn't perfect? Who said everything wasn't perfect just the way it was? This hadn't come out of a little bottle of nail polish; this was already in her. It was her nature, and it just took a little tiny thing like this to wake it up. Maybe cellulite and flab were some of those lies Bea mentioned. Maybe "Be Beauty" wasn't such a strange instruction after all.

After the kids were in bed, I picked up the sandals and put them on. I tried prancing around like Megan, but I felt stupid. I had to admit, though, my toes looked pretty cute in them. Maybe tomorrow I'd wear them to work. Maybe I'd even wear a dress. I mean, there was no law against dressing up, was there? And it's not like I'd be on my feet all day. Quite the opposite. So why not?

CHAPTER ELEVEN

Beauty Backfires

Wearing a pretty dress to work on a random Thursday morning when my typical uniform had been baggy khakis and wrinkled button-downs for as long as I or anyone could remember was a fairly radical act. First, it wasn't easy. I had to find a dress in my closet that fit and looked good, and for some reason, that entailed trying them all on and leaving them scattered across the room (not that I had so many dresses, but it had been so long since I'd bothered to even look at them I could barely remember which ones fit. Or even used to fit). And I'm not even going to discuss the quest for appropriate undergarments here. Then there were a whole lot of other things that needed to be addressed: leg shaving, hair-styling, eyebrow maintenance, makeup. I was beginning to regret ever painting my stupid toenails. My kids had this book, *If You Give a Moose a Muffin*, about the whole pile of crazy things that need to happen because you gave a moose…well, you get the point. I felt trapped in the same absurd domino spiral. Thanks a lot, Bea.

I almost gave up the entire idiotic idea, but since I'd gone that far (and it turned out I didn't have any clean khakis anyway), I went through with it. You really should have seen my kids' faces when I came out of the bathroom. You know how they say "their jaws dropped"? Well, that about summed it up. I felt like I was wearing a chicken suit.

"Don't just stand there staring. We've got to get going. We don't want to be late, do we?" Really, it was a bit unnerving. I mean, it was just a little sundress. And some makeup. And high heels.

I was beginning to feel stupid.

"Mommy?"

"Yes, Justin?"

"You look pretty."

I felt a little less stupid. Actually, I wanted to scoop him up and kiss him. So I did. He squirmed out of my arms, as I knew he would, but it seemed he wasn't in quite such a hurry to get away from me as usual. Or maybe I imagined it. Megan just stared at me, all the way to school, and when I dropped her off at her classroom, she didn't want to let go of my hand. She pulled me down so she could whisper in my ear.

"I love you."

Driving the rest of the way to work, the traffic didn't even faze me. I usually listened to NPR or some talk nonsense with lots of traffic reports, but today, instead, I just wanted music—loud music, happy music, stupid eighties pop music I could sing to. The sun was shining, and I was wearing a pretty dress, so what if it was a few years old—I didn't want to listen to bad news. Crawling down the 10 freeway at twenty-five miles an hour, I was singing at the top of my lungs. People must have thought I was nuts, but I didn't care. I was being Beauty. I smiled at them, and a lot of them smiled back.

No one at work believed I was dressed up for no reason. They assumed it was for a man, a date, a party, a something. They kept trying to pry it out of me.

"So, what's his name?" and "Anyone I know?" Like that. All day. I finally gave up and just smiled like I had a secret. Like I was the Mona Lisa or something. I mean, I did have a secret, but it was for sure not what they thought. I was dressed up because some nutty old lady had sent me a letter, and I painted my toenails just to see what happened next. And there was something in there about a moose.

It was weird, though. That it was so impossible for anyone to believe a person could want to dress up a little just for herself. I mean, it made me feel sad. Because that was the truth of it, for me too. Until that day, I'd only ever dressed up for special occasions, and special occasions were only really special if there was a man involved. It was something to think about for sure.

Many, many times over the next few weeks, I reread her letter for some kind of clues about what it meant to "Be Beauty." I didn't think she really meant wear makeup and high heels all the time. It didn't make any sense with the rest of the letters, all that stuff about the dark cave, begin again, or any of it. But there was definitely something there. Of course, I didn't keep dressing up for work every day. For one thing, I just didn't have enough pretty clothes. I had to admit, though, that it had felt totally different to be me on that Thursday. Like I had a different relationship with everyone. The way I'd felt before Rick, like I was available to people—the people in the other cars on the way to work, the people I passed in the hallways, everyone. I felt friendlier, a little less like I was hiding out, trying to be invisible. I sure didn't want to become some shallow, manicured, Los Angeles stereotype—another trophy bimbo like Tiffany (Who, me, bitter? What would make you think that?)—but maybe I had gone a little too far to the other extreme. I mean, I really had let myself go. It's funny, all those voices in my head telling me what was wrong with me hadn't been able to get me to take care of myself; they'd just made it worse. Something to notice there. Be Beauty was a different voice entirely. I got my hair cut. Started paying more attention.

Still, I didn't think Bea had been talking about my hair and makeup. I didn't think she really meant anything on the outside. It seemed as if she was actually talking about something deep inside, sort of shining through. But I think I felt it when I dressed up that day, like I was rising to the outfit, somehow. I think it helped me find the place in me that was a little lighter, a little friendlier, a little less frightened. Maybe it wasn't the outfit or the makeup or even the toenails, but just the fact that I had put some effort and thought into, well, me.

The last part of the letter was pretty clear. Notice how Beauty feels to me, sounds to me, tastes to me, looks to *me*. Begin to invite it into my life. Hmmmm. Since all her other letters encouraged me to write things down, and this was way more fun-sounding than fear, I decided to keep a separate journal just to capture my thoughts on Beauty. To find out what I actually found beautiful, to notice it, to make a record of it. To really discover what was beautiful to me—my unique personal version of Beauty.

A long time ago, someone had given me a fancy little blank book. It was this tiny thing from India or somewhere, covered in orange silk with ribbons sewn on it. I thought it was pretty, but I'd never had anything to write in it. It seemed a little too precious to put the grocery list in. It was perfect for this.

So for the next month, almost, I tried to keep track of everything that struck me as beautiful. And everything that felt ugly—just for comparison. Just to notice, like she always said, without any judgments. To discover what these things felt like in my body. I looked at colors, listened to music, touched things. It was pretty cool, like being on a scavenger hunt in my body and in my life. I decided not to worry about the part about how the world needed me to do this, other women needed me, whatever. I didn't understand it; it was a little creepy, but I just figured she liked to talk that way. Or maybe I was afraid it might actually be true. I didn't want that kind of pressure. I was having a hard enough time with the baby steps.

So for a month, I didn't even try to make sense of her big picture, I just got very, very curious about what exactly was "my Beauty." And the funniest thing happened. The more I focused on Beauty, the more I found it in the most unusual places. The more I really looked for things in me and around me that truly felt beautiful, the more I found. Every night, I'd write down what I noticed that day. Then I even started carrying the orange book with me everywhere so I could write things down when I came across them during the day so I wouldn't forget. I caught myself appreciating the weirdest things: the delicate shades of green and brown in the decaying leaves on the street, cloud formations and subtle color changes in the sky, the different smells that came in through the car window as I drove by. I could smell a lot of things I had never bothered with before. Pleasant or unpleasant, it didn't really matter. I noticed them. Who knew I had such a good nose?

And I also started to notice that so many of the things I usually thought were "pretty" really didn't interest me at all. Most of my clothes, for instance. A whole lot of stuff that I'd gotten because Rick liked it on me just didn't feel right. The colors were not the ones that I was discovering I loved, and they didn't fit the way I wanted them to. They were clothes for this image of someone, but not me. I don't know if I knew yet what exactly "me" was, but it was getting easier to notice when it wasn't right. And the more I paid attention, the more uncomfortable I was whenever I wore something that wasn't "me." I kept dragging bags of clothes to the Goodwill drop-off. At the rate I was going, I'd soon be down to three outfits, none of which would be right for work.

My clothes weren't the only thing that didn't seem to fit. I got more and more uncomfortable everywhere in my life. Work was the worst. Sitting on my butt under fluorescent lights looking at a computer screen made me want to tear my hair out. I just couldn't find anything beautiful about my job.

Everything started bugging me. But the worst of all were my own words and thoughts. I'd catch myself saying things that weren't mine. I found myself complaining or swearing, something I'd definitely picked up from Rick. Or I'd voice an opinion about something that was just a mimic of what someone else had said. As soon as those things were out of my mouth, I felt really uncomfortable. I could feel them just hanging in the air. I discovered I didn't have many of my own opinions. I also discovered I didn't have that much to talk about if I wasn't complaining, and complaining sure didn't feel beautiful. I wasn't even sure anymore if my thoughts were even mine or if they came from those same old rattling voices in my head I'd been trying to notice. When I considered them in light of "Beauty," a lot of them just, well, weren't beautiful.

By the end of the month, I was walking around in a fog of sensitivity. I could hardly get dressed, speak, think, anything, without being aware. I didn't even know what to eat anymore. At first, it had been wonderful, but it had become too much. Too much stimulation, too much to notice everywhere. I felt like I didn't have the capacity for it. I just wanted to shut down. To tell the truth, it started to piss me off. I didn't have time for this nonsense. I wanted my old life back—just normal, you know. Okay, my sad and lonely and un-beautiful life, but normal. I wanted to eat a bunch of ice cream and brownies and popcorn and watch other people on the TV, but none of that felt right anymore. Be Beauty. Yeah, great. You know that movie, *The Matrix*? I felt I'd definitely swallowed the wrong pill. I didn't know how to go forward, and I couldn't go back. I felt awful, and I wanted to quit, like I always did. I decided again that the old bat was nuts and this whole thing was stupid and what I really needed was a break. Or at least brownies. I was about to snap. The next letter came just in time.

CHAPTER TWELVE

Soul Survival

Dear Grace,

On the quest for your particular expression of Beauty, you may see things slip away. Many things the world and even your own history hold dear become noxious. Despair not, for the dark spots are the secret gateways of the light. You must pass through them to get into the garden. Yes, it will cost you something. It always does.

You will perhaps not be able to find distraction as easily as before, and you may long for a certain slippery oblivion of habit. The gatekeeper is demanding this small sacrifice of you if you are to be allowed access to a far greater and more satisfying life. This time passes, and soon you will be able to freely choose anything, even, on occasion, those things which now trouble you. You are simply becoming aware. Awareness is often uncomfortable. Freedom has consequences. My mother said, in her inimitable way, "The truth will set you free, but first it will beat you repeatedly about the head and shoulders." Ah. Yes.

It is important that you nourish and shelter your soul, as important as nourishing and sheltering your body. You must start small. Build yourself a haven, a temple to your own particular delights. One tiny space to call yours, exactly yours. A retreat from abusing yourself with things and thoughts that aren't beautiful to you. A place where your soul will respond to your desire for wholeness, gentleness, safety. A place where you will unfold your full self and breathe deeply. Start small: an altar, a closet, a cushion. This is not decoration. This is survival. Soul survival. Do it now. Do you know the Spanish for survive? Sobrevivir "to live above it." You will find life on top of it. Begin again.

—BB

* * *

The letter was on plain white paper and signed like that: "BB." Double B. Be Beauty? BB. Betty Boop? Beatrice Blasphemous? Who was this woman? I didn't even know her last name, though I was starting to think she had some kind of spy cam aimed at me. Maybe this was all some kind of weird reality show, and I was totally being set up. I mean, how could she know what I was thinking, how I was struggling, how much I longed for trash TV and junk food? How badly I wanted a chocolate brownie? How it irritated me to notice that these things weren't "Beauty" and yet still I craved them? I was sure this proved I was a total loser in the "Beauty" department. But there was a ray of hope. Didn't she write that someday I would be able to choose anything? Maybe even brownies?

Okay, I knew I could choose them anytime, and if you want to know the sordid truth, I had been sneaking them here and there anyway. It was my little rebellion, especially in the last few days, when it had gotten to be too much. It was an angry teenager's response, a "Forget you, you old nag. I can do whatever I want. Who do you think you are?" kind of thing. But I had to admit, it wasn't her I was fighting. She'd never even mentioned brownies. I was the one who felt crappy when I ate too many brownies, and I always ate too many. It was I who'd decided they didn't really fit in with "Be Beauty." So it wasn't her fault if I couldn't have them. It was someone else's voice I was fighting, my mother's, probably, though I don't think she ever really said anything specific about brownies either. It was like I'd put together this idea of who I was supposed to be at all times. And I kept score of how much I failed at it and wrapped it up in the perennial disappointment I felt I had been to my mother. When I looked closely though, I couldn't quite put my finger on the actual proof of her disappointment; it was more a constant sense of it. And the brownies? Well, I ate brownies because I liked them, even if I knew they weren't good for me. She didn't have to say, "Don't eat *brownies*," for me to know I shouldn't. Anyway, didn't mothers always try to keep you from getting fat by telling you not to eat stuff like brownies? Maybe it was just part of their job. I was the one who used brownies as proof of what a loser I was and beat myself up for it. I kept trying to prove myself to my mother, even though she was dead, and then I'd get so sick of failing all the time that I'd just go off the deep end and eat a whole package. Just to prove she couldn't control me with her damned disappointment.

Disappointment. That was the real problem. I had been nothing but this big disappointment to my mother. And no matter how hard I tried to live up to her ideals, I couldn't do it. So I hid it—all that shame. I ate brownies (and a lot of other things too) in secret. I don't think I had even admitted it to myself until this "Be Beauty" experiment had begun. I had this all-or-nothing deal going on in my head with my mother. Either I was busy working hard to prove her wrong or I was ashamed because I was proving her right. Either way, she was still running the show. I was a puppet. It was just some kind of giant, residual, slimy mess that kept playing itself out all over my life—in this particular case over brownies.

For crying out loud, why did something so simple stir up all this yucky stuff? I found myself pacing the floor, crumpling her letter in my fist. Like a caged animal. Again. I was angry and struggling to make sense of it all. This nutty old kook, these letters and how deeply they affected me, spinning me off into a fresh hell over brownies, of all the stupid things. I mean, for crying out loud. There was no mention of brownies in the letter. None at all. I really did feel like an angry teenager. I felt misunderstood, lonely. I wanted my mother. And I didn't want to admit it. I wanted someone to hold me. Too bad for me. My mother was dead. I figured it was probably just as well too. She had never been the comforting, nurturing type.

Although, apparently, neither had Bea's mother. What was that quote of hers? I found it in the crumpled letter: "beat you repeatedly about the head and shoulders." Yikes. That cracked me up a little. I mean, it's funny how we don't think about old people as being anything but old people, but they were once children and they had mothers. Although it was a little tricky to imagine, I could almost see this even older version of Bea telling Bea the truth would beat her in the head. I tried it out in a little-old-lady voice, sucking on my teeth, "Well, this is the thing, sonny…" (little old grannies always said, "sonny," didn't they?) "Yep, that's right, sonny-boy, the truth's gonna set you free, but first it's gonna knock you upside the head." Real cute. Making fun of an old lady's mother. I smoothed out the letter and looked at it again.

"Start small." Well, that was pretty standard Bea advice. I guess there's no other way to do it. Start small, begin where you are. Begin again. Breathe. Tell the truth. Maybe I was beginning to get the hang of this. And then: build myself a haven. Okay, what the heck did that mean? I looked around my living room. That stain on the carpet now made me smile. Nice. But there was no place for a haven there. The kids used the whole thing to play in and mess up. I didn't think it would work. My bedroom? Maybe, but I could not see how to start small in there. I mean, it needed a complete overhaul. New bedroom set, paint, everything. It was awful, just a total mess in there. I'd never even finished unpacking some of the boxes from moving in. They were still stacked in the corner. I suspected I was keeping it that way to make sure I was never tempted to bring anyone in there, if you know what I mean. Not that I'd have really wanted to, not with the kids around. Of course, the kids weren't the real issue, but frankly, I didn't want to face the real issue at that moment. I left the bedroom in a hurry. I refused to open that messy can of worms, not right then.

I wandered back out to the living room, past the bathroom. Thought about it for like one second, but we all shared the bathroom, and well, it wasn't gonna happen. The kitchen?

Yuck. A haven in there? Between the endless dirty dishes and "What's for dinner?" whines, I didn't think so.

That left only one option: the lanai. Where I'd gone to write my first pages. I battled the sliding glass door and jiggled the screen until I got it to open. I had to get that fixed. But I didn't know how to go about it. I wondered if it was covered in my condo agreement. I doubted it. It seemed I was on my own for anything that actually broke. I was about to spin off and go look up the paperwork, write a letter to the condo board to complain, you know the drill—anything but follow the simple instruction to build myself a haven, but I caught myself and let it go. Start small. Begin where I was, busted door and everything. Okay.

The moon was rising. Or maybe it was setting; anyway, it was low in the sky up there, and I could smell just a hint of night-blooming jasmine, I didn't know from where. But it was also chilly and a little damp. So I went and got a blanket. And a pillow. And a candle I found on the way. Warm slippers. I came back out onto the little porch, cleared off the one functional chair, lit the candle and set it on the rusty barbecue, wrapped myself up in the blanket, and sat down. I fidgeted for a minute, trying to get comfortable. I was trying to figure out what to do next. And then it hit me that there was nothing to do in that moment except sit. Breathe. The night air was lovely. The moon was beautiful, floating up there. I was okay, warm enough with the blanket, comfortable enough; the candle was flickering, keeping me company. The street noise was just far enough away that I didn't have to really listen to it. No helicopters for the time being.

I wrapped the blanket really tightly around myself and held on to the pillow. Bea's letter and brownies, my mother, and even my imagined picture of Bea's old mother were swirling around my head, and I felt it again, that longing for my mother to hold me, for someone to wrap around me and make it safe for me to relax. Was I really so lonely? So sad? I did miss my mom, I guess. Though I didn't know if it was my actual mom I missed or some idea of a perfect mother who would make it all better, make me all better…whichever it was, wrapped in that blanket with the moon rising (or setting?), I wanted her.

I wanted her soft hand on my forehead. My mother had such lovely hands. But no, I wanted more than that, I wanted to curl up in her lap and have her be bigger than me and make it all better. I mean, I had this life, and it was an okay life, I guess, and I did have these (mostly) adorable kids, who somehow seemed to love me in spite of everything, and I knew I was the grown-up now, but, dammit, I wanted to be small again and not in charge of so many things. I thought when I got married to Rick that he would handle some of the things, that life would be easier. Yeah, I guess it was pretty naive. It had never gotten easier. Life had just gotten harder and harder, and there was no one, ever, to make it better.

My mother was already sick by the time we got married. She hated Rick. I could tell, but she would never come right out and say it. She probably knew it wouldn't do any good, even if she did. Her hating him would only have made me more determined to marry him. She did try to warn me a few times, but I wasn't listening. I was so mad at her—for being sick at all, for having such a horrible disease that scared me so much. I hated that she was so sick at my wedding that everyone was focused on her instead of me. It was supposed to be my day; she was supposed to be taking care of me, paying attention to me, not the other way around.

I knew that wasn't fair, but I felt it anyway. I mean, my mother took care of everybody, all the time, until the very end when her body just gave out on her. And we just expected it, that she would always do everything for us. She did it in her controlling, bossy, condescending way, and we hated it, but we counted on her. She just gave and gave and gave. And to hear her tell it, she never got anything back. We were always letting her down. Nothing was ever quite enough. So I guess we sort of tuned her out, went numb to her endless complaints. We protected ourselves by not listening. My dad just left, but my sister and I didn't have that option, so we stayed and took what she gave and became immune to the endless instructions on how to do every single thing the right way. Which was, of course, her way. I knew it was her way of loving us, of giving to us, but I couldn't stand it. It felt as if she was force-feeding me her love and wrapping it up in guilt. I gagged on it but couldn't stop taking it.

I always thought that was why she got the cancer: she just gave until there was nothing left of herself to give, so her body built those tumors to fill in the holes where she'd been giving it all away. Then when the doctors cut her breasts off to get the tumors out, she just gave up. After chemo and radiation, when she was so tired and she had nothing left to give, she still would not let herself accept anything from us, so there was really nothing left for her to do but die. End of the story. Her story. Give till it kills you.

So how could I dare sit there and be mad at her for not taking care of me on my wedding day? Or any other day, when it was her caretaking that killed her? I knew I should stop thinking like that. It didn't help. Besides, it had to be more complicated than that. You didn't get cancer from being a mother, no matter how badly you did it. The doctors said it was just a disease, an unfortunate circumstance. Maybe environment. Maybe heredity (great). Probably just dumb luck.

But some part of me didn't buy it. I was certain that that woman sacrificed herself until it killed her, and she had trained me to do the same thing. I'd been fighting it and scared of it and resigned to it and really mad about it. But somehow, I'd never questioned that to give like that, to give until there was nothing left, was the right thing; the noble thing; the mature, responsible thing. I believed it was how a mother should act, no matter how much I had hated it. It was another of the ways in which I would never measure up.

But this crazy old lady was asking me to do something completely different, and somehow, I was determined to do it. That was why I was out there in the dark; that was why I was holding that pillow. Because I hoped that, just maybe, Bea was right. There was a core of me that was mine alone, that wasn't meant to be given away, and it was so beautiful that it was worth finding, worth expressing, and maybe even worth loving. I desperately wanted it, and I was willing to do what she asked, no matter how crazy it seemed, just in case it was true. I was so sick of myself and even sicker of being sick of myself that I was willing to try it.

But weirdly, even inside my determination to challenge the rules that seemed to come from my mother, I still wanted the comfort that only she could have given. Pure and simple, I wanted my mommy. I was a mother, so I knew a little about those "magic mommy powers," which could "make it all better." What I didn't know was how long they'd last. Would Megan turn against me like I'd turned against my own mother? Would we grow into polite strangers? I prayed she would never ignore or tolerate me the way I'd ignored and tolerated my mother. Would she find herself someday sitting in the dark somewhere missing me? Wishing for just one more time in my lap? Would Justin curse me someday for trying to control him? For dying? I mean, I knew I'd die eventually, but would I have to leave them when they still needed me? Would I be able to teach them what they needed to know before I was gone? Would I be able to learn it in time?

The night was clear, and I could finally tell the moon was setting. It was much lower now. I hated that—how could the moon set when the night was so young? What would light the rest of the darkness till dawn? How dare the moon go out before its job was finished? How dare a mother leave her children when they still needed her? When I still needed her?

As the moon slipped into the marine layer and out of sight, I began to cry. Silent sobbing into the pillow. Wrapped up tight in the blanket, alone as the night grew colder and darker, I cried like the abandoned child I was inside. Cried in helpless rage against the bitter loneliness of it, for the mother I'd lost and, worse, for the mother I'd never actually had. The one I wished I could be but fell short of being so many times, in so many ways. I cried at the ugly unfairness of being left alone by my own mother, my husband, my father, by everyone—everyone except this strange letter writer. This one person who seemed to believe I was capable of something different. Capable of making up a life that was more wonderful and exciting than the one they'd all prepared me for. A life where I could be somebody beautiful, magical, and interesting. A life where I actually mattered.

The tears finally cried themselves out, and even without the moon, the night was sweet. Softer, somehow. I blew out the candle and went to bed. As I was drifting off to sleep, I could swear I felt my mother's presence there, felt her hand on my forehead. She seemed to want to tell me something, but I couldn't hold it. I slid into a deep sleep.

CHAPTER THIRTEEN
A Couple of Cans of Paint

The next morning, I found myself looking at the lanai while the kids were eating their cereal and toast. With a little elbow grease, it could be pretty nice out there. I decided to start cleaning it out in the evenings after I got home from work, just to see if I could make sense of it. It couldn't hurt.

So I went back to noticing what I thought was beautiful, this time in the context of creating a little haven for myself. My refuge, a sanctuary on my tiny balcony. It was really pretty fun. Everything was possible. I looked at colors as if they were my very own amazing discoveries. I started making notes in earnest. Bit by bit, I began to clear away the old trash. The kids helped me throw out the junk that had accumulated. They really seemed to get into the idea of Mommy having her own special place.

Well, that is, they got into it after I promised to create a special place for each of them as well. Justin was building himself a fort in the corner of the living room, and Megan was getting a "princess bed." It took me a while to figure out that she was talking about a canopy bed. I wanted her to have it, but there was no way I could have just gone and bought her one. Even at Sears, they were over two hundred dollars. So I was making it with some old flowered sheets I stapled to the ceiling around the back and sides and a sheer curtain from the thrift store across the front. I liked it for her because I was starting to wonder how long I could keep them in the same bedroom, and I really couldn't afford to move.

I found I enjoyed being "fun mommy" instead of "grumpy mommy." It was good to have a family project. Somehow, I'd forgotten that I could do projects with the kids without Rick. It had never occurred to me to take something like this on by myself. I'd always deferred to Rick in terms of what we should do. The truth is, of all the projects we'd planned to do as a family, this was the first one that was actually happening. That was something to notice. The kids and I were having fun, being creative, and they were certainly enjoying their new private spots.

And my own refuge was starting to take shape as well. I tossed the barbecue, since it was rusting through and pretty gross. I hated using it anyway. Barbecuing had been Rick's deal. I took the bikes downstairs and locked them in the garage. I had to be a lot more careful parking, but it was worth it, because we actually started using them again since they were easier to get to. I put the plastic chairs in the alley, and someone took them, even the broken ones. I was glad that someone else might be using them; it felt less wasteful than just throwing them away.

At last it was empty. I went out there with a cushion from the couch and all of my notes about beauty and thought about what I might like to have, just for myself. I decided not to worry about what I could afford, not right away at least. I just thought about what would make me happy, what would feel like Beauty to me, what my soul required for it to feel safe and gentle and loved. I thought about colors and sounds and smells. I thought about texture, about what would feel good to me.

It felt odd. I had never been any good at decorating or anything like that. But something was helping, something I'd kind of figured out from everything Bea had sent me. It was that somehow I understood that I didn't have to do it right. It didn't have to be perfect; it could just be one thing at a time. And it was just for me. I didn't have to explain or justify it to anyone. I started to have some ideas. And then I had some more, and they were contradictory, but I didn't worry about that yet. I just wrote them all down in my little orange Beauty notebook.

I told you I wasn't the creative one. That was my sister. Susan's house always looked perfect. She watched all those shows on TV, the decorator shows, the home-makeover shows. I was just happy if my place wasn't too much of a wreck. And I got very nervous about committing to things and spending money. I had been in such a panic when I tried to choose curtains for my bedroom that I finally just put some old blankets up with thumbtacks and left it at that. Pretty pathetic, I know. And then life just kept coming at me so fast, and I was so tired after work and everything, that a whole year had gone by and I had never put up anything else. So the project on the lanai was a pretty big deal. It took a while. Susan came over and saw it empty like that one day and asked me what was going on. She thought I must have had a leak or something.

"No, I'm, um, I'm actually..." I didn't know how to say it and wasn't sure I wanted to.

"Mommy's making herself a special place, just for her private time. It's a project. Like my princess bed. Wanna see my princess bed, Auntie Susan?" Megan, bless her little heart.

My sister turned to me with big eyes and this hungry expression, like I was chum. "In a minute, sweetheart. Why don't you go get it all ready, and I'll be right there." Megan raced off to prepare for her audience with Auntie Susan. She worshipped her. Whatever I was in for it now.

"You're making a what?" She was moving in for some kind of attack; I could smell it, but I didn't know what it would be exactly.

"I don't know, just a place to hang out, you know, read the paper. Whatever." I wasn't about to tell Susan about Bea, the letters, "Be Beauty," any of it. She'd never let up until she had the whole story. She'd keep at it until she'd either talked me out of the entire thing or made us both think it was her idea in the first place. I don't know how she did that, but she always did. She was just that way—like Mom was. Most of the time, I just let her tell me what to do and how to do it. And then I either did what she said, or pretended to do it at least. Sometimes, though, I just dug in my heels and did nothing at all. It was my version of a tantrum. Like the curtains in the bedroom. Susan had several kinds picked out for me. I just resisted. But this one thing I wanted all for myself. I didn't want her help or even her advice. And I didn't even care that she would probably have been right, and she probably did know better about things like this. This one was mine. All mine. And she wasn't going to get her claws in it. But I could tell she was going to try.

"That's wonderful, Gracie. You should let me help you with it. I have tons of ideas. You know I was just saying to Phil this morning that we should redo our south terrace this spring. You know, the one with the roses?"

Of course I knew. I knew every inch of her house; she'd made sure of that. Everyone in four counties knew the intimate details of the "South Terrace." It was on the local garden tour. As far as Susan was concerned, it was the entire garden tour. I nodded warily.

"Well, I was looking through this magazine the other day, and they had just the most adorable patio ideas, and, well, yours is a little smaller than the ones they were working with…" I caught the pause, the little snub. I guess she just couldn't resist. "…but we could totally modify them to fit this space…" She was walking toward the sliding door. I had to stop her before she got her hooks in it, before she took over and I was just dumbly nodding and smiling and she was doing what she loved to do: controlling everything, doing it her way. She was like a well-oiled machine, slipping into action. You had to admire it really, but I had to do something, anything, and fast. She was struggling with the door. "…You really have to get this fixed first, you know. You should get rid of it. Sliding doors are so early eighties. You could take it out and put some nice French doors—"

"Susan," I tried to pretend I was going to help with the door, but really I was trying to keep her away from it. "Susan, don't you think you should go see Megan's bed? She's waiting for you."

And she was, bless her little heart. The miniature traitor who'd spilled the beans to Auntie and nearly ruined everything was standing in the doorway, hopping from one foot to the other, waiting as patiently as she could muster at her age. Megan had appeared to save the day.

"I thought you said you were *coming*." Megan aimed it at Susan, but I knew from the sidelong look she threw at me that she believed I was keeping her beloved auntie away from the very important bed-business. If only she knew the truth. I would have given anything to get Susan on to the bed-business. Or any other business frankly. Why was it so hard to stand up to my big sister? Even on something as simple as my own lanai? Even now that we were both, theoretically, adults? I wanted to pull her hair and tell her to mind her own beeswax. To stomp my feet and yell. Real mature. Thank God for my six-year-old girl.

I finally got Susan to leave it alone by telling her I couldn't do anything without approval from the condo board (which may or may not have been true, but I had zero intention of asking them) and by promising to study her magazines for ideas. I knew it was her way of helping me, but it made me want to *scream*. I always felt helpless when she was around. Her voice was definitely one of the ones I carried in my head, mostly telling me I couldn't do anything without her. Was I ever really going to grow up?

So I took her decorator magazines—I swear she must subscribe to *all* of them, piled them behind the couch, and kept going with my little project—my way. It may not have been exactly the "start small" I think Bea must have meant, but nonetheless, it was giving me a lot of pleasure. First, I chose colors. I went back and forth between soothing greens and beiges and electrifying orange and blue. I kept thinking about my Mexican escape fantasy. I really liked the bright colors. My life seemed so dull. Everything was beige, khaki, blah. I decided to go for it. I mean, it was nobody's business anyway, right? It was just paint, and I could paint over it if I needed to, and besides, I knew my sister would never have chosen anything so unusual. I hoped it would scare her off entirely.

I went to Home Depot and spent over an hour in front of their paint colors. Finally, I just took an enormous breath and did it. I picked a deep rich orange they called "Dragon Fire" and this amazing shade of blue, "Cobalt Flame." It was a lot of fire for a sanctuary, but I thought maybe my soul was bored. I just got a quart of each; the balcony was really small, and I figured it'd be enough—and it cost less money in case I chickened out and threw both cans away. I bought brushes and a small roller, drop cloths, everything. I wanted to be ready. I knew if I had to stop for any reason, I might lose my nerve.

While I was there, I also went into the garden section and got some plants. A couple of tall ones with lots of leaves and a night-blooming jasmine that I thought would be great climbing on the railing. I knew this was tempting fate. I'd never been able to keep anything alive, not even the cactus I'd had in fourth grade, but Beauty was calling and with it the sweet smell that had come to me that night of the setting moon. I let the Home Depot lady help me with soil and fertilizer and the right kind of pot. She was very sweet, and besides, they have this great thing where if it dies, you can just bring it back. Not that I would have. I never brought anything back. I was too embarrassed, but it was nice to know I *could*. I carted the whole project home and up the stairs. Rick had the kids until six, and I didn't want to waste one minute.

But the second I got it all out on the lanai, I froze. My mind went crazy with thoughts. What was I doing? I couldn't do this by myself. These colors were ridiculous anyway. Why didn't I just go with a cream color like Susan would? Shabby chic—something normal? And I couldn't just paint it, I mean, didn't I have to prepare the surface or, I don't know what, something...?

"Take a deep breath," she'd tell me. I know she would. "Begin where you are. Write if you need to."

Write? Now? Where was that coming from? I had all this paint stuff. I'd spent all this money; the kids would be home in a few hours. I didn't have time to write anything. "Write. Tell the truth about yourself. Be brave." It was as if I could hear her voice in my head. It seemed nutty, but somehow, it was easier than picking up the paintbrush. I went and got my book and a pen.

Right there in the middle of the mess, I filled seven pages of "I am afraid that..." Turns out I was afraid of making a mess, of doing it wrong, of being wrong, of being stupid, of being ugly, that everything I did was bad and ugly, that Rick would see it and make fun of me again, that I would be humiliated because of my color choice. That I'd be kicked out on the street. It was so much; it was crazy. Just picking up a paintbrush, no, to tell the truth, not even picking it up, just thinking about picking it up brought up so much fear. It was more than fear. Some of it was downright paranoid.

Finally, after I'd written it all down, I could almost laugh at it. I mean, really, it was just paint. I was an adult. I owned this cruddy little condo, and Rick was a shithead anyway. All this stuff was leftover from other times: the kindergarten teacher using my picture to show everyone how not to draw an elephant; that pink dress I'd wanted so badly only to have the boys call me "Pepto-Bismol" for the whole next year; Rick always calling me, "white trash," and finally leaving me for Miss Manicure. All of it was from some other time and yet it had me totally stopped. I was whipped. I mean, I don't really want to admit this, but I actually cried while I was writing all this gruck.

But once it was all out on the page, something happened to it. It kind of lost its power. I was curious about what would come next, so I kept writing. I was afraid that I didn't know anything about Beauty, that I didn't have it in me, that Bea was wrong about me. I was afraid that if I were true to my own notion of beauty I'd turn out to be a weirdo, some kind of kooky hippie freak. I was afraid that if I didn't keep telling myself I was ugly before anyone else could do it, I'd be shamed and humiliated. That if I stood proud in myself, I'd be a target. That men would hurt me, or at least laugh at me like my daddy did when I told him I wanted to be Miss America. I couldn't bear that ever again. Awful and true (though I hated to admit it), but kind of out of left field, right?

And then came the really weird stuff: "I'm afraid that if I really thought I was beautiful, I would be different. I would walk differently, act differently than I do now. I wouldn't put up with anyone being mean to me. I'd be powerful. Men would want me, and I'd ignore them. Everyone would want me, but no one would like me. I'd be stuck-up. I'd be mean..." On and on and on it went like that.

Where the heck was all this crap coming from? It was as if I was just afraid of everything, all over the place. Afraid of doing it wrong, but then also afraid of doing it right. I was afraid of being ugly and afraid of being beautiful. Afraid of being powerless and, at the exact same time, afraid of being powerful. Most of it didn't have anything to do with painting a porch. I was glad I had done this kind of writing before, so I had some idea that I wasn't just going nuts. And it didn't matter that my free time was going by, because if all that stuff was sitting underneath my being able to even pick up a paintbrush, I guessed I might as well get at it. I mean, who knew what else it was keeping me from…

Finally, it felt like I had gotten it all out. For the time being, at least. All those wacky forward and backward fears—at last, there was a lull in the staccato race of words and then a pause. A quiet minute and then it appeared. The question. The question it seemed I'd been longing to answer all of my life. It seemed to write itself on the paper.

"Who would you be free to be if you weren't afraid?"

Wow. Where did that come from? Not afraid? Of any of it? Of doing it right or wrong or any of it at all? Who would I be free to be? The pen was flying now. "I'd be free to paint anything any color I wanted. I'd be free to be happy. I'd be free to be playful, to be wrong, to make mistakes. I'd be free to wear clothes that suited me, to smile at strangers and flirt with men. I'd be free to say yes. I'd be free to say no. I'd be free to eat what I want, to do art if I want, to stand up to my sister. I'd be free…" and it went on and on and on. Finally, one last thing: "I'd be free to Be Beauty in the world. To be exactly myself and not care what anyone said or thought about it. I would be free to love myself and everyone else. I'd be free to *be*. And that's Beautiful. To be exactly me."

And I got it, at last. What it was she'd been talking about in her cryptic way. It was all about being exactly who I was, doing exactly what I chose to do, in the way that I found most lovely. That pleased me, because it seemed like all the things I did, for any reason other than because they felt beautiful and right to me, were done out of fear. I was afraid of everything. I was afraid of orange and blue, and yet look at me—I chose them, "Dragon Fire" and "Cobalt Flame." To burn away the fears and leave me free to be my beautiful self—at least in this spot. This would be my sanctuary. And if it was too scary to take into the world (I could already feel my shoulders scrunching up a little at the thought of how my sister might react to this new idea), I didn't have to. This could simply be where I began. Right here on this little porch. It was quite a notion. That I might be free to exist without all these fears. Bea always said, "Be gentle; start small; begin where you are." I didn't want to start small; I wanted to rip forward, burn everything that kept me afraid, tear through it all, but somehow, I knew that today, just painting in blue and orange would be plenty.

That it was actually quite a lot. I pried open the cans and stirred the alarmingly bright colors.

I had pretty much planned to paint the stucco walls with the orange and the concrete floor with the blue. I figured it would rub off the floor, but I thought it would look, I don't know, "weathered." So I started there. Walls orange. Even I could figure out not to do the floor first. I dipped my brush in the fiery paint. And I knew I should paint the corners first, work my way outward, and use the roller, being very careful and worrying about "coverage." But I didn't want to do it like that. It was my wall. It was my sanctuary, and I didn't want to do it "right." I wanted to do it my way. I had a loaded paintbrush, and I wasn't afraid to use it. I put a streak right down the middle of the wall. It was shocking, like a gash. I painted it into a flame. Well, my version of a flame. A flame-like streak-thing. And I made swirls coming out of it. Fireballs. Starry Night meets kindergarten fleur-de-lis. Or something like that. I liked the way it wasn't smooth, how some of the old beige stucco was showing through. I swirled and flamed and rubbed it off here and there, and I liked it.

Then I took the blue and made some swirls with that as well. Added some little flourishes. Some splats. It was getting all over me: my hands, my jeans, my hair. Orange and cobalt and the kind of dirty brown they made when they mixed too much. But it was pretty warm out, they were drying fast, so not too much dirty brown, and I was having a blast. It was mine to do, mine to mess up, mine, mine, mine. I did both side walls. They were mostly orange, swirls and flames with the blue as accent. I painted blue around the door, blue railings. The floor was last; I rolled it out with the blue and stood back. Yikes. I wasn't sure what I'd done. It was getting dark. Rick would be bringing the kids home any minute. I closed the door and pulled the blinds over it. I guess I'd just have to see it in the morning. I cleaned up the mess as best I could and got in the shower.

The water rolled over me, and I found myself looking at my paint-crusted hands. The paint was sticking pretty good around the cuticles; the spatters seemed embedded in the hairs on my arms. Orange bits, blue bits—emblems of this amazing new possibility I'd stumbled on. What if none of those things I'd been writing out, none of those fears that kept me stuck in place were real at all? What if they were just the "story" of my life, the inner conversation I entertained myself with and used to keep myself from risking anything? Sure, I believed a lot of that stuff. But if none of it was the truth about me, about who I was or what I could and couldn't do in any moment, then that question was really, truly, enormously…I didn't even have the word for it. Just the question, over and over again: "Who would I be free to be if I wasn't afraid? If none of that garbage was true?" Because maybe it wasn't.

What if I just used all of it to keep myself stuck? I mean, just maybe I wasn't even really afraid of any of those things. They had all happened in the past, if they had ever actually happened at all. A lot of them had never really happened at all. I was just afraid they would. And I'd survived all of them—the few that did happen at least. I mean, there I was in the shower with all this paint on me, and two hours earlier, I'd been so afraid I couldn't even open the cans of paint. I was living proof.

I felt very alive in that moment with the water spraying me, feeling the slight breeze from the open window. Everything was very specific. I could feel each drop of water, really smell the fresh, cool evening air. The slippery soap was delightful, the way it allowed my fingers to slide over the little droplets of paint on my arms, like brilliant raised freckles. I didn't want to wash it off. Maybe I just wouldn't. Besides, it was kind of stuck. In the end, I did scrub most of it off, but I "accidentally" left some around my cuticles. I didn't know why. I just kind of liked the way it looked. The way it made me feel. Unusual. Different. Special. After all, it was my body. It was nobody's business.

CHAPTER FOURTEEN

My Haven

In the morning light, my little creation was...well, different. But I liked it. The colors were very intense, but not too bright after all. When I brought out the plants and put them against the walls, it really was pretty cool. Tropical. Not like anything else in my life. It made me want to keep going with it. To really make it special. What more did I want? A really comfortable chair, yes, and some candles. A lot of candles. Maybe some kind of other lights too. Little sparkly Christmas lights? And what about a fountain? Could I get myself a fountain? Why not? It was my place.

It became a scavenger hunt. I took the kids on an adventure to Chinatown. Treats for them and me: rice candy, those wonderful greasy sesame balls, paper lanterns, bamboo, a little fountain for the corner, a bead curtain. I was going all out. I found a huge old wicker chair at the Goodwill and painted it blue. I got a cheap rug from a guy who had them spread out on a construction fence on Venice Boulevard. Fake sheepskin—fluffy for my feet and easy to bring in if it rained, but it almost never rained. Big, comfy pillows for the chair. A little trunk to keep my journals and papers in and to put candles on. It took a couple of weeks, but it was coming together.

The kids were really going for it as well. Justin's fort was now made out of a refrigerator box we'd gotten from the local appliance shop. He'd used my leftover paint on it, and it had become quite a thing of...well, it was definitely an eye-catcher. Megan was putting pictures of princesses all around her bed and was forever draping and redraping the Mardi Gras beads she'd gotten on our Chinatown adventure. Mostly Justin was okay with having her girly stuff in their room—unless she ventured too far into his "territory." I'd never realized how creative they were or how much delight they would take in claiming their "space." I guess I'd always been so busy trying to make them clean up their "messes" so the place would be acceptable (to my sister, I suppose, or the ghost of my mother) that I'd never really allowed them to express themselves. I had to admit it was way more fun this way, creating with them rather than fighting them all the time.

Come to think of it, I enjoyed my kids a lot more these days. And they didn't seem to squabble so much. Everyone was happier now that we each had our sanctuaries to work on. Bea may or may not have had kids of her own; she certainly hadn't written any specific child-rearing advice, but it was amazing the transformation around our home. Be Beauty. Make a haven for your soul. And invite your kids to do the same. Maybe that was part of what she meant about being a salvation for the world, or however she said it. I mean, what was I doing but teaching my own kids by example how to Be Beauty in their own lives? I sure hadn't been taught that.

My mother never took a minute for herself, let alone carved out a place of her own. I mean, the whole house was her domain, and she wanted it just so, but I never ever got the sense that that was for any other reason than to look good in case company came over or the neighbors or maybe just to make her feel everything was under control. Nothing was out of place. The world may have been falling apart, but the house was impeccable. But it was never any kind of joy. It was work, pure and simple. Especially after my father left and we moved to Culver City. No more Blanca. We couldn't afford a maid. Weekends were "clean the house" days. Laundry, scrubbing toilets, vacuuming, mopping, everything. And then it was all about keeping it perfect all week. Living on tiptoes.

So I had been doing what I was taught: keeping the house clean, looking good Well, I'd been trying to anyway. The trouble was I was kind of a slob. I hated housework. So I just was a little disgusted with myself most of the time and got mad at the kids for making it worse and madder at myself for yelling at them, and while it wasn't always completely awful, you can pretty much see how it went. But now that we were creating havens, things didn't seem to get quite so out of control. Justin was keeping his fort the way he liked it, and the toys, for the most part, stayed inside of it. Megan was constantly improving her little princess suite, and I was very careful to keep my little haven clean and restful. I noticed that keeping it tidy was easy...well, easier. Okay, it was at least more rewarding. I was doing it for my sake, so that I could enjoy it, not out of some obligation to the tyrant in my head.

My haven. Early mornings, I had taken to getting up before the kids so I could have some time out there. And late nights, after they were in bed, after I finished the dishes and all the other chores, I would find myself out there with a candle, with the jasmine blooming. Yes, I'd actually managed to keep it alive, and it was blooming on the railing. I'd sit and breathe and listen to the night. I found I preferred to be out there instead of even watching TV. I'd squish down in my chair, wrap up in my soft blanket, and drink a cup of chamomile tea. Sometimes I'd read, but mostly, I'd just sit. I'd think about the day, or I'd think about what I might want to do next, or I'd think about Beauty...I'd make some notes in my journal or I wouldn't. It was a nice time. It lasted about three weeks. Then I got distracted.

CHAPTER FIFTEEN

Free Fall

I met him at a party. A friend of my sister's was having this little get-together. It had seemed like a nice idea when she invited me. After all, I didn't get out much. But when the day came, it was almost more than I could manage. Rick, in one of his famous last-minute maneuvers, had backed out of taking the kids for the weekend. An unexpected business trip. Sure. Whatever. He was notorious. And it was never on a weekend when I had nothing planned. So I had the kids. And they were cranky. It was hot. I was going to bag the whole thing, but I was sick and tired of being a flake because Rick had let me down. I called to ask. My sister's friend Rachel said to go ahead and bring the kids, it would be "lovely." She was English. They talk like that. Also she has no kids, or she'd have known that there would be nothing lovely about a couple of bored kids at a grown-up party.

I knew it might be a disaster, but I really wanted to get out of the house. And I had said we would come, so we piled in the car for what should have been a quick trip down to Redondo Beach. Now I'm sure if you aren't from LA, you probably think taking the kids to a party in Redondo Beach on a hot, smoggy Saturday afternoon in August would be a treat. First of all, you'd think it was, well, on a beach. But Redondo, though it did technically have a small stretch of beach near the refinery, was one of what we call the "Beach Cities," where the roads are steep, windy, and confusing and where what were once quaint cottages are now giant monstrosities built right on top of one another with no yards at all. There's extremely limited parking, and the actual beach can be miles away. But that's not the worst of it. To get there, you had to drive the 405 freeway. I heard once that the 405 in Los Angeles/Orange County was the most congested freeway in the country. Quite possibly the whole world. And it is. But you'd probably think—well, this is what I thought, at least—it's Saturday afternoon, no problem. Just take a look at the Thomas guide, hop on the freeway, get to the party, piece of cake. Yeah.

An hour and fifteen minutes later, after the road construction and the SigAlert—Los Angelese for "big ugly traffic mess"—after we'd found the address, after we'd then found a parking place only three blocks (and two hills) away, we staggered into the party. Justin already wanted to know when we could leave, and I wanted a drink.

Honestly, I wanted several drinks, but I wasn't going down that road, not at three in the afternoon, not with kids in the car. So I settled for one glass of nice cold white wine once I knew the kids were more or less all right. They were torturing Rachel's cat, I think, but not making too much noise about it. My sister wasn't even there after all (it figured), so I only knew Rachel barely and not another soul. But I managed. I was talking to Rachel's current boyfriend. He was a nice guy, droll, you know? Funny in that sort of my-life-is-ridiculously-worse-than-your-life kind of way. We were laughing about our stupid jobs, and the wine was starting to work its magic. Sometimes, I really think I should drink more. Actually, I only ever think that at the party where I'm drinking. The next day, it no longer seems like such a good idea. Still, it was a nice way to relax after the drive, and I was laughing and thinking he was sort of cute, which was okay because he was Rachel's boyfriend and therefore totally off-limits and safe, when this man very pointedly sat down next to me.

I'd seen him when I walked in to the party—he was not the kind of man you wouldn't notice—but I hadn't paid too much attention. My first thought was to get the kids settled, and my second thought was to get that glass of wine. I know you're probably thinking I'm some kind of a lush. Really, I'm not; it's just the kind of day it was.

But this guy was so handsome, in that arrogant, polished kind of way. He was the kind of man I knew better than to fall for, the kind who wouldn't be interested in a single mom with two kids, the kind with a trail of broken hearts behind him. In short, the kind I liked best. So I (wisely, I thought) ignored him and went for the cold wine and chatting with the nice, safely off-limits boyfriend of the host. But suddenly there he was sitting right next to me. Waiting until I spoke to him. So close I could almost feel the warmth of his body, and it had been a long time since any man had been sitting that close to me on purpose. I could smell his cologne. I wasn't wearing any. I hadn't even thought to put any on.

I tried not to be self-conscious, tried, in fact, to be completely disinterested, but I was acutely aware of him. And myself. Not certain why he'd be sitting next to me. But maybe it wasn't so weird really. Even I could tell I was more attractive since I'd started being a little more relaxed and happy. And I was wearing my favorite dress. It suited my figure, and the blue set off my eyes. But I wasn't wearing it to attract a man. In the beginning of the whole "Be Beauty" experiment, I'd thrown away almost all of my clothes. I'd only kept those things I absolutely loved. And I'd been careful since to only buy things that I felt really suited me, no matter what anyone else thought of them. So I was only able to wear clothes I loved, and since this was a party, I had felt like dressing up—a bit, at least. I'm sure

I was a little wilted by then, but I knew I'd looked pretty good when I walked out the door. It still didn't make a lot of sense, though. I mean, this guy was really good-looking, you know? A ladies' man. And I know he had to have noticed that I came in with two kids, obviously mine, and even though I hadn't been on many dates since I got divorced (okay, three. In a year and a half. Three first dates, no second dates, okay? Any other questions?) I had already learned that a woman with two small kids was not what most men were into, not the interesting ones anyway. Sure, the ones with three or four kids of their own, who just wanted a new mom for their brood were, but I really wasn't into taking that on. So all of that was going through my head as I was trying to be nonchalant and listen to Rachel's boyfriend's next story and trying to hold my wine glass in just the right, "It's no big deal; I go to parties and drink wine all the time" kind of way, when of course, I went to take a drink, missed my mouth, and dribbled wine down the front of my dress. Great. Just great.

Maybe he hadn't noticed. Of course, he noticed. Okay, I told myself, just try not to panic. Simply put the glass down and get a napkin. Where's a napkin? Why wasn't there a napkin? Okay, breathe. Don't act flustered. Act normal. Well, no, don't act too normal, then he'd think I spilled wine on myself all the time, that I was some kind of special ed case. Okay then, just act somewhat normal. Just don't cry, please. Make a joke about it. Yeah, that's it. I'd think of something funny…in this lifetime…it was coming…I'd just…

"Having one of those days?" Mr. Gorgeous was smiling at me, holding out a napkin. Where did he get that? Maybe he carried them around in case just this sort of thing happened. Maybe he was used to it happening. Perhaps women spilled wine on themselves whenever he was in the room. So often that he thought it was normal. That was probably it.

"Yeah. Can you tell?" I took the napkin and patted my bosom self-consciously.

"Only a little. I'm Steve. And you are?"

"Grace." I noticed his eyebrow inch up the tiniest bit. "I know. Probably wishful thinking on my mother's part." He laughed.

"Well, Grace, it's extremely nice to meet you."

So that was how it started. How it went from there was sort of a blur. He picked me up for lunch in his convertible; we talked on the phone. I asked my sister to watch the kids while we went to dinner and a movie. He was always brilliant and clever; I was usually clumsy and tongue-tied. He was charming with the kids; they were suspicious of him. I had a permanent case of butterflies in my stomach. There were e-mails, lots of e-mails.

And then there was the kissing.

I thought I'd forgotten how to kiss. I know I'd forgotten how much I liked it. Steve made kissing a sacrament. Well, that's what it felt like to me anyway. I could have happily kissed him for a month—nothing else, just that electric, exquisite dance of lips and breath and tongue and fingertips on faces and...well, you get the picture. Or maybe you don't. Kissing Steve was like nothing I'd ever done. Nothing I could remember at least—not that I could remember anything much whenever he was around. If it could've stayed at the kissing, I think I'd have been saying I was in love. I'm not certain I wasn't. But it didn't stay at the kissing. And that's where it started to fall apart.

I don't want to bore you with the details. I can't even whine about it being a train wreck or that I didn't see it coming. I did. He had mentioned her right away—more than once, I might add. His ex. Not wife, just girlfriend. He'd never been married, of course. She was the one who'd left *him*. The only one who'd ever left first. The girl who had his heart, the one who'd made him laugh, feel alive. The one I wasn't. I figured: who was I to complain? I was still pretty wrecked over my divorce, maybe we could commiserate, help each other through it. I even thought it meant we had more in common. He mentioned her less after we started the kissing, and when it moved beyond kissing, one night when the kids were at Rick's, after a candlelit dinner at his apartment, well, I thought I was ready.

But he wasn't. I guess he was still hung up on her or maybe too tired or maybe it was the wine. Or maybe these things just happen sometimes. I didn't know exactly; I'd never encountered it before. Rick may not have been the most considerate of lovers, but he was always, well, up for it. But I'd read enough articles in the women's magazines to know it was an awkward, difficult experience for him and not to make too big a deal out of it. I mean it wasn't like we couldn't try again. In a month or so. Whenever I could get another night free. Whatever. I hadn't been with anyone but Rick in ten years. I guessed it could wait a while longer. I might not even have known what to do with someone new anyway. But still.

I was disappointed, but it probably would have been fine if he hadn't gotten all weird and defensive. Telling me how it had never happened before, how maybe he had a stomachache...my perfume gave him a headache...maybe the salmon...etc., etc. And although he didn't exactly say it outright, it was sitting there all the time. *This* had never happened with *her*. That was the real message. I got it loud and clear. I got dressed and drove home. He didn't see me out.

And when he stopped calling, I added some more to the story about why he didn't want me. Details of my own. Specific ways I was sure I was not as good as her. Particularly my body—I had lumpy thighs, saggy breasts, a belly. I even became self-conscious about parts of me I'd never much thought about until they started putting those ads in the *LA Weekly* about the surgeries you could now have done to "rejuvenate" them. Apparently, there were things wrong with me I had never imagined. Never even considered. But those ads were popping up everywhere. I wondered if that was the real reason Rick had left me: maybe I was grotesque. Maybe after two kids, I was no longer giving him pleasure. Maybe I needed one of those surgeries. And while I was at it, maybe I needed a Brazilian wax (I was not sure exactly what that was, but I was pretty sure it would hurt), a boob job, a personal trainer, and I thought I'd better throw in a face lift and some Botox just for good measure. It probably would have cost the entire equity in the condo. But I figured I could get a loan. My sister would help. I was seriously considering it. I wasn't that old, but I'd had two kids. Not small kids either. Bowling balls. I mean, maybe I was disgusting down there. Everywhere. Maybe I grossed men out.

I found myself wanting to buy a porno magazine, just to see what I was supposed to look like. So the next day, believe it or not, I actually did it. I just walked into a 7-Eleven and bought one on the way home from work before I picked up the kids. It was a huge mistake. For one thing, I could have died of embarrassment when the kid behind the counter asked me if I wanted anything else with this sleazy "I know what you need" look. For another, I had to get rid of it after, where no one could see it. But the worst was in the middle. Where I looked at it. After the kids were asleep. In the bathroom with the door locked. Then I was certain no man would ever want me. Now I knew what they did in those surgeries. I kept looking at the pictures, looking in the mirror, trying to make sense of it all. I'll spare you the specifics, but let's just say I didn't look like those girls. I mean, the basic parts were in the same places, but well, you know: Porsche versus minivan. Heck, Mack truck. I wrapped the magazine in a brown bag, took it to the kitchen garbage, and dumped a whole pan of leftover Costco lasagna on top of it, just to make sure no one would fish it out. Okay, to make sure I wouldn't fish it out. Then I made a pan of brownies from a mix I had been saving for a special occasion and sat on the couch watching the FOX 10:00 rape, murder, and gang war news and ate the whole thing.

I'm not kidding. I ate the entire pan. I hated myself every bite, and I did it anyway. Maybe I could just get so fat and so disgusting that the whole issue would never come up again. Maybe I could just keep my mouth full of sugar and chocolate and forever wipe away the memories of kissing from my lips. Maybe I could fill the empty hole inside me once and for all.

The hole that was so big, so stretched out, and not from the kids—from the empty aloneness of it all. I couldn't even cry.

After the news, I went back into the bathroom, stood in front of the mirror, under the ugly green light and picked at every pimple I could. Every tiny clogged pore. Nothing was safe. I kept at it. I finally went to bed without even brushing my teeth, just for spite. Because so what anyway? Maybe they'd all fall out. Maybe I'd get oral cancer and die. Maybe I should take up smoking. Drinking. Crack. Why not? I mean, who'd care? I was disgusting and ruined and saggy, and I was going to have to sell my home to get myself fixed up, so we'd wind up on the street, and then I'd be a tight, firm, smooth, hairless, buxom bag lady with two kids. No, I wouldn't even have the kids. My sister would take the kids. She'd go to court and declare me unfit. I would be. I could just see myself, standing on an off-ramp with a cardboard sign: "Will work for plastic surgery." Yeah. I knew what kind of work. That was obvious. In the *Weekly*, the ads in the front were all for the plastic surgeons, and in the back, they were all for hookers. Paying it off. I felt really sick. And not only from the brownies. I tossed and turned all night.

More and more days passed. Weeks. Summer was long over. My thirty-fifth birthday came and went. I told Susan I had a date, just so she'd take the kids and I could stay home and cry. Steve didn't even call. After all the torture I was putting myself through over that son of a bitch, I'd still hoped he would. If he would have just called and wanted to see me, I thought that would fix it. How messed up was that? But I didn't expect him to. I knew why he didn't. It was because I was the grossest thing since moldy bread. Maybe because the whole thing hurt so much or maybe I finally just got angry, but I swore off all men. I decided they were shitheads, shallow scumbags who just wanted to bone perfectly groomed nineteen-year-olds. Steve was just like Rick, just like all the rest of them. I didn't know who to hate more, them or me. I was disgusting, pathetic, old, and of no interest to anyone. I might as well join the convent. Or eat my way to oblivion.

So much for "Be Beauty." I had taken a headlong tumble down the backside of that hill. My "sanctuary" languished. Plants turned brown, the fountain dried up, the rug got dirty. I never had fixed that sliding door, and it was just too much trouble to even open it. I watched TV at night and slept in until the last possible minute in the mornings. The kids bickered. So much for my lovely life.

I felt like I was letting Bea down, and that made me mad at her. Meddling old cow. It was ridiculous. I was letting myself down, further and further. And I still hadn't heard from her. Maybe she was dead. Maybe she somehow knew how far I'd sunk and had given up on me. Good. I never asked for this. Any of it. I told myself I had been doing just fine until she came along. Yeah. Sure. I was doing fine then. Just like now. But at least before, it had just seemed normal. There was no shining possibility to make it seem so horrid by comparison. Thanks a lot, Bea—for nothing. I was pretty pissed off about it all. Besides, I'd gotten rid of all my fat clothes, and it wouldn't be long before I'd have nothing at all to wear. Great. Just fucking great.

Finally, I was so miserable, I couldn't take it anymore. I didn't know what else to do. Fast, before I could change my mind, I wrote a single word on a plain white postcard and mailed it to the address in Albuquerque. One word: "Help."

CHAPTER SIXTEEN

Stumbling Stone

Dear Grace,

Do you think that because you have failed somewhere, or even many, many somewheres, that you are a failure? That nothing you have is of any worth, that you will fail always and everywhere? Is it enough to make you consider giving up? Do not resist your perfection simply because you know all too well your wretchedness, your failings. Yes, you are wretched, of course you are. And yes, yes, you stumble again and again over the same stone in your path. You know the one. You know exactly. Yes, that one. That same rock wearing a new name, a new suit. That one. No? Look closely. Recognize it? Did you perhaps notice yourself dropping it there so you could stumble over it? No? Pay closer attention. This is the nature of it all. This is being human. This is how we grow.

Did you think that one day you would be finished being yourself? Think that you would be done learning your specific lessons? That one day you would wake up and get out of bed and be someone other? That you would be "all better?" What if you are never to be cured of this being Grace-like-that? What if these lessons you are learning, these stones you keep dropping in your path, are actually so perfect for you that they will be with you an entire lifetime? Could you own them? Play with me for a moment. Experiment. You can choose later. Can you make friends with your lessons and stop resisting them? Could you refrain from kicking the stone? Would you, if you knew that to fight it merely wedges it deeper into your path? Resistance merely causes more pain.

What if the stone was not your enemy, but your true and beloved teacher? Consider that it is your kick causing the pain, not the nature of the stone. It is simply your stone, placed there by you yourself so that you could experience it. No matter what or who the stone is wearing today, it is simply your same old stone, your dear friend. Could you find the willingness, today, for the merest second, even in the midst of your agony, your broken-footedness, to stop for an instant and sit with this old stone? To rest against it without rancor? To greet it as your old friend, your teacher? Yes, here you are. Again. Now.

Just for a moment, and today, if you can, will you pick up the stone and hold it to your heart? Look closely; study it without knowing what you will find. It is the same, and yet perhaps, like you, it is evolving, slowly shifting. Those pathways, those contours, some are becoming more deeply etched and some, perhaps, filling in with disuse. A few new cracks appear, some new wrinkles, but it's still the same stone. No judgments. Just look for a moment. Carry it with you before you toss it back—maybe further out, maybe not. Go ahead and put it down before it becomes too much. It will be there next time, as long as you need it.

Yes, next time. You will come again and again to this place. This place where the only thing you can do is take the next breath, and the one after, and even that will seem like too much. Many times, you will return to the breath, to the page, to the dance, lugging this old, heavy rock. Many times will you return to this weight. You will begin to give voice to its particular texture, its scraping roughness, its unbreachable darkness. Good. It is your teacher in this time. Come to know it. Cease to resist it.

When you no longer resist, it seems lighter. Perhaps it is lighter or perhaps it is that you are stronger. You may even find it begins to soften. Or you do. It doesn't matter which, and though it may never go, it can become your guide, your signpost. You can use it to notice where you are on your journey, on your particular path. When it becomes too heavy, perhaps you will throw it down to block a way you are no longer willing to go. You will see it there, and know: Ah yes, I know you, old friend. I will choose otherwise. A new lesson, a new opportunity. Your stone itself, once you truly recognize it, will guide you into new territory, if only by marking the old.

There is no right way to do this. There is no deadline. You are not engaged in this life merely to finish it. As long as there is breath to draw, you won't be finished. Every time you reach a destination, another appears, just beyond the horizon. There is no arriving, only traveling.

Yet do not think there is no urgency. This moment is an urgent and important matter. This precious moment is all you have. This one and then it is gone to the next. If you fall into the seductive trap of resisting yourself, rejecting this moment, this experience, or this feeling because they are not the "right" ones, because you are in your own suffering skin at this moment, because you are not someone else, then you are wasting precious moments of your exquisite and only life.

This precious moment may be the one where you have discovered yourself sprawled flat on your face with that damned rock leering at you. Do not resist. Do not dramatize it. Do not think you could have or should have known better. And do not for a second think it is a different rock or someone else's doing. Pick it up and bring it close. Brush off the caked mud and residue of the specific details and discover that, yes, it is your stone. You see, there? Those contours, that history? This is your own perfect stumbling stone; this is where you get to begin again; this is where you learn compassion. This rock is how you find your way home. This rock is your key to love; without it, you will have no access to your heart or anyone else's. This is your key to the cave.

—B

* * *

The letter was postmarked Miami. It arrived two days after I'd sent the postcard. She must have already mailed it to me—maybe even on the same day I'd written for help. How did she do that? I read it on my porch, in my dusty and unused sanctuary, with the morning sun on my legs. On my frighteningly white legs: unshaved, unloved, peeking out from the bathrobe, dying for some affection; like the rest of my neglected body. I felt stubborn and spiteful, unwilling to believe what she had said. This was not a rock; this was a...what? A disaster. Just when I was doing so much better, I'd let myself fall for a man. Then he'd dumped me because I wasn't sexy enough for him. Period. And that made him a shit and me pathetic, end of story. Rock, schmock. That woman was off her rock-er. Ha. Even my jokes were pathetic.

I heard the kids getting up. Running for the television, fighting over which cartoons to watch. Saturday. Another Saturday. It was already the middle of October. Time was racing past, and I hadn't even been paying attention. I'd been lost in my constant internal litany of how disgusting I was, alternating with a few outspoken rampages about how shallow men were and how hard it was to live in a town where all the beautiful people had been coming for a hundred years and breeding, and now their gorgeous daughters and granddaughters with their perfect tans and their perfect Porsches and their perfect, augmented bodies were running around ruining it for the rest of us. Add the occasional rant about the impossible beauty ideal/plastic surgery/women's magazines...Anyone would have thought I'd become a raving feminist. It was a smoke screen.

I was just another bitter, jilted woman. And I was jealous. I hated the beautiful ones because I wanted to be them. It was awful. I had started to alienate people. My sister didn't return my phone calls. I was really miserable and determined to stay that way.

But I was absolutely certain I was right about it. This stupid town was so plastic. I'd never wanted to come here anyway. My dad had gotten a job with McDonnell Douglas here when I was eight, and so we moved. It was the beginning of the end of my parents' marriage. We'd settled into this big new house in Beverly Hills. Joined the country club. We had left this sweet neighborhood in Dayton, Ohio, where I rode bikes with the kids and played kick the can and king of the hill in the vacant lots, where I skinned my knees and made tree forts and played with my best friend, Renee, until dark, and didn't even own a dress, to a house with a gardener and these heavy, horrible curtains and white carpet you were afraid to even walk on and a country club with kids who had everything they never wanted, so they just hung around and smoked pot and made out in the bushes.

My mother went a little insane then. She was determined to fit in, so she tried her best to out–country club the country-clubbers. She wore these fussy little dresses and got manicures, and we had a maid, but we weren't allowed in most parts of our own house so we wouldn't make a mess. We had to wear stupid scratchy clothes and not wreck them by riding bikes or whatever, and I didn't know it at the time, but we were going deeply into debt to keep up these appearances. My big sister was fine. She was cute and funny and didn't like to ride bikes anyway. She made friends with the right girls and talked about the right things, and they had a great time torturing me. I was alternately their pet, the one they dressed up and made do little shows with them, and the outcast scapegoat who took the heat for everything.

One day, I really needed to hide from them. I knew they had cooked up something for me to do, and that it would get me in big trouble. I could tell from the fake sweet way they were calling me. I found myself in the kitchen with Blanca. She barely spoke any English, but she could tell I was in mortal danger. She took pity on me and let me hide in the pantry, and when my sister and her friends came in, all innocent, looking for me, she shooed them out with a torrent of incomprehensible Spanish and a ferocious waving of the arms. She was my hero. I started spending all my time in the kitchen with Blanca. She took pity on me, taught me *un poquito de español* and, best of all, fed me lots of treats. We made cookies and, yes, brownies and even that amazing *pastel de tres leches*, which is like the richest cake ever invented. I felt safe with Blanca, and when the fighting began, I imagined going home with her when she left in the evenings. I didn't know where she lived, only that it was a long way on the bus, but I was sure that no matter where it was, it was better than my house. I started asking her to adopt me, take me into her family, or even back to Mexico someday. She always smiled and pushed the straggly hair out of my eyes. Called me *mija* and told me that someday, I would certainly visit the beautiful floating gardens of Xochimilco, but for now, God had given me the job of taking care of my family. She told me how they would suffer if I left them. I didn't believe her. But it helped, somehow.

Later, after the money was gone and my father was gone and Blanca was gone and finally even the house was gone, I would take out a picture book Blanca had given me of the sights of Mexico City and stare at the amazing flowers of Xochimilco, the little boats full of orchids and smiling brown people and imagine finding her there, in a little cottage full of flowers making brownies and cake and letting me stay forever.

Blanca. I hadn't thought of her in years. I wondered what had happened to her. Did she ever think about me? Did she wonder what became of the frightened little fat kid who lived in the too-big house? The girl from Ohio who had no idea why she was suddenly in Beverly Hills, and still, even all these years later, had never figured it out? Another Los Angeles minidrama. She'd probably forgotten all about me. About that short time so long ago. I'm sure she had her own problems to deal with. Lots of them.

The sun was getting hot; the kids were rottimg their brains out with television; and there were a million things to do, but I wanted to sit out a while longer. I never thought about the Beverly Hills time if I could help it. Though for my mother and my sister, it had been some kind of Golden Era, which they had loved to relive in detail. The good days.

Afterward, we moved to the house in Culver City, a small bungalow, sort of vaguely Spanish, with dark wood floors and dark wood trim around the windows, and my mother tried to recreate the feel of the big house as much as she could. She made it as formal as possible, just in case her country-club friends came to visit. They never did, of course. But the house was ready, just in case. We had a gardener, but no maid. I was the new maid. My sister was too popular. My mother was too upset. I was the one scrubbing the house to perfection for the guests that never came.

My dad left McDonnell Douglas and took a job with Boeing in Seattle. My mother said she wouldn't go to that dreary, rainy city, so he went without us. I figured he didn't want us anymore. There were lawyers and papers, and my mother's eyes were red. There was always a bottle by her bed, and he was gone and that was that. We'd see him when he passed through LA. I'd loved my daddy, but something in me closed up tight after that. His wife still sent Christmas cards and gifts to me and the kids, but we never made much effort to see him.

By the time he left, the treats with Blanca had taken their toll. I was what my mother tactfully called "chunky." My sister was "blossoming," and I was "chunky." Chunky and bucktoothed. Chunky and buck-toothed and very alone. My mother, in her infinite "wisdom," had made the schools skip me up a grade so my sister and I could be in middle school together. I think she just didn't want to have to bother with two different schools, schedules, buses, everything. Never mind that I would have to work twice as hard to do half as well. Since I was a girl, it didn't really matter about my grades as long as they weren't too embarrassingly bad. Never mind that I would never catch up, ever. It wasn't convenient. So I missed fifth and went into sixth.

A new school and a new neighborhood, but I was still the scapegoat of my sister who had made it her mission in life to be one of the popular girls. I was an embarrassment to her, a liability, and since she couldn't make me go away, she had to find a way to distance herself from me as much as possible. So she became the leader of the "Pick-On-Grace Society." Actually, they didn't have a name, at least not one I knew of, but that's what I called them because it was what they spent most of their time doing. POGS, I called them for short. I spent most of that year hiding from the POGS.

POGS. You know, that's actually kind of cute. That I had a name for them. My one friend—another outcast named

Heather—and I called them that. "POG alert!" we'd announce when they were coming. We had an alert/warning noise: "Ehng, ehng, ehng, ehng," that we'd adapted from submarine movies and the Emergency Broadcast System. My sister really hated us then; we were so "immature." Well, of course we were. We were just kids. I was ten years old. Duh. I liked remembering something fun for a change: hiding from the POGS, racing around the neighborhood on our bikes. Bikes were okay again, now that all of our fancy clothes were outgrown. It didn't matter to me that I was fat, as long as I could stay out and play until dark and my mom left me alone about it.

Dammit, Bea. What did any of this have to do with rocks? Stumbling over the same rock. That was what she'd written, that it was the same rock, and there I went on this whole childhood memory thing, and I didn't buy it. I never whined about my childhood. I mean, we all had crappy childhoods, right? So what? At thirty-five, I was miserable, flabby, ugly, and pathetic—so of course I had a crappy childhood. That didn't take a psychologist to figure out. And my sitting there feeling sorry for myself while my kids rotted their brains on cartoons and their teeth on Sugar Puffs was not going to help things any.

Rocks. What a bunch of BS. I didn't trip over a rock. I just fell for the wrong man. Again. Any man was the wrong man, apparently. At least any man I'd fall for. Okay, I was getting a little hysterical. Breathe. In. Out. In. Out. I was there, on the porch, and there was nowhere to run. I didn't think she was right, but maybe she was. Maybe there was something I wasn't seeing. I knew what she would say. Begin again. Be where I was. Angry. Ugly. Scared. Get a pen. Write it down. Take my temperature. Tell the truth. I guessed it couldn't hurt. How much worse could it get?

I got a pen and my journal, stopped to put water in my little Chinatown fountain. Turned it on and listened to the familiar soothing gurgle. Watered my plants. It looked like a few of them might pull through. I plumped up the pillows and shook out the rug. It wasn't much, but it was better. Like someone cared. At least a little. And then I wrote about it. I told the truth. What's true was: I was angry. I was sad. I was lonely. I was disappointed. I was afraid. I hated him. Which him? All of them—Steve, Rick, Andrew from the second grade, Eric from the seventh. My father. All of them. All the ones who'd made me feel fat and ugly and unlovable. And the POGS. My mother. My mother for never telling me I was beautiful. Even if I wasn't. She was my mother. I should have been beautiful to my mother. To both my parents. I should have been beautiful and not something hideous to be fixed. Not compared and teased and sent to fat camps to fix me. Not something to be ashamed of. I should have been valuable. I should have been precious.

Bea used words like that all the time. *Precious.* She seemed to think my life was precious. That I was worth cherishing. She said it was my Beauty that mattered, and I knew somehow that she didn't mean my looking pretty. She seemed to think I was okay, no matter where I was at in my mind. In my life. But what did she know really? I hated myself, when I got right down to it. When I stopped and thought about it. Which I tried not to do. I ran around keeping busy, distracting myself so I wouldn't have to think about it. And the other truth, the scary one sitting underneath, was that I didn't feel like my life was worth living if I was fat and alone. I didn't feel I deserved to be alive. And yes, of course I loved my kids, and of course I would never have done anything stupid, anything that would have hurt them, but it just didn't feel as if I was worth anything by myself. Nothing I did was enough to make up for it. To make up for being the fat one, the ugly one, the one nobody wanted.

And even though I finally learned to play the game, lost the weight, did the whole ugly-duckling-into-swan routine—even finally managed to snag a "catch" like Rick—I was still, always, being chased by the POGS. I saw them everywhere. In the magazines, on billboards, walking along in their little velour sweats with rhinestone studs spelling out words like "princess" across their perfect little butts. They were everywhere, and I still wanted to hide from them. I hated them. That's what was true. I was still afraid they would torment and humiliate me like my sister and her popular friends. Back then, after I'd transformed myself into someone acceptable, I'd almost felt safe, hiding behind a starved-thin body and a very thick layer of makeup. I could almost convince myself that I was okay. I tried not to pay any attention to the feeling that it wasn't really mine. That one day, I might just wake up and be the same old disgusting Grace again. I told myself it was worth it.

But I suddenly realized, sitting in my fiery little sanctuary, that by disguising myself like that, instead of protecting myself from the POGS, I had become one of them. I was the new chief of the POGS. They had eventually gotten bored and moved on. They probably didn't even care about me anymore. I was the real POG. I attacked myself more than they ever did. And I did it mercilessly. No part of me was safe, not even parts the POGS could never see. Was this my rock? The thing that was with me always? This need to disguise myself, to cover up what I saw as the truth about me, that I was actually so hideous that I must be taunted, battered, ridiculed into submission…Was this my stumbling stone?

I would have thought it was picking men who'd leave me or some other pop-psychology thing. But maybe that was just part of the bigger story, the "Grace is disgusting and barely deserves to live" epic that had been playing itself out since we'd come to Beverly Hills. Since my dad left and the money ran out. Like his leaving was all my fault. Because I got fat. Which was, of course, what I believed. I mean, I guess I knew better, at least in my mind. I knew it couldn't have really been my fault; it just all happened at the same time. I couldn't really have had that much power to change the course of my entire family history with a few too many brownies. But it certainly was the preferred topic. Dinnertimes were nightmares. They watched every bite I took, every little chew. There were no more desserts. Not for Grace; she had a "problem."

It just got worse and worse. I started sneaking food. I was hungry all the time. And lonely and sad. I'd use my allowance to buy Hostess Fruit Pies, frosted animal cookies, anything sweet. Heather and I would eat them in our hideout behind the garage. And her mom always made us cookies. I ate to spite my family, my stupid life, to prove they couldn't boss me around. I ate because they couldn't stop me. I ate to fill the bitter hole they bored into me with something sweet. Until it all changed.

I guess it would have happened sooner or later. I mean, we all have to go through that first heartbreak, right? For me, it was in seventh grade. The big-deal all-school dance. And I didn't get invited. I mean, I guess I shouldn't have expected to, but there was this guy, Eric, and we were buddies, or I thought we were anyway. And well, I really liked him, I thought he liked me too. I was sure he'd ask me. He didn't. He asked Stephie—little, cute, perfect Stephie. Of course. How could he have stood to be seen with me? I was pretty sure I was the only girl in the whole school who wasn't asked. Even Heather was going to the dance. With geeky Toby, the one with the crew cut we laughed about who threw frog guts at us in biology. And I would have given anything to be going to the dance with him in her place. The night of the dance, I watched my sister get into her lacy Gunne-Sax dress, put on her makeup, fix her hair, and leave with her "date," the super-cute Brian, captain of the swim team. As my sister swept out the door, looking like a fairy-tale princess, I imagined she was laughing at me. That the whole school was. Fat Grace, who'd want to see her in a party dress?

My mother tried to help. She told me that it was just baby fat, and I would probably outgrow it. And if not, I could certainly find a boy who liked me for my personality. She said maybe it wasn't so bad not to be a pretty one. That the one thing I could always be sure of was that if a boy ever did like me, it would be because of my personality, not just because I was a pretty girl. But not to worry, I would probably outgrow it. I don't remember exactly how she said it. But that was the gist. I could tell even she didn't believe a word of it. And then she went into her room, turned on the TV, and drank until my sister came home.

I was inconsolable. I lay on my bed and sobbed. This "comfort" from my mother was worse than all the times when she would yell at me about sneaking food. There weren't enough fruit pies in the world to fill that hole, and somehow, even I knew it. I had finally gotten the real facts of life talk from my mother. My fate was sealed. I was not only fat; I was ugly. And no boy who wasn't blind would ever like me. I was in middle school. I already knew normal boys didn't care about personality. I was doomed to a life alone. I might as well become a librarian. Or an undertaker. It was over for me. Unless…

And that was it. No more fruit pies. No more sneaking food. I was not going to be the ugly kind of girl with personality. Somehow, I was going to change. I would be like my sister if it killed me. So I swallowed my pride and asked the POGS for help. They must have been thrilled to have a pet project. To have a pet, was more like it. Now I needed my own scapegoat, and Heather was it. I think I believed it served her right for going to the dance without me. Whatever it was, I was determined. I was going to be pretty, and I was going to be thin, and I needed to turn my back on everything that went before. I hate to think about how mean I was to her. But I was going to be the kind of girl that boys liked. The transformation took quite a while, and it wasn't easy. There were lots of times when I really missed my friend, but I had chosen my path. I had become a POG.

CHAPTER SEVENTEEN

Shameless

Well, Bea, if this was my stone, at least I knew where I got it. What was that old line, "We have met the enemy and he is us." Yeah. POG alert! POG alert! POG alert!

I wrote those words again and again in my journal. And then I put it away. I took a shower, and while I was soaping up my thighs, the old familiar monologue about cellulite started up. I made the warning noise out loud. "Ehng...Ehng...Ehng...POG alert!" It was stupid, I know, but it felt good to fight back a little. And it stopped the monologue in its tracks. I decided to try an experiment: a POG-free day. I wasn't going to worry about rocks or stones or any other cryptic Bea stuff. But I was not going to POG myself for one whole day. I was going to do the things I would have liked to do before I became a POG. Just for today. One simple Saturday. See what happened. So I rounded up the kids and took them to the Santa Monica Pier. We went on rides, ate ice cream, and played games. We went in the ocean even though we weren't dressed for it. So what? Things wash. The kids had a blast. I did too.

It wasn't really a POG-free day, though, not remotely. There were POG attacks all over the place, but I just dodged them, Sunday too. I took the kids to the beach again. Why not? Who knew how many more nice days we'd have before winter set in? We played the whole weekend, and I dodged those mental POG attacks. Some hours, they came so fast I couldn't even keep up. It was almost funny. It was like the days when I was first getting to know the voices in my head, but in action. More fun. I felt I was uncovering some buried part of myself, some wild child I'd been before I covered her in shame. She was feisty, spunky, and she knew when people were being mean to her; she even knew when I was being mean to her, and she didn't like it. She was shameless.

The kids were so tired they went to bed almost right after dinner. I wandered around picking up the place, putting our sandy, wet clothes into the wash, and thought about the day. I kept coming back to shame. Or more specifically, being *shameless*. What an interesting word. How did it get to be that we used that word to keep people, especially girls and women, in their place? I mean, what was wrong with being without shame? Un-ashamed. How was that wrong? I guess without shame you were a danger to society. You would be uncontrollable. You'd be a problem. Maybe you were fat, or some other thing they didn't want you to be, and if they couldn't shame you into behaving yourself, all would be lost. Shame-less. But what if all of that was backward? What if it was the shame itself that could destroy you? All those POGS—my sister, her friends, my mother, and then the worst one of all: my own self—all those POGS were using shame to make me behave myself, to make me fit in, be what they wanted, keep me from causing any trouble. They said it was for my own good. But was it?

I mean, yeah, it was probably better that I was not totally obese, probably good that I got braces on my buckteeth, that I learned to fit in and be nice…It was certainly better for society, and I never would have gotten Rick to notice me, so my kids wouldn't have been born, so I guess it was better for the survival of the species and all that, but did it have to be shame that kept me in line? Wasn't there any other way? All these phrases kept swirling around in my head. "You oughta be ashamed of yourself." "Have you no shame?" "Shame on you, young lady." I mean, what the heck did all of that even mean?

What was this thing, "shame," anyway? I was pretty sure it was from the Bible. Weren't you supposed to feel shame when you committed a great sin? Shame was like embarrassment, only worse. Bigger. I suppose in terms of really big sin, like murder or something, it might have been useful. But around my house, it was a way of being. I was ashamed all the time. Ashamed of my very self. Whatever it was that made me uniquely *me*, somehow that was the source of shame. My body—big shame there. My feelings—hide those away in shame. My failures, my weaknesses, and even some of my strengths, all shameful, if they called attention to me. Teasing, taunting, nagging, picking on...all called me into shame. The whole thing congealed into this horrible background of shame, which kept me hating myself, judging myself, comparing myself to everyone and always coming up short.

But there must have been a time before shame had become the tyrant running the show of my life. I know it. A time when I didn't always worry first about how something would look or what people would think or say. A Grace before the POGS. Before they won. That Grace had known what she wanted and hadn't been afraid. She knew who she was, what she liked and didn't like; she was fearless and feisty and fun and fabulous. She peeked out sometimes. She let herself be known sometimes, like during the best moments of the Be Beauty experiment. I recognized her like a half-remembered dream.

Was that the point of Bea's letters? All that wild woman stuff from the beginning? What if shame itself was the stone? And what if maybe there was another way, Bea's way. She'd never shamed me. She'd never ever said anything was wrong with me or had to be changed. She'd never told me to reject anything about myself. She only said to pick it up and hold it to my heart. Shame itself? POG-ness? All of it? Begin again, she'd say. Start where you are. Make friends with it all.

But the slow, gentle approach wasn't fast enough. I wanted it back, *now*. My wild self, my whole self. I didn't want to take the long way. Forget that. I wanted to be alive again! I wanted to be the Grace before shame, Grace before the Fall. How biblical. Sunday school stuff. Talk about shame. Eat this apple and suffer forever. I was tired of suffering. I wanted to kill the POGS—all of them. Especially the ones in my head. Why did I have to make friends with them? I wanted them to go away! Forever. The truth was, I didn't want it her way, her tender, gentle, understanding way. I wanted it the other way, the very thing she said not to want, that—how did she put it? Right. To be cured of this being myself. To wake up and be somebody else. No, even that wasn't quite right. I didn't want to be somebody other; I wanted to be me, only without shame. Shameless. Free. Why couldn't I just be free?

I wanted to rip off my skin, rip off all the years of hating myself, of holding myself back; to rip off the job that I hated, the life that I hated, the city that I hated. I wanted to run away and see the world, to be the wild woman I'd never been because I was too busy being what the POGS thought I should be. Pretty. Nice. Sweet. Sexy, but not too sexy. Not a slut sexy. Just appealing to men who would save me. I didn't want saving. I wanted to be wild and powerful and interesting and colorful and intense and all the things nice girls weren't supposed to be. I wanted to be passionate, and I wanted it that minute! I wanted to be *shameless*! A wild animal. I wanted to answer to nobody at all.

Yeah, right. As if. I was pacing like a caged animal. Again. There I was again, pacing the living room while the kids slept. My kids. As if there was any way I was going to run off and become a wild woman; a shameless, passionate, powerful wild woman. Right. How would that go over at the day care, the PTA meeting, the DWP? I needed to get a hold of myself. Needed to get to bed. It was late, and there was work tomorrow.

But this wild Grace, peeking around the corner at me, daring me to let her out—she was so strong. I couldn't imagine sleeping. I ached for this…this possible way of being. I wanted to be shameless, free of shame, to live in a new way, a way I couldn't even quite imagine. I could only sense it, around the edges. If I tried to look at it directly, it would slip away, taunting me. It was very late. I went to bed, but I lay there for a long time, fighting the urge to rip off my skin, my sheets, to run naked across the desert…sprouting fur, and fangs, sharp claws and leaping, twisting free in the air…or maybe that was part of the dream, the restless, wild dream that kept coming, all night. Shameless.

CHAPTER EIGHTEEN

The Fight Is On

Of course, I was tired the next day, and everything got on my nerves. My stupid, boring desk, the gray carpet and the gray half cubicle where I had to sit and sit and answer the phone all day long, all of it. When I'd started this job, we'd had a different system. The main line would ring, and we could choose for ourselves if we answered it. It was even kind of fun back then. There was this column of lights and the line ringing would flash and whoever wanted it would answer it. We all shared these flat desks in one big open room. It felt like we were part of a team. If I needed to go to the ladies' room or get a drink of water, I just went. I knew the other gals would manage it. I was usually bored, so I picked up as many calls as I could. Some of the older ladies who'd been there forever hardly answered any calls, but we didn't care; it was just part of the whole picture. They did the filing, which I hated. There was a natural ebb and flow. It was human. Some days, a person just couldn't handle too many complaints; she just couldn't take it. So she could let the others do it. It allowed for us to have days when we had bad cramps or couldn't concentrate or just needed a break and to pick up the slack when you'd see one of the other gals was having a rough time. It was like a family. Okay, I admit, sometimes it was like a really dysfunctional family, but most of the time, it worked pretty well.

Then management had decided to upgrade, and we got stuck in these awful little cubicles, and the calls were routed, and you had to just sit there and wait for yours to come. You had to officially notify the main desk before you went to the bathroom between breaks or got a drink of water, and they kept track because these activities were frowned upon. I couldn't see anyone else, couldn't roll my eyes at anyone when I had a really nasty call, or put a funny one on speaker. The days dragged on and on, and I had no control over anything. I hated it. Even though it had been almost three years since the "improvements," I still hadn't done anything to my cubicle. At first, it was my little protest. Then my personal life went to hell, and I just didn't have the energy. Somehow, Be Beauty hadn't made its way to my cube. I had a calendar, my kids' school pictures, a big purple plastic cup for water, which I filled on the breaks, and that was it. Some of the other gals had brought plants and put up posters. Management wasn't too keen on it, but they didn't hassle us all that much. As long as we did our job and didn't talk to the union reps, they didn't much care.

To tell the truth, the place felt like a prison: gray carpet-covered cubes, fluorescent lights, they'd even covered the windows that used to let in so much daylight. Climate control, they'd said. Yeah, like in your coffin. I'd walk out of work blinking like a mole. I never had any idea what the weather was. Not that it changed very much in Los Angeles. Usually sunny and smoggy. But on the few days when it rained or on those scorching Santa Ana wind days, it would have been nice to have some connection with the world. But nobody else seemed to mind it. They liked the AC.

I knew I should be grateful to have such a good job. It came with full health benefits, paid vacation, scheduled raises…I could take the test for supervisor anytime, but I'd never bothered, even though I'd been there so long. I just didn't want to move up there. I still felt like it was my in-between job. But it paid the mortgage on the condo. Mostly, I was fine with it. But on that particular Monday, when that wild Grace had kept me squirming all night, the gray prison was wearing me down.

The sensation of wanting to rip my skin off continued all day. I told them I had stomach problems and spent a lot of the day in the "bathroom." Really, I went to the roof. We weren't supposed to, of course, but one of the meter readers had showed me how to get up there. This guy, Joe. I liked the meter readers, but since they came in and went home earlier than I did, I didn't often see them. They were out all day. But I used to see

Joe hanging around the parking lot after work, waiting for his buddy Larry. I think they were roommates. Larry was a lineman. They were pretty cool. Larry had tattoos on his arms. I think Joe used to have a little crush on me, to tell you the truth. He would always come over and talk to me.

And once, last year, or maybe it was already longer ago than that…anyway, it was a beautiful sunset, and he insisted on showing me how to get up to the roof to see it. I wasn't sure I should go with him alone and even less sure about breaking the company rules, but it had been right after I'd finalized the divorce and I was feeling reckless. So I went with him. And he was right; it was incredible. The sun was setting over all the downtown buildings, turning the sky every shade of pink and orange, and the moon was rising on the other side. It was a sliver of a moon, just the ghostly outline, barely over the horizon. We just stood there, taking it in. Next to each other, our shoulders almost touching. I think he was about to say something or maybe take my hand, but it was too much. I was too fragile from the whole Rick thing, and I knew I was going to have to rush to get my kids in time, so I just fled. I regretted it now. I still saw him around sometimes, but he barely acknowledged me anymore. It was my fault. I had avoided him after that day, and then with the divorce and everything else, I'd just tried to forget about the whole thing.

Until I pushed open the door that said: "Roof—Emergency Access Only. Alarm Will Sound," and waited, heart pounding, for the alarm, which didn't sound, and then propped it open with the broken chair leg the way Joe had shown me. And there I was. Alone with the sky and the wind and the sun beating down on my head and the cigarette butts (I guess I wasn't the only one who came up here to hide) and myself. *Thank you, Joe,* I thought silently, *for showing me this place.* I should find him and thank him in person. I would do it, too, the next time I could.

But for now, I just walked to the edge of the building. It was a wide, raised ledge. I stood there breathing deeply. I felt free and happy and trapped and miserable all at the same time. What was going on here? What had that one conversation with that wacky old woman unleashed in me? I felt like Alice down the rabbit hole. Like I couldn't ever go back, but I didn't know what forward held either. Was I really supposed to throw my whole life away and become a wild woman? And do what, live in a cave? What about my kids, my job, my…my what?

That was the question. My what? This life that stretched out before me, what was it, exactly? A long line of little minutes, of driving to work, sitting in a gray cube, driving to get my kids, driving home, making dinner, watching some TV, and then doing it all again the next day? And then they'd grow up and get married and probably divorced, and they'd have the same boring gray life, and so what? So on every other

Friday, when they got their paycheck, they could go to a movie? Scrub the bathroom on Saturday? Church on Sunday? Okay, so I didn't go to church, but you get my drift. Why not church? It was as good as anything else. Standing there, breathing the forbidden air of the secret roof, feeling the Indian summer heat ripple off the asphalt, smelling the tar where it was oozing from the cracks, with the sun on my scalp and the wind in my face and knowing that before too many minutes had passed, I would give up again and go back to my cube and toe the line—this was the almost totally certain future, the endless, pointless, monotonous, only future I could see. There was no room in this predictable future for the wild woman who taunted me, who'd laughed her way through my dreams.

There, on that roof, a great battle was being waged inside me, and the outcome was uncertain. The smart money was probably on the same old Grace, hounded by POGS, getting by and withering away, but it was too early to leave the stadium. Not even to try to beat the traffic. The game was on. Predictable Grace may have had in her corner the weight of habit, the home-court advantage, and the screaming POGS, but the wild woman wasn't going down without a fight. She had gotten a toehold, and it was too early to call it.

CHAPTER NINETEEN

The Body

Dear Grace,

Where is your body in space? In this moment? Do you know, really? Do not dismiss this question without at least a quick check. Do you know where each joint is, and how it is? Each tendon? You race through your days, using this body like a slave, yet how well do you know it? How well can you love it, if at all? You may crave freedom, power, beauty in your life, in your outer world, but until you find it/choose it/grant it in your very own body, you have nothing at all.

Start in this moment, this now, this breath, and discover something you haven't noticed before. Become aware of some sensation you have neglected. Is there a pain in your left knee? Is the strap of your brassiere digging into your shoulder? What is really happening between the second and third toes of your *left foot? Become curious. Take a tour of your sacred temple, right now. Close your eyes and begin at the top. Just notice. This is your home; this is your base. Your first and last heartbeat and all of the ones between are sheltered in this container, this corpus, this you. How well do you know it? How much do you listen to it? It is wise and will teach you if you let it. It is your access to freedom; it will guide you into the life you are beginning to claim for yourself. It is your experience of life itself; isn't it therefore worthy of a few minutes of your attention, every day?*

You think you simply "have" a body. That this is "your" body, as if "you" were someplace else, some being separate from this cluster of cells. But where, then, would you be? What? Who? The ancient philosophers' conundrum—if you can perceive of yourself, then who is doing the perceiving? Leave the debate for the philosophers. You are woman, have brought forth life from your womb; you need not bother with the question. You and "your" body are not separate; that is a story made up to control you. This story that your body is distinct from the real you, that it is somehow traitorous and must be controlled, is not of your making, and it is not the truth. You have believed that bodies, and especially yours, must be disciplined into submission, starved, or carved. You ignore your body unless its protests grow too annoying, too inconvenient. Then you allow it to be drugged or mutilated, placed into the hands of "experts." You have accepted the story that your body is the enemy, that its rhythms, its natural shape, cyclic changes, its needs, desires, and its wisdom are nothing but problems to be managed, controlled, solved.

Your body—your "self" in specific earthly form—has much to contribute, and it is time you learned to listen. Time to honor this partner, this vessel that is constantly being created in your image. In the image you have allowed for it. Will you pause now to discover it?

This ship, which has agreed to carry you through your earthly days, has one purpose only, to express itself as fully and as perfectly as it can. And what is the perfect expression of itself? Why, nothing more than the perfect expression of you. You are not separate. Every single molecule is nothing but the perfect manifestation of everything you are. And as such, as the greatest artwork you have made, it is to be cherished, adored, honored. It is, in this moment, *exactly as it is, perfect. It is perfection itself. Right now.*

Oh, I know you are protesting furiously. "Not this body!" "Not like this!" "Not until I fix it, until I make it perfect." But, my beloved, you must know, somewhere in you, that no fixing would ever be enough. It is the nature of a body in physical space to be specific unto itself. The body is constantly being remade, reshaped, reinvented. It is perfect in its state of constant transformation. To judge anything that is continually becoming as if it were finished is cruel. And to hold it to standards that are not part of its unique plan is also cruel. This body is being built according to the design you have for it. And no other blueprints exist. I promise you, no matter its current expression, it is perfectly adhering to your design.

So love this wondrous creation. Its workings are largely unseen; its magic, which propels you through every day of your life without much of a thought; this is all part of your design, your path, your particular choice of a life. Marvel at your opposable thumb. What a wonder. At your tear ducts. Your toenails. Marvel at the process that exchanges breath for blood and pushes it back out to feed the trees. Can you imagine anything more wonderful? If you seek perfection before adoration, you will achieve neither. If you adore first and recognize the perfection of specificity, you will have both. As with everything ever made, your body is the perfect expression of itself now. Explore and adore first and allow your delight to lead you to the choices that best support this beautiful house.

Yes, delight will make you whole. You are so angry at your body for betraying you. For looking the way it looks, acting the way it acts, and not as you think it should. You think if you simply heap enough rejection and damnation upon your body, it will begin to behave. You do not know that your body is already behaving itself perfectly, in perfect accord with the abuse. Your body, free of your torture, free of overload and poison, desires only to be strong and true and supple and joyful. It desires to be healthy and whole and perfect. It is made for pleasure. It has many, many systems in place to clean and heal itself; it has wholesome desires, which get buried. The exact way your body is today is the exact way you have created it to be. And this is cause for celebration, not despair!

Your body is exquisitely designed for pleasure. Designed for nothing else but to experience life. Why not start today?

En-joy yourself.

—B

* * *

It was waiting for me when I got home from work. I was surprised to get two letters so close together. I was exhausted. What I really wanted was to sit down and have a beer. And I don't even like beer. It was unseasonably hot. Traffic was hell. My job was tedious and horrible, and if I kept sneaking up to the roof, I was probably going to get fired. I hated my life. Loved my kids, but they were driving me crazy. There was a direct connection between my lack of patience and their bad behavior. We'd gone to Panda Express for dinner. It was their favorite Chinese food and my standby when I just couldn't face the kitchen. Everything was okay till the ride home. Who took who's what, or broke who's what or whatever it was—I didn't know, and I didn't care, and it went downhill from there. They were fighting over everything. I told them to shut up and go to bed, and then I stormed out onto the little porch and slammed the door behind me. Well, that's what I wanted to have done. I certainly would have slammed it if it hadn't stuck. I screamed at the door. I rattled it and pulled on it and pounded on it, and it just got more stuck. Like my whole stupid life. I could hear the kids crying, and I didn't even care. I was crying too. We were one big sobbing family. Great. That there would be days like this, I guess I knew somewhere in the back of my mind when I'd been longing for children. But you never really knew what you were in for, did you?

The frustration finally burned itself out. I gave up on the door and went back inside to soothe the children. We all climbed in my bed and made up stories together. We took turns imagining the "worst day ever" until we made ourselves laugh. I let them fall asleep there, in their clothes, without even brushing their teeth. I figured one night wasn't going to do too much damage, and I just didn't have the strength to begin the nag. I left them there in my bed and went back out to my little sanctuary. At least it was starting to cool down some. I picked the letter out of the bills and junk mail, lit a candle, and sat down to read it.

At first, I couldn't even follow it. I was too distracted; my mind was spinning. I was agitated and tired from not sleeping. What was she talking about? The body? My body? This body, a temple? Sacred? The Panda Express was taking its toll. I felt bloated and thirsty and just too heavy to do anything at all about it. My head kept dropping. Maybe I needed to sleep on it. Maybe it was just a lot of BS anyway. Delight my body? Designed for pleasure? My body just wanted ice cream and brownies and to be left alone. I blew out the candle and took the letter inside. I left the door stuck open but shut the screen. Megan and Justin were sleeping at right angles on my bed, and I just didn't think I could lift them. I got a blanket and slept on the couch. For the record, I didn't brush my teeth either.

CHAPTER TWENTY

Wild Grace

The wild woman danced through my dreams again. I saw her in front of some kind of round structure. It was some kind of tent, but not at all a teepee. More like a dome, I guess, but low, almost a cave. It seemed to be made of animal skins and was glowing red from the inside. She was tending a fire, and when she saw me, she bared her teeth. She seemed to be taunting me. Daring me to come closer. I would not. I stayed in the shadows, my back against the trunk of a huge tree. The wild woman was wearing a cape or a robe that seemed to be made of many colored velvets and silks, tattered and ragged. Her hair was long and crazy—black and white tangled together, with wildflowers and leaves woven in. The full moon was rising, and she turned to face it, ignoring me. She raised her arms to the moon, and the robe fell away from her. Naked, she began to dance for the moon. She seemed to be calling it to rise with her very dance. I watched as she swayed, swirled, alternately tender and caressing and then suddenly wild and terrible, pulling the moon up into the sky and also drawing it down as if to fill herself with its power. The music was the rhythmic stamping of her feet and a long, low sob that woke me when I realized it was coming from my own throat.

I got up from the couch and went back out on the lanai. The moon was out, not full, like in the dream, but just a little less than half, enough to make out the face of the man in the moon. I raised my arms to it, I don't know, hoping, I guess, to get some taste of the power and sweetness of the dance I'd been watching from the shadows of my dream. I swayed back and forth, a little. I felt my feet on the rough floor shuffle and stamp, but it was a pale sound, an empty sound, an empty gesture. I dropped my arms. Who was I kidding anyway? I was just a white girl trying to raise my white children and survive my gray cubicle life.

I didn't have anything wild and mysterious in me. I was afraid of the wilderness, of wild animals and snakes and spiders. Whoever this wild woman was, she wasn't me. I felt something drain out of me, like all my juice. I sat down on the hard floor and started to sob—just great, heaving sobs, not even for any reason I could name. Just this misery at being so trapped, so white, so bored and boring and hopeless.

Where on earth did I go from there? I couldn't keep this up, this one-step-forward-three-steps back mess. I was so tired of it. Ben had opened the window to some kind of wild world, something I never knew existed, and I thought I wanted it, really I did, but I was so scared; I kept stumbling, and then I just wanted to quit, give up on myself, to abandon the whole thing. What was it going to take to get me out of this pattern? How could I manage my life and my children and my job *and* this messy journey I seemed to have started? I felt like giving up. I didn't know how to do this. The problem was I also didn't seem to know how to not do this. I couldn't go back, and I didn't know how to go forward.

I must have dozed off there on the floor, because I felt her arms around me and heard her voice. *"There is no place to go, you see. Nothing is wrong at all. You are simply returning home to your secret, precious cave, and you have discovered that you have been away for far too long. You have left your most sacred private sanctuary unguarded while you attended to the world. Are you surprised to find that robbers have desecrated the place? You left it to them. Are you surprised that they do not want to surrender what they now consider to be theirs?*

"Did I ever tell you it would be easy? A direct route? No, my beloved, this journey, this reclaiming is messy; it is at once inner and outer, for yourself and against. Yes, against yourself, for these robbers who have upended the furniture, scattered your jewels over the floor and sold them too cheap on the open market, these devils who would rather see you half or even wholly dead than strong, lovely, and powerful, they are not separate from you.

"There is a contrary force inside all women, an equal and opposite contrast to our life-creating power, and this is our death-bringing power. Women are not just the bearers of life; we are also the ones who sing over the dead, who usher them into the next world. It is we who face without flinching the ebb of life, we who mark each moon with the blood of life's unfulfilled longing for itself. And until that intricate dance of life and death has finished bleeding itself through a woman's body, your body, that death force can be turned against you, against your very soul, unless you have staked that territory for yourself.

"This is not a child's journey, nor a maiden's. It is even beyond the initiation of motherhood. You have passed all of these. This is the stage between mother and crone, a station of woman only to be entered by choice, with willingness and unflinching courage. Only you can make the choice to become the queen. This potential is calling you; it led you to me. The path is laid, and you have chosen to walk it. You are reawakening yourself, but first, you must see what your sleeping has cost you. What you feel is the discomfort of facing the desecration of your cave and choosing to face squarely the task of reclaiming it.

"Do not be overwhelmed. There is much to celebrate here. It is good news that these robbers are not some alien force; that they are your own power. They are actually the gatekeepers whose duty is to protect you and keep you from harm. They have simply been left too long alone. They took over the place, marked it as their own, and now guard it against even yourself, as intruder. They have ceased to recognize their

mistress. You must stand tall and inform them. It is yours now to claim your position and put them back on their posts. This will to destroy yourself is a perversion of your own power. You have taught them well. By diminishing yourself, by giving away your power, by handing over the keys to your life, your love, and your joy too easily and too often, you showed them that it was your will to be destroyed. They have been helping you achieve your aim. Can you see this? They have only been doing what you asked, and they will respond, though perhaps slowly, to new instructions.

"You are on the path, and it is steep, but this is good news, not bad. Few are given the desire to come this far, fewer still the fortitude. You are closer than you think."

I awoke with a start, feeling a warmth leave me, almost certain I could smell something. Patchouli? The echo of her soothing voice was fading…Was I imagining the whole thing? It may have been just a dream, but it was as clear as one of her letters. All of it, even this horribly trapped feeling, this fear, and even the rage, everything was as it should be. There was no place to go but home. And I was already there. I went inside and closed the door behind me. It slid easily into place. I crawled into bed with my kids and slept soundly.

CHAPTER TWENTY-ONE

Back to the Boardwalk

Something had to give. I was tired of this back-and-forth, this push and pull. Either I was going to surrender myself fully to this "Path" Bea kept talking about, or I was going to have to stop altogether, throw out the damn letters, and just get on with my regular life. Somehow, I had to choose. Get on the boat or off it. I didn't know how to *do* the path, exactly, but even I could tell that my resistance was wearing me out. I needed some time to myself to think about it. I dropped the kids at school and called in sick. In all the time I'd worked at the DWP, I had never taken what they call a "mental health day." I'd always been too worried I'd need the day if I was really sick or the kids were. But after the night I'd had, I took it. I wasn't sure what I was going to do. The thought of just going home and sleeping all day was very, very appealing, but I nixed it. If I was going to play hooky, I wanted to make the most of it.

Instead of going home, I drove to the beach and walked along the boardwalk where I'd first seen Bea. I'd never been there so early in the morning. On a workday. It was a different world than the Saturday afternoon tourist scene. The homeless people were just waking, packing up their makeshift beds, loading their entire lives back into shopping carts. It was a whole community I'd never seen up close. They were laughing and giving each other shit and grumping and sharing cigarettes and paper bag mystery bottles. The shopkeepers were hosing down the walkways and setting up tables; the artists and vendors were staking out their spots, their wares neatly bundled onto rolling carts and wheeled suitcases. I'd never thought about what a lot of work it must be to haul all that stuff out every day and pack it back up by sunset.

Though it felt weird for me to be there, I wasn't questioned. I was just part of the morning milieu, another piece of American Dream flotsam washed up here on the left coast. This was as far west as you could get, the extreme end of the New World: Venice Beach, California. The air was chilly; the sun was streaking the sky pink and yellow. It would warm up soon. Then the clouds would roll in off the water, and the day would pass in a typical beach haze. There are no seasons here, not really. Nothing much to mark the passage of time, yet still it passed.

It had been almost nine months since I'd followed Bea into that little café, seven since the first letter arrived and set my world on its ear. A gestation period, certainly. But what was cooking in there? I pulled my jacket a little tighter and crammed my hands deeper into the pockets. It wasn't the outside cold I was feeling so much, just a need to be tightly wrapped. Swaddled like an infant.

"Hey there, pretty lady." It came from a small group of men standing around a bench. I looked up and then away in a hurry. I'm not one to talk to a whole group of men.

"Oh, come on, Mama, we ain't gonna bite you. Whatcha doin' this fine morning? Why not stop a minute? Say hello."

I hesitated, considering. I was playing hooky, after all, feeling a little reckless, and besides, it was broad daylight, my kids were safe in school. Why not?

"Hello." Even to my own ears, my voice sounded weak. But I said it.

"Now that's more like it." The speaker was taller than the others, half sitting against an iron bench. A muscular black man—sorry, African-American, shaved head, maybe forty, forty-five. I can never tell ages. Good-looking and wearing clean black workout pants, tank top, and a windbreaker. His pals were younger: a skinny white kid with dark, lanky hair and piercings; another white guy who looked like he'd probably clean up to be a nice Orange County surfer boy—except that he seemed to have no interest in ever cleaning up—and a younger African-American kid, early twenties, in nice jeans and a leather jacket, looking nervous. Or maybe I was the one who was nervous. I checked my watch: 8:43 a.m. The whole day to myself. I could spend a few minutes talking to these guys. My sister would have a heart attack if she had any idea. Good.

I moved a little closer to the group. The tall man stood up. He was so graceful in the way he moved. "I'm Al." He walked right up to me and held out his hand, his eyes locked on mine. "And this is DJ, Johnny, and Carlo. You are…?"

"Grace." I shook his hand. It was warm and strong.

"Grace." It hung on the air. "Well, Grace, the boys and I were just about to go into this fine establishment and get us a cup of coffee to start this morning off right. Join us?"

My eyes followed his gesture to the "fine establishment." It was the very same café I'd followed Bea into, though it looked dark and desolate right now. A lone busboy was taking chairs off battered wooden tables; it smelled of bleach and had that old grease and coffee grounds feel of dive cafés everywhere. Funny how different it had looked in the afternoon sunshine, with the checkered tablecloths and little vases of carnations and happy, sun-pinked tourists vying to share the weirdest thing they'd seen on their first trip to "Hollywood."

Open With Love

And though I suspected I might be buying the coffees, I felt strangely relaxed at that particular moment in the company of those men, well, one man, at least, and the boys. All bets were off, it seemed to me, before 9:00 a.m. on Tuesday on the Venice Beach boardwalk. So that's how I found myself at a table for four (Carlo had kind of slunk off when I'd joined the group) drinking coffee with total strangers.

Al paid for the coffees. I was sure it was going to have been my treat, that this was some elaborate panhandling exercise. I was wrong. I'd been wrong about pretty much how everything would go that day. I had expected to be sitting in a gray cubicle answering complaint calls right now, after all. Funny how fragile my fixed life actually was. How close I was at any moment to a completely different life, and no one, least of all me, ever noticed. How close I was to a shopping-cart-on-the-beach life or…or perhaps any kind of life at all. I was always so careful, making sure I did it right, that I didn't mess up, that I was the same each day, and protecting against any cracks, that I didn't even know what was out there. I thought I knew what was possible for me—or more to the point what was *impossible* for me—but maybe I actually had no idea at all. I was lost in this thought, feeling the coffee warm me and kick my brain into gear, when I noticed that the guys were looking at me. Uh-oh. What'd I miss?

I must have looked a little panicked or something, because they all burst out laughing.

"What?" I tried to be cool. "What?"

"We were just trying to figure out where you're supposed to be right now. It sure ain't here. That's all," Al finally said. "My man DJ here thinks you killed your husband and left him face down in his eggs. Johnny thinks you walked out and left the kindergarteners reciting their ABCs, and when they get to Z and you aren't back, there's gonna be hell to pay."

"And you?"

Al smiled. Big brown eyes crinkled at the corners. "I think you killed your husband first and then left the kindergarteners alone."

"When, how…" I looked from Al to DJ to Johnny "…did you figure all this?"

"Yo, I told you she wasn't paying any attention to us. We could've totally jacked her purse or something. Lady, you got to be more careful." DJ looked at me and then at Al (who just raised one eyebrow) and then back down to his cup. Johnny just looked out at the water and drank his coffee. I tried to figure out if he was serious about the purse. I had hung it on the back of the chair. I felt for it. Al was watching me. He smiled and shook his head a tiny bit. It was just a joke. I was safe here. I relaxed and left it where it was. The joke was on me. The square white girl. As usual.

"So how'd you do it," DJ finally asked, leaning in close to me, "rat poison?" Johnny choked, spraying coffee out his nose all over the table.

"Man! Watch it, dude! Shit." There was a scramble for napkins; we were all laughing now, and the nasty looks from the busboy only made us laugh harder. It was like I was back in school, cutting class with the bad boys.

Only I never actually did cut class with the bad boys. I'd sure wanted to, and I was certain this was exactly what it would have been like. I liked it. I was having fun, and I didn't care what anyone thought, especially not the busboy. Maybe it was time Grace learned to break a few rules. Lighten the heck up.

The coffees were finished; I could tell the boys were eager to get out into the morning action. A few regular-looking people were straggling in for breakfast. The tables were all set up. Things were beginning to get moving on the boardwalk. Time for me to get back to the question that had brought me out here in the first place.

Johnny and DJ spotted a couple of friends on skateboards and took off after them. Al and I stood in front of the café, awkward, doing that thing I dread so much it sometimes makes me not want to talk to anyone: the see-you-later shuffle. How do you get out of it after?

"Uhm, thanks for the coffee, Al." I reached to shake his hand. He took it and held on.

"I don't know who or what you had to kill to get to the beach this fine morning, pretty lady Grace. I just know you need to come down here more often. You got friends you don't even know yet. You got a life you been forgetting. You got something else too." He looked deep into my eyes. "You know what it is. Right here." He touched himself on the chest, then pointed at my heart, kissed my hand, and let it drop. Before I could say anything at all, he was gone, sauntering down the sidewalk like a big cat. A panther or a tiger—slow, so smooth. I watched him go, but he didn't look back. I wanted to run after him and ask him to tell me more, what he meant, how he knew. But I just stood there and watched him walk away. Then I turned and walked straight out onto the sand. All the way to the water. I kicked off my shoes and socks, rolled up my pant legs, and went into the waves.

CHAPTER TWENTY-TWO
Stuck in the Mud

The water was cold, the sand too rough on my tender feet. When was the last time I'd come to the beach alone and walked in the water? I lived so close, too. Fifteen minutes, including parking. What the heck was the point of living in Los Angeles if I didn't even go to the beach? Oh yeah, mostly I was working. Mostly I took care of the kids, took care of the house, took care of, well, everything except me. I was struck again by how fragile my solid life actually was. How close to the beach, even on a Tuesday morning. A big wave took me by surprise. I was wet to the crotch. I laughed out loud. It was all so ridiculous. I'd met some nutty old lady, and somehow it had led to coffee with strange men and walking barefoot in the water on a Tuesday morning when I should have been at work. But so what? Whose life was it anyway?

That, I guess, was the question I'd come here to answer for myself. Somehow, I knew I was at a major crossroads. I suppose I had been since the letters had started coming or maybe since

I'd asked her the question or even since I'd laid eyes on her. What had happened to me on that day? Was it really the sight of Bea that had changed me? Or was I already hungry for something? I rather suspected it had already been there. I might have passed her or someone like her a thousand times and not even noticed her. Of course, I had been looking for something. Something different.

I wondered if all old ladies had this kind of weird wisdom hidden away in them. The ones you saw in Los Angeles were—well, it's funny. You hardly saw old ladies in Los Angeles. It was like there was a code, an ordinance. Women did not age here. They disappeared. Or they dyed their hair and had various procedures. I can't tell you how many times I'd been standing in line at the bank, at Costco, somewhere, and I'd see some woman, and out of the corner of my eye, she would seem, I don't know, mid-thirties, maybe. Sometimes younger. She'd be wearing a short skirt or workout clothes. Super tan, super thin, with perfect high boobs, tight skin, blond hair, makeup; everything. I'd look away, but something would stick in my head, and make me look again, and I'd realize with a start that she was probably closer to sixty than thirty. The hands, maybe, or the skin at the throat. The voice. It was like the times when I'd see a transvestite. S/he might look really good, but something in my stomach just wouldn't sit right. Something would just be off. And my brain would start doing flips trying to work it out with my body. I would be really unsettled until I figured it out. The same with these Barbie-doll old ladies. They were really common here. We joked about it, my friends at work, my sister, and me. But they scared me. We thought they were pathetic; that's what we said, but really, weren't they just trying to do what we all wanted to do—keep it at bay? Trying not to become some sad old hag in a walker? Keep their man, their looks, their power?

You saw a lot of these older women in LA, more than you'd know, even. If forty was the new thirty, and fifty was the new, well, thirty—how do you think that happened? It wasn't just a natural occurrence. But what had happened to sixty and seventy and beyond? I doubted that those women had anything like what Bea wrote about to me on their minds. When would they have had the time? It had to be a lot of work—not to mention money to maintain it: trainers, tanning, manicures, surgery, facials, shopping. Be Beauty? Well, I guess that was one route.

But what about the other kind of old lady? The grandma kind? Whenever I saw any, and that was very rarely, they seemed to spend all their time complaining about one thing or another while fumbling in enormous ratty handbags full of wadded-up tissues for exact change. Slowing down the line. I didn't have a grandmother. I had had a couple, before we left Ohio. But they were both gone. My kids had one. Rick's mom was still alive. She lived in England and had been there since Rick was a kid. He grew up in boarding schools. She flew over every couple of years to see the kids. Sent them sweaters or tins of cookies at Christmas. She didn't bake them herself. She was an imperious, tiny thing, more likely to command a regiment than bake a cookie. I thought they tasted like dog biscuits, but the kids liked them. So that was another type of old lady. Yuck. I was glad to be away from her.

I'd been walking and thinking and thinking and walking without really noticing. I was nearly to the jetty. The water seemed much warmer now. Either my feet were numb, or it was warming up. Or both. I preferred to think in either/ors, but so often it turned out to be both. Or some other thing I hadn't considered. Toxic algae bloom warming the water for example? Yuck. I always wondered about this water. It was a mess. The surfers were always sick. Last year, the beaches were littered with dead jelly fish. Huge piles of slime. Red jellies, bits of them everywhere; with yellow rings in the center and long tentacles. I was afraid to go near them. I didn't know if they'd still sting. I never did find out what killed them. Was it some kind of chemical leak from the refineries? Red Tide? Mass gelatinous suicide? Who knew? I was pretty certain the scientists had some theory, but did anyone actually know these things? Perhaps it was simply time for them to die. The balance of the ocean had shifted, and they were no longer adapted for it. Something had to give. I wondered about the jellyfish that might have survived that time. What had they done differently? Was survival simply a matter of dumb luck? Or did certain creatures manage to adapt? Was there any choice to it? Did you get to choose if you wanted to evolve? Or even notice?

I stopped walking and watched the waves coming, going. In, out. The sand dissolved away from under my feet as the water receded. It pulled me off balance. I changed my footing, adapted to the changing sands. Was it choice? Reflex?

Had something shifted in my life that I was trying to adapt to or was I myself the force that seemed to be pulling the foundation out from under me?

Wasn't it Freud who said it? "What do women want?" If so, he was on to something. That was the only important question in all of this. What did I want? That was why I was at the beach on a Tuesday. The struggles I'd been having, all the back-and-forth, up and down, yes and no—it all came down to this: what kind of life did I want to have, and what was I willing to do to get it? That was Bea's question from the beginning: "Are you willing?" And I had said yes. Of course, I'd said it with no idea what I was agreeing to, but I had said it. Did we ever really know what we were agreeing to before it played out? And there I was in the water, asking the question again, but deeper. With a little more understanding of what it meant to be willing, what it might cost, what it might bring. Not a very clear understanding, even after all that time. But a little more.

And the thing that made it such a tricky question was that there was no one asking it of me but myself. Most of the decisions I made were based on other people's opinions. You know, "What am I supposed to do? What do you think? What do you want me to do?" My kids, my husband, my mother, the POGS...I chose based on what would win their approval, how to best keep them happy with me, what would keep the love coming. But my mother and husband were gone, and I knew that the POGS now lived in my own head. And frankly, I was losing interest in what the POGS thought or what the neighbors or my co-workers or even my sister thought. It came down to me at last. This was my only life. And all my choices were actually mine to make. They were all there, even if I didn't stop to notice. Just like the beach was there whether I went to work or not. In the very same way that I could suddenly see right through my life, through all of my possible lives, even the imaginary husband dead in the eggs while the kindergarteners kept on reciting, I could suddenly see that there was no one right way. And no wrong way. Just other ways.

I saw that I could choose to throw all of Bea's letters in the trash or I could quit my job or I could work hard and get a promotion, or I could run away to a yurt (what was a yurt, exactly?). I could become a stripper, a bag lady, a corporate honcho. I could get married again and have more kids. Or just have more kids without getting married. Or not. I could even just stay there at the beach and watch the days come and go until I forgot who I ever was. Rick would take care of the kids. Probably. He'd have to. My sister would—I don't know what, but she'd do something. She always did. No one could stop me, really, but the shocking thing was that none of it mattered at all. In a hundred years or even less, no one would even remember. In a thousand, all trace of everything I knew would be gone, and at the rate we were going, the planet itself might be nothing but a dead crust by then.

More waves broke, more sand slipped out from under my feet, sinking me deeper in place. By not moving at all, I was becoming part of the beach. Up to my ankles, I saw what was happening. If I didn't move, nothing would change except I'd get deeper and deeper in. It would get harder and harder to extract myself. If I kept moving, I'd travel along the surface of things. Mobile but shallow. Unconnected. Neither seemed satisfactory. If I stayed in one place, I'd become embedded. How far was that from petrified? Centuries, I guessed. From turning to stone, that was. But what about the other meaning of petrified? So scared you couldn't move? How long did that take? To become frozen in place? So embedded in my idea of a life that to shed it would be impossible? How close was I to that?

I was afraid I might be pretty close. But I didn't want to move just to be moving. I mean, change everything and go do what, exactly? Shake free from my steady life and run along the top, skim the surface? Okay, maybe sometimes I wanted to do exactly that. Especially when it all seemed so stagnant, so predictable. But really, what? Run away from my children and spend my time hanging out at the beach with the DJs, the Johnnys, the Als? Drink coffee with strangers, bum change, or worse? Sure, I'd have the freedom, but at what cost? But neither did I want to stay stuck, petrifying slowly into stone.

What did Bea want from me? What exactly was she pointing the way toward? Something entirely different, I suspected. Something that wasn't an either/or, but something that maybe I still couldn't wrap my brain around. She talked about the cave, about coming home to myself. Surely that was embedded, right? Deep. Very deep. But did it have to mean stuck, like the routine day in, day out of my life? Sure, routine was safe, yes, comfortable even, in its way, but so stuck. My life felt stuck. It was totally dependent on my making the same moves every day. My job depended on my not coming to the beach on Tuesday. But my job, my steady life—that was certainly not my cave. It was not the center of me; it was not any kind of home, and it was not truly so safe at all. Anything could disrupt it. I could lose my job. People did. Lots of them. Or I could get sick so

I couldn't work. Another big earthquake might take out the whole city. Anything. What would I do then? Who would I be?

That was a question, for sure. And perhaps a big part of the answer Bea wanted me to find for myself. Not just what did I want to do, no, it was something bigger than that. Who did I want to *be*? Who could I be, separate from the container of my life, distinct from the voices in my head that were always telling me what I should and shouldn't do? That was what she was always trying to get to the core of, wasn't it? Who was I? What did I love? What did I fear? What was my expression of beauty in the world? If I were deeply enough embedded in that, so deeply connected it couldn't be destroyed by anyone, not even those demons inside of myself, then it wouldn't matter what I did or didn't do; I would never be trapped, no matter what my outer life contained. I wouldn't need the details of my life to tell me and the world who I was. I would be able to define myself. I could even change my definition if I outgrew it. Or if I just wanted to. But what about the day-to-day structure? What would happen next? How would I know what to do with myself? Okay, so I wanted to be anchored in the core of myself, but what the heck did that look like? Who did I want to be?

Up to my ankles in wet sand, I forced myself to start walking forward. I wanted to make it all the way to the jetty. It wasn't very ambitious in the greater scheme of things, but it was a start. The sand released its suction grip, and I went slopping and slapping along. The sun was higher now; it was getting hot. I was tired of all the thoughts. How on earth was I supposed to answer any of these questions? What did I want? Who did I want to be? It was so much easier not to ask these things. I wondered if I was losing it or if everyone thought about this kind of thing, and for some reason, I just never had until I met Bea. Now a wild dancing woman haunted my dreams, an old lady wrote me letters, and I'd met Al and his pals on the beach doing whatever it was they did all day. And there were a million other choices, sitting there all along, right outside my point of view.

I think I'd been hoping to have some blinding revelation, some flash of insight that would make it all clear. A lightning bolt that would change my life and I'd know exactly what I wanted, exactly what to do next. And I'd hoped it would be something good too, really exciting. Maybe even dramatic. I mean, I'd called in sick from work. I had this whole day without the kids, and I wanted to be a new woman at the end of it. Sort of like what the ads made you think would happen if you went to a really good day spa or on a cruise. I hoped I'd come back a different person. I wanted to change everything. Why not? I wanted to have a glamorous, exciting life for a change, some kind of wild, passionate life, but all I was doing at the beach was getting stuck in the sand.

Yeah, stuck in the mud. The quagmire. I was thinking, endlessly thinking, and still not quite figuring it out. And I was starting to get really pissed off at myself. I was afraid I was wasting it all: my day off, my whole life. It had to matter, didn't it?

I walked faster, losing my breath with the pace of my frustration. The waves just kept doing what they did. Up and back. In and out. Never getting anywhere either, but somehow they didn't seem to care. What was the point of it all? I wanted to be moving forward, going somewhere, doing something important, not just this endless back and forth. I wasn't a wave. I wanted to get somewhere.

CHAPTER TWENTY-THREE

To Be Happy?

I walked until I couldn't keep up with myself. I was nearly running. I was out of breath, gasping for air. I was closer to the jetty, but no closer to any answers. What did I want? What did I want? The question kept repeating, as relentless as the waves. I stopped and sat down. I was already wet through, so adding some sand to the mess wasn't going to matter at this point. I just sat there and felt the sun, sat there and watched the water come and go and come again. I watched the little shorebirds with their toothpick legs run down to the water's edge, plunge their beaks into the sand three or four times, and then race back as fast as they could to beat the incoming wave. I couldn't tell if they ever got anything to eat. They must have, because they kept at it. Like the waves, again and again. Talk about a pointless life. Run, dig for food, run. Repeat. But it was the only life they had. These birds didn't ask themselves these awful questions. What did they want? They just did what they did. It was so simple. Had we humans really needed to evolve to the point where we'd lost our instincts? Eat, mate, nest, raise young, die...life was pretty straightforward if you were a bird. How different were we really? Couldn't it be that simple for us? Why did I keep complicating it? I hugged my knees to my chest. I knew a huge part of me would rather just die and get it over with. I hated to admit it, but when my mom died, I kind of wished it had just been me. I was going to die anyway; why keep all of this drama up in the meantime? We were all going to die in the end, and except for the kids, it just didn't feel as if what I was doing in the meantime mattered that much. I suppose I was depressed. But I couldn't talk about this to anyone. They'd freak out and think I meant I was planning to kill myself. I wasn't, of course. It wasn't that big of a deal—just this constant sadness that made it hard to keep myself excited about anything for very long. There just didn't seem to be much point in a whole life spent running down to the water, sticking your head in the sand, running back up, and then doing it all over again.

But did the birds need a point? What if they were perfectly happy doing it that way? What if they actually enjoyed it, the feeling of the water, the sand, their legs running? What if they loved their lives? What if that was all they wanted, some water, some sand, and the joy of their own legs, feathers, beaks? What if they knew it was enough?

Could I ever be like those birds? Could my life, just like it was, be enough? I suddenly knew what I really wanted. I wanted to love my life. Even more than that, I wanted to love myself. I had always wanted a man to love me, because then I thought I would be loved all the time, like I'd hoped my mom would love me, like I'd always wanted my dad to. I'd tried to get that love from Rick instead. I'd learned to jump through all the hoops. I had dressed for him, dieted for him, did anything and everything to make him happy. I was a good wife, a good mother. And he had left anyway. He took all that work, all that effort, and left. All I had ever wanted was to be loved exactly the way I was. But it had seemed impossible. So instead, I just kept trying to change myself into whoever they said I had to be to get their love. I was tired of it.

That was the core of the thing Bea was trying to get me to see, wasn't it? The same big rock that I kept dragging around with me. It was all of that doing whatever it took to get their love. Trying anything that I thought might work. And refusing to give any love to myself was just my way of trying to get myself to behave. I thought I could hate myself into being a better person. It hadn't worked. I was just the same person, doing the same things, who hated myself.

What did I want? I wanted to be happy, to love myself, to have some kind of joy in my life. Okay, a lot of joy in my life. Maybe I even wanted to have some fun, what about that? Even if it was just for myself, just for me and the kids, and there was never any man at all, I wanted to love myself anyway. Love myself because no one could take that away from me. I wanted to want to live. To know that my life mattered because it was mine. I wanted to love the feeling of the sand and water and sun and my strong legs and have it be enough. I wanted to choose my life, to inhabit each moment, not just bide my time trying to be good until I died. I was going to die anyway, whether I had any fun or not, and no one cared at all. The shocking truth was that no one really cared if I skipped work and had coffee with strange men. No one cared if I did anything or didn't. But I wanted to care. I wanted my life to matter to me. I wanted my life to please me. That was what I wanted. I wanted to go through each day like it mattered. To treat myself like I mattered. To be interesting to myself. I wanted to really live my life, not just get through it. I wanted to live like Bea did.

It seemed like such a stupidly simple thing. I wanted to be happy. And it seemed totally selfish too. How could I be worried about a thing like that? I mean, what about world peace? Ending hunger? Saving the whales? Shouldn't those things be more important than my personal happiness? But at the same time, it also seemed like such a little thing, not nearly selfish enough for this TV world, where what I was supposed to want was fast cars, a glamorous career, a sexy body, lots of money, all of that *stuff*.

I started to giggle. I mean, I really cracked myself up. Look at that, I had gone from world peace and hungry whales to a sexy new Porsche in ten seconds flat. But how different were they really? Wasn't the point of any of it to be happy? At the bottom of it, wouldn't that be why I'd want any of that stuff? Could I even really care about the whales if I wasn't happy? I sure wasn't helping them any like this. I didn't have enough energy to save anything. And would it matter how fast I could drive if I didn't enjoy it? But what did it take to be happy?

I felt a little ridiculous when I realized that I was fretting about all of this while sitting in the sand at Venice Beach on a Tuesday morning when I should have been at work. Half the planet would have given anything to be where I was at that moment. More than half, probably. And the only reason I wasn't happy was that I thought I should be somewhere else, someone else. I thought I should have bigger answers to bigger questions. I was always unsatisfied, always looking outside for love, for beauty, for pleasure. That may be the only thing that separated me from the toothpick-leg birds, running up and down and up again. They didn't think they should have been somewhere else, doing something else. What was there not to be happy about, after all? The sun was shining, the waves were gentle, and the sand was getting warmer.

And I was hungry. I looked at my watch—nearly noon. How had that happened? I started to get irritated. My free day was almost half over. What had I accomplished? I'd gotten totally wet and muddy and finally come to the monumentally ordinary conclusion that all I wanted was to be happy and love myself. And so what? The minute I looked at my watch, the recriminations began. The panic set in. I looked again at those tiny birds. Did they ever get discouraged? Did they ever have even a moment of doubt? I recognized what was happening, and I refused to give in to the habit. This was a POG attack, pure and simple. One moment of weakness, one glance at my watch, and they were back, like wolves at the door. No wonder I felt like I was going nowhere with the whole Bea thing. It seemed like one step forward and two back. But maybe, just maybe, it was two forward and only one back. I could now see the POGS coming, recognize them. Even consider for an instant that they might not be right about me, that they might be…well, just POGS after all. They didn't have to run the show. Wasn't that something? Wouldn't it be considered progress?

How would I get free? If what I wanted was to be happy and love myself exactly as I was, then I could see that this was what I was up against. The battle was inside me, not with Rick or any other man. The challenge was mine. If it was going to happen, I'd have to challenge everything about how I had managed myself in the past. It seemed like a lot of work for such a simple goal: to be happy. And it looked like there was nothing at all in it for the whales. I wondered if it would be a tremendous waste of energy. I really thought I should have a more meaningful goal in life. It didn't seem like enough. But what if it was not only enough—what if it was actually a lot? I guess it seemed juvenile. "I want to love myself." But what if it was actually important? And worth committing to?

Committing to? I guessed that was the core of it, the missing piece. I kept trying these Bea things on, and liking them even, but then getting distracted and stopping. Maybe this whole thing was going to take something more if it was going to stick. Like a commitment. Commit to myself, like being married. To myself. For better or for worse. No backing out. No stopping, no matter what. I mean, everyone knew a relationship was hard work sometimes. A marriage took work, that's what they said. Why would a good relationship with myself be any different?

I had loved being married. I had absolutely loved the feeling that at last, something was real, someone was mine, and I was safe. It was this wonderful glow. Of course, it didn't last very long. I wanted so badly to have that feeling again. But the marriage hadn't worked out, so I assumed it wasn't real after all. I had never been safe with Rick. I supposed it was just some kind of bubble I was in. When my marriage fell apart, my whole life had fallen apart.

Or had it? Maybe it had fallen apart a long time before that, and I just hadn't noticed. I couldn't actually remember a time in my entire life when I felt as if my life was together, not really.

I had thought marrying Rick would fix it. Would make me okay somehow. I thought being married would prove to me and the world that I was lovable, desirable, worthwhile. I kept trying to make Rick prove those things to me, but no matter what he did or didn't do, I never for one minute believed it myself. In fact, I remember disagreeing with him whenever he said anything sweet about me. I'd thought it was modesty. I'd thought it wasn't nice to think well of myself. I was a nice girl, and nice girls were demure and never vain or arrogant. But that was just self-defense. After the POGS, I made sure to put myself down before anyone else could. It seemed easier to take that way.

What a bunch of garbage! No wonder I was so miserable all the time. Did those birds ever bother with anything as absurd as that? Could they have enjoyed the feel of the water and the sand if they were busy putting themselves down about the shape of their legs? It was absurd. And yet that was exactly what I believed I was supposed to do. The day my daughter and I painted our toenails, she ran around showing them off. She was just loving being in her body; she had no shame, no fear. It bugged me that I had noticed this before and then forgotten again. It seemed so circular. I felt as if I just kept going round and winding up in the same place. What was the deal with that? Was I not moving at all or was it something else? I stared at the ocean until my eyes blurred. I was hungry, but I didn't want to move, not yet. I was breathing deeply, watching the waves, in, out, in, out. Like the planet was breathing. Maybe that's exactly what it was doing. In, out. Breathing.

I heard this dumb blonde joke once. A blonde walks into a beauty parlor wearing a walkman with earphones. The stylist does his best, but finally he needs her to take off the headphones. He gestures to her to take them off, but to no avail. Finally, in frustration, he yanks them off her. The blonde stares at him in shock for a minute and then drops dead. Confused, the stylist listens to the earphones: "Breathe in, breathe out, breathe in, breathe out." Cute, right? Too dumb to remember to breathe. Except that I felt like the blonde in the joke—as if I'd forgotten the simplest things that would keep me alive. As if I would even forget to breathe. I sure kept forgetting to breathe deeply. To notice. Bea kept having to remind me. Begin with the breath. What was the big deal about the breath?

The waves continued. In, out, in, out. The birds ran down and back, down and back. But they were much farther away than they were before. The tide had been going out. It was so subtle I hadn't even noticed. The tides go in and out every day. Twice, I think. There are the little waves that break on the shore and then the big wave of the tides. Giant breaths, in, out, in, out. And what about the moon? Doesn't the moon control the tides? I never understood how, but somehow, the moon controls the tides. And the moon waxes full and then wanes, once a month. A giant breath indeed. And the moon goes around the earth, and the earth goes around the sun, and it was all going in circles. Everything was coming closer and then moving away. In, out. I bled and then refilled, and then bled again. Almost like a breath. My body just did what it did, this monthly breath, this tide, this waxing and waning…I was getting dizzy just thinking about it. I was sure Bea would have some weird mystical thing to say about all of this waxing and waning, this breathing, these tides. I felt as if I was right on the brink of figuring it out for myself, figuring out something important. But it kept slipping away.

CHAPTER TWENTY-FOUR
Time to Eat. Again.

I was really, really hungry by then, and I just didn't have the right equipment to go stick my head in the sand to get my lunch like the birds did. But I had some cash, and the boardwalk was right up there. That was the human version. We stuck our cards in a cash machine, got money, and then ran into a restaurant and got fed. And then we ran back to the cash machine and started over. Maybe we were not so different from the birds as I'd thought.

As hungry as I was, I really didn't want a slice of pizza or a burger or any of the usual beachy junk food. I knew there was a restaurant a little way up that had healthy food. I never took the kids there because it was a little pricey, but it was my holiday, and I decided to treat myself. I got a table outside, right on the boardwalk, watching the people go by. Some guy was playing guitar and singing Beatles songs. At least he was mostly on key and not too loud. He was way better than that guy in the turban who carried the amp on his back. Yikes. I ordered a spinach salad with salmon on top. And a lemonade. My pants had dried while I had been sitting in the sand twisting my brain in knots about life, the universe, and everything, so I wasn't too much of an embarrassment. True to Venice Beach form, the haze was rolling in, but it did keep the sun from being too hot.

I don't usually like eating in restaurants alone. I felt too self-conscious, as if the waiters must feel sorry for me because I didn't have a date, or sometimes, I thought they must be pissed because with only one person, there'd be only half the tip. But I was really hungry, and it was my vacation day, so I didn't care much. I had a lot on my mind. It was all still pulling at me. The thing with the tides and breathing and bleeding and, well, all of it. It was on the tip of my tongue, like a name I'd forgotten. The food came, and I started just wolfing it down the way I always did, trying just to get through it fast, get it over with, get out of the restaurant in a hurry. Eating just to fill up the gnawing hole. Again. Then it hit me. It was all exactly the same. Circular. Or maybe more of an oval, building up and then going over the top and back out the other way. Eating. The food goes in, goes through its processes, waste goes out, and then you have to bring in food again. I couldn't just eat once and be finished any more than I could breathe once and call it good. I slowed down and carefully chewed my salad. I actually spent some time with the flavors.

Open With Love

Why did I think I could learn something once and then never have to think about it again? Why was I surprised and frustrated that it hadn't all changed in some blinding flash of understanding? Bea kept saying it, "Begin again." And again and again…but did it mean nothing was changed? Was it just a pointless exercise of doing the same thing over and over? Or was the change happening even though I had to begin again? What was really happening with the tides? It wasn't as if nothing changed there. The sand washed away and washed back a little differently. The beach changed.

Well, not in Los Angeles, actually—in Los Angeles, we spent hundreds of thousands in tax dollars to dredge the sand, shore up the beach, rake it clean, and bulldoze it, all to keep it from changing. Because of the million-dollar condos along the coast and the tourist dollars, the beach must not be allowed to erode, to change. Kind of like the women, spending whatever it cost, doing whatever it took to make sure time didn't erode the landscape. Wow. Yikes. It was everywhere. Humans against nature.

But in other places, natural places, the beaches changed. Heck, even sand was formed by the tides, right? Whole mountains got ground away into sand, and then the sand deposited itself somewhere else. Eventually, didn't the sand itself compact, form new rock, an island, maybe? It took a very long time, but something changed a little bit with each and every wave.

And it was the same with eating. I mean, if it didn't matter at all because I always had to eat again in a few hours, if it really was a pointless, repetitive exercise, if nothing in my body was changing, then it wouldn't matter what I ate. So long as the calories were enough to keep me alive, beyond that, it wouldn't matter. But it didn't work like that. Even I knew it. I mean, I could eat junk food once in a while and still be okay, but if I ate too much of it, for too long, I could really tell. I just didn't feel right. And I bet if that was all a person ate, after a while, she'd really get sick. So even though I had to eat again and again, it was changing something in my body, somehow leaving a residue each time I did it. Well, that made sense, actually. Because my body used the food to build new cells or whatever—however it did it, it used the food to do that, right? And then the cells stuck around long after the food was gone. So even though I had to eat again and again and again, each meal was leaving a residue.

Was it the same with all of Bea's letters? All those things I learned and "forgot" and learned again? All the times I felt I was right back where I started—staring down a warm pan of brownies, for instance; every time I thought I was a total loser because I really should have known better—maybe it was just time to learn something again. What if nothing was wrong with me, and it was just time for dinner. Or at least a snack? Perhaps it was all a normal part of the cycle of learning. Of this "being human," as Bea would say. No matter what I ever had for lunch, it seemed totally gone by dinner. But the residue remained. Was my mind the same way? No, it was more than my mind; it was like…what? Something more than that, because Bea was definitely trying to get me in touch with more than just my "mind." It was something deeper than the endless stream of thinking. It was more of, I don't know, my "essence."

So even if I seemed to forget—even if my mind did actually forget and then remember these same simple ideas, and even if I seemed to be at the same place again and again—was it possible that some residue was being left? That some change was happening inside of me, maybe too slow for me to see, like the tide going out? Would it be like the tides, when I would look up after a while and it would be clear that something was definitely different? Maybe whole mountains inside me were being worn away to sand.

I was almost finished with my salad. It was delicious. I stopped thinking just to enjoy it—chewing, tasting, swallowing. Knowing that my body would make good, healthy cells from this good, healthy meal, from the fresh air of the beach. That even though I might blow it and eat junk food tomorrow, this moment wasn't going to be wasted. This meal would leave a residue. Everything left a residue, became a part of me until it was ground away, used up, released. I thought about how Bea had said people left a residue as well. Their words became part of us, and there was no use resisting it. That must be part of the cycle as well. People came into my life and left a residue. Yikes. And I thought chicken McNuggets were bad. If everything and everyone was leaving a residue, and I really was committed to being joyful and happy, I could see that it would become very important to pay attention to what I was taking in. Wow.

I skipped dessert because it just didn't seem that I wanted it. Maybe I'd have a popsicle later. Or maybe not. Or a coffee. Or not. It was my day. I could have or not have whatever I wanted. What a cool feeling. I paid the check and left a generous tip. I was feeling generous. I was feeling really happy actually. I even gave the Beatles guy a buck in his guitar case. He was pretty good.

CHAPTER TWENTY-FIVE

I Do

I wandered into a little clothing shop with belly dancing stuff. Incense, jewelry, and flowing skirts and scarves. Bea would probably have adored that kind of thing. I loved the colors and the smells, but it had always seemed too hippie-ish for me. My mother and Rick had both preferred to see me in tailored clothes. They didn't approve of anything too flashy, anything that would draw attention to me or my body. "Nice girls just don't dress like that." Who the heck was doing the talking anyway? My mother was dead, and Rick was gone. Not just gone, he had gone with that flashy blonde—and she was anything but a nice girl. In fact, she was exactly what I'd been trying my whole life to make sure I wasn't. She was spoiled and vain and sure of herself. She was proud of herself and dressed specifically to show herself off.

I bet she never, ever contradicted Rick if he told her she looked good. I had to admit that just the thought of him and her still made me a little queasy. But I forced myself to think about it anyway. It seemed important to notice something. I had spent my life trying so hard never to look or act like a "spoiled little princess" and that was exactly what he had left me for. Okay, I had to admit I wasn't being fair; I didn't know her well enough to say what she was really like, but it was certainly how she came across. Men seemed to love that kind of girl.

"Be Beauty. Notice what pleases you. Attend to it. Be Beauty in the world. Your own Beauty." Something like that, anyway. Bea kept saying it again and again. She told me to be in my body, to notice what I loved. To attend to myself. To choose Beauty. I could choose to love myself. Choose to love even the parts I didn't approve of. Be tender with myself and the world. Was it Bea speaking now or me in my head? Begin again. From the very beginning. Be willing to be in this moment, right now.

I was in front of a rack of colorful skirts. Long, swirly skirts. Skirts that swayed to the touch and sparkled in the light. Skirts with elastic or drawstring waists. Adjustable. Comfortable no matter what size I was that week. Not tailored, no need for control-top hose or diets. My body breathed with its cycles. Larger and smaller, often within a single month. My hands kept returning to this beautiful turquoise skirt. It had silver sequins stitched along a hot-pink flower pattern. It felt like silk. I looked at my dirty khakis. I was sick of khakis, of sensible shoes, of trying to disappear. I wanted to stand out. I wanted to be the spoiled princess for a change. I wanted to spoil myself. I wanted to run around and love myself and not care who knew it. Why had I stopped before? The "Be Beauty" time had been fun. Cycles, I supposed. The tide had gone out. I needed to fuel up again. I needed to keep practicing. I had a mountain of shame inside of me, many years of hiding out, and it would take a few tides to grind it down to sand, to build an island somewhere else. An island of freedom and beauty—my own inner Tahiti.

Maybe it would take my lifetime to catch up with these new ideas. Bea had pointed out the path, but I sort of wandered around a bit before I got on it—or stayed on it. Well, one step back, two forward. This was a "Be Beauty" holiday, and I was going to try on the skirt.

So I did. And then a simple velvet top to go with it and a wonderful embroidered jacket with a fuzzy collar. And my body didn't look bad at all. It looked feminine and curvy—not like the gross, overstuffed sausage I often thought I saw in the mirror. Those clothes, those shapes went with my body; they didn't try to compress me into some other woman's ideal shape. I even picked out some jeweled sandals. Well, they were flip-flops, really, but with beads and sparkles sewn onto the straps. Comfy and pretty. The skirt was quite long; the sandals only showed when I walked.

I had them put all my old clothes into a bag so I could wear the new ones. Then I chose some earrings and even a bracelet. This was what I'd been hoping for at the water's edge. Dramatic and different. A new me. The girls in the shop had been great. They kept telling me how fabulous I looked and assuring me it wasn't "too much" or "over the top." Of course, they had tattoos and tongue piercings, so maybe they weren't the best judges, but I didn't care. It was nice to be with the girls, nice to feel cared for.

I walked out of the shop feeling like a gypsy, like a girl playing dress up, an artist, a queen, and a fraud, all at once. Weird. But not bad. I tried to walk tall, the way Bea had walked down the boardwalk. No, not like Bea, not at all. Like Grace, walking tall. My head was still swimming with thoughts. I kept noodling over the idea of committing to myself, to this process. I checked my watch, on guard for another POG attack. It was after three o'clock. Another hour or so and I'd have to go back to my real life. What would the kids say about this outfit? They'd know something was up. I'd be busted for skipping work. How could I teach them to be good citizens when I was out playing hooky?

But what if I didn't want to teach them to be good? What if I didn't want my daughter to grow up like I had? For my son to turn into another Rick? Uck, what a thought. But he would, wouldn't he? It was all he knew. It really was up to me.

Open With Love

If they were going to have a chance at another kind of life, any chance at happiness and freedom, they would have to learn it from me. I owed it to them to learn how to be free, how to be happy. If I didn't, I was just going to hand my unhappiness on to them, like my parents had handed theirs to me. That was a weird twist on what I'd always thought was right and proper. I thought the plan was you had to sacrifice for your children; you had to suffer so they could have a better life.

What if that was nothing but a big fat lie? What if the only thing you owed your children was to teach them how to be happy? How to love themselves? And what if the only way to do *that* was to love yourself and be happy? Then that would have to be my highest duty—my real job as a parent. To love myself and make myself happy. Why not?

I was pretty sure tooth-brushing and looking both ways were still in the job description—not to mention the birds and the bees. But walking along the boardwalk on that Tuesday afternoon, I realized it. I understood something all the way down to my heart. This was it. My whole job as a parent, as a human. And I had this sense that I had already known this, that I had figured it out before, maybe a long time ago, but that I'd forgotten it. It felt like a déjà vu. Perhaps it was like breathing, like eating; I just had to keep on doing it, remembering and forgetting many times. The lesson would always be the same. My job was to be happy in myself, maybe even joyful.

Nothing more and nothing less. It was tiny, and it was unbelievably huge, and it was going to take everything I had. It was an enormous commitment. And no one would be there to hold me to it; no one cared if I pulled it off or not. They probably didn't even want to hear about it. Everyone was too busy dealing with their own stuff. My happiness, my self-love was no one else's problem. It was no one's job but mine. And my whole life—and probably even my children's—was riding on it.

But what did I really mean by happiness, by joy? Not some kind of plastic pop-a-Prozac happiness, with everything glossed over. No, I wanted a deeper joy, an all-encompassing, good-bad-and-ugly happiness. Peacefulness, maybe. Or contentment. But not just some feeling that might come and go. Deeper than mood or preference, this was more solid. Like marriage vows, "in sickness and in health, for better or worse, for richer or for poorer..." all that stuff. No matter what. You didn't expect the poorer, the sicker, or the worse, but you vowed not to abandon the person.

No matter what. Rick had broken those vows. I guess I had too, though it was tidier just to blame him. I still felt really guilty about it. I had never forgiven myself for blowing the marriage thing. I felt like such a failure. Because I had meant it when I said it. It was supposed to be forever. I was afraid to stop punishing myself for it, because if I did, I might want to try again. I might fail again. And I couldn't handle that. No way.

Not that I'd even had a clue what forever was. And what business did I have making vows like that to another person? Or expecting him to make them to me if I couldn't even commit to myself? I had sold myself out. If I refused to love me, how could I begin to think I knew how to love? How could I ever be happy if I kept hating myself and refusing to forgive myself for failing at marriage?

I caught my reflection in a shop window and didn't recognize myself. In all that thinking, I had forgotten about the outfit. I almost giggled. I was in front of a Native American shop. I liked the music they were playing, so I went in. The pulsing down beat of the drums made me want to move. I found myself walking in time with the beat and thumping my feet. I hoped no one would notice. I wanted to dance but didn't want to embarrass myself or to make fun of their traditions.

A young man with a long ponytail was watching me from behind the counter. He had beautiful brown skin and huge black eyes. He smiled. I smiled and looked down. He turned the music up, and came out from behind the counter, dancing with me. He caught my eyes and held the gaze. I couldn't look away. He pounded his feet in time with the drum, almost like his feet were playing the rhythm. His chest moved back and forward. His shoulders and arms pulsed lightly like a bird, tracing the lyrical tones of the flute. I could feel my face burning, but he never took his eyes off mine. He was encouraging me with those eyes, pulling me in deeper, letting me know I was safe, that it was okay to be dancing in broad daylight with a perfect stranger.

Well, why not? It was that kind of a day. No one knew me there. No one would have recognized me in that outfit anyway. No one knew anything at all about me. Least of all me. I could be the wild woman for the day if I wanted. It could be me, dancing easily to the deep drumbeats, my arms moving lightly with the delicate flute. We danced all around the small shop, past colorful blankets and statues of wolves, eagles, and salmon, carvings in wood and stone. Something was burning in the corner, some kind of smoky incense. As we danced past it, he cupped his hands to catch the smoke and then spread it over himself. I hesitated then did the same. It smelled sweet but natural, some kind of herb. I hoped it wasn't illegal. I felt my body moving, my breath coming faster. I didn't care about anything. I was alive, and it was good to be alive. My skirt swirled. The sequins flashed. He never took his eyes from mine, and he never spoke. My eyes unfocused a little bit, and I seemed to see us somewhere else, moving around a campfire in the dark, wearing beads and fringe and carved masks. His body moved like a bird's...He seemed to become the bird, an enormous, powerful bird of prey...We were in another time, another place.

When I blinked, the vision was gone, but the sense of it hovered still, like a mist around the edge of the normal, daylight things. Finally, the music faded away. He stood before me and touched his heart, then gently reached out and touched mine. Just like Al had done. Was this some kind of secret code?

Then, without a word, he went back behind the counter and returned to work. He was sorting silver chains, untangling some kind of necklaces. I stood still for a full minute, gathering myself. It was almost as if I had imagined it all, as if our dance had been part of another wild-woman dream or as if the dream was taking over my waking life. I shook my head. The sweet smoke was still wafting from the table in the corner. I went to it. Small bundles of grass wrapped in brightly colored cord were stacked neatly. "Sweetgrass: very good for calling in the ancestors, spirits, and guides," read the hand-lettered sign, and next to a smaller pile of thick-leafed gray-green bundles another sign read: "California White Sage: for cleansing and purifying the body, mind, spirit, and the environment." In front of the bundles, from inside an enormous, magnificently iridescent seashell, rose a delicate plume of smoke. A burning bundle. Sweetgrass, for calling in the ancestors, spirits, and guides. Maybe that explained the vision. I looked back at my dance partner. He was still working on the chains. I cupped my hands around the rising smoke as we had done earlier and washed it over me, breathing deeply. I took some more and waved it over my heart. My heart sure seemed to be getting a lot of attention today.

I wandered around the store and found myself in front of a jewelry case. Inside were all kinds of turquoise rings in silver. They reminded me of Bea's ring. Hers was turquoise with an enormous pearl. She wore it on her ring finger. I wondered again if she was married. That got me thinking about my failed marriage, my fear of making the same mistakes, of risking it again. I was really afraid of putting my heart into someone else's hands, of having him take it with him when he left—like Rick. Like my father. Like so many others. Were any of them true love? Whether they had been loves or just girlish crushes didn't matter. I'd given them my heart, and I don't recall any of them giving it back.

I caught myself before I slipped into a good old "poor me" session. The notion was ridiculous. My heart was beating right there in my chest. It was nothing but a figure of speech. No matter how much it hurt sometimes, my heart had not been stolen from me. It had never been broken. It was still there, beating steadily in that deep, secret cave Bea kept referring to. It was mine. I was the one who kept forgetting to keep hold of it. I'd always sold myself too cheaply to the first bidder and then assumed my heart was safe in his care.

My heart. There had to be some other way to love. Could there be a way to share something without giving it away? Without neglecting myself? Could I love someone else without abandoning myself? I thought it must be possible. But…well, it was probably a moot point, since there was no one around to love. I stole a quick look at the handsome man sorting silver. Nah. Whatever that was we had shared, it wasn't any kind of happily ever after. Just a Tuesday afternoon rain dance. Or something like that. I felt a little warmth where he had touched my heart, where Al had touched it so many hours ago. It felt like love. Some kind of love, anyway—not the anxious kind I thought I knew about, but a simpler kind of love, love for the person right in front of you, sharing the journey. Not the usual "I will trade you this if you give me that" kind of love. Just a here-and-now love. What if there were all kinds of love, and they were all real? Maybe there was plenty of love in the world if I would just open my eyes and stop thinking I knew what it was supposed to look like.

I was really drawn to one ring in the case. The band was simple; the stone was smooth greenish turquoise, wrapped in gleaming silver. I must have been staring at it for a long time because suddenly he was there, opening the case, taking out the exact ring, slipping it on my finger. My ring finger. I hadn't worn a ring there since I'd given Rick his diamond back. My lawyer had said I could keep it, but I didn't want it; I didn't ever want to see it again.

The turquoise was beautiful. It sat perfectly on my hand and seemed to warm up immediately. It was dramatic but not ostentatious. It was the color of my skirt, the color of the clear waters off my imagined island paradise. It was perfect. I felt myself trying to resist. "It's too expensive," the voices were saying. "You can't wear that on your ring finger. What will people think?"

I just stood there, breathing, letting them have their say, not fighting them or reacting. The chatter slowed. I stood there with my hand on the glass, taking it all in, smelling the sweetgrass smoke and the ocean breeze from outside, feeling the gently beating drums calling my feet to play.

The ring was no ordinary piece of jewelry. It was a wedding ring. I knew if I bought that ring—standing there in that dress, on that amazing, not so ordinary Tuesday, that window into all that was possible on the other side of my daily habits—if I bought the ring and wore it out of there, something would change in me. Or maybe it already had. I felt my heart beating in my own chest, where it belonged. I recited vows in my head. "To love and honor and cherish, for better or for worse, in sickness and in health, richer or poorer, till death did me part." Until death itself took me out of my body, my churning mind, until the end of my life. Was that a commitment I could make? Was it one I could keep, no matter what? Could I become married to myself, from that day forth? Could I forgive myself and Rick and God and my father and try it again another way? Me for me forever? With this strange, lovely man as my witness?

Open With Love

Would I take myself, from this day forth, no matter what, for always?

He never said a word. Just looked at me, holding my hand with the ring gleaming there on my finger. I'm sure I was imagining it, but I felt he knew exactly what was going on in my mind, in my heart. His eyes were quiet strength, completely present, and I knew he would not think better or worse of me whatever I did. I could have walked away from that moment, walked away from the ring, away from the possibility it held. I could have walked out of that shop, shed those new clothes, returned to my safe, predictable life, and no one would ever be the wiser. It was entirely up to me, and there was no right or wrong answer. That was true freedom. The choice was mine and mine alone, and no one even knew I was making it. Except perhaps the lovely man, that gentle, dancing soul, whom I would probably never see again. And his eyes held no judgment, no answers, only that strange, unfamiliar love I had noticed before. I felt completely loved in that moment. I also felt utterly exposed and seen in all of my confusion, all of my fear and frailty. The unusual feeling was simply what it felt like to be totally present.

And I felt such a wash of love coming from inside of me as well, such a wave of pure feeling it threatened to engulf me. In that moment, I loved him, that total stranger, but more than him, I loved all of life, throughout all time. I loved how my life had gotten me to that precise moment and could not have been any different, could not have happened any way other than it had, or I would not have been standing there. I loved Bea for opening the door, but I also loved Rick and everyone else that it had taken to break me wide open on that precious Tuesday. I was suddenly grateful to Rick and even Tiffany and all of the others. I saw that they had served me well, that we were all part of an exquisite, complex dance, and that it was perfect.

I felt tears filling me up, spilling out of my eyes, and still I did not look away. Even with tears pouring down my face, I was not ashamed. I was loved, and I loved. I was part of all that had come before and all that was coming next, and it was not just a horrible mistake. I was not a horrible mistake. I belonged here, somehow. I belonged on the planet, and I belonged in that shop, and I belonged in that moment and in my life and in my body. I was alive with my own stretching, pounding heart. There was nothing I needed to escape from or to, and there was nothing missing and no place I needed to get to. Everything was perfect as it was, and yet, at the same exact moment, everything suddenly became possible. Out of this incredible sense of love and peace, the whole world and everything and everyone in it opened up completely.

"Yes."

"Yes."

Open With Love

"*Yes*! I *do*. No matter what! Always." It was my voice I finally recognized, saying these things out loud, these vows, these yeses. Yes to life, yes to love, yes to freedom and forgiveness, *yes* to happiness and joy, and yes to the ring and the dance and my own body and each magical Tuesday, which I suddenly saw could last a lifetime. *Yes!*

I was laughing and crying and hugging that lovely stranger and choosing to own that perfect ring as a symbol to myself of forever. Outside the sun was setting and the sky was all the colors you'd hope for. I paid for the ring and walked out onto the sand and raised my arms to the sun just as it slipped below the watery horizon. And as loud as I could, I said, "*Yes!*"

And then the day was over. With the sun's passing, it was time to get the kids, to make the dinner, to manage all the bits and pieces of my regular life. I felt a chill wash over me. What exactly had I done? What did it all mean? What would happen next?

As I made my way back to the car, back to my life, back to where I had come from only this morning, I was swept with alternating bouts of joy and terror. Of both excitement and a paralyzing sense of danger. It was intense, and I was keenly alive. I felt everything, smelled everything. I tasted the damp air as a dog would. I saw the faces of all the people I passed, saw the colors of the lights coming on; everything was so vivid.

And I saw Al, leaning against a brick wall, as I turned up the street where I'd left my car. At first, he just glanced away, but as I watched him, he looked back and recognized me. His face slowly broke into this huge smile; he put his finger to his heart, pointed at me, and then gave me the thumbs-up. I smiled back. Yes, thumbs-up for sure. So much love everywhere. I'd never even noticed it. It was all around me, all the time. Simply waiting for me to stop and see it. I decided to take the kids out for dinner. This was a night to celebrate.

CHAPTER TWENTY-SIX
Till Death Do Us Part

Lying in bed that night with all of Bea's letters spread around me, I thought about my delightful day. The kids were in bed, exhausted after our celebration. I'd taken them bowling, of all things. We ate in the diner, which they loved, and shared a big ice cream sundae. Then we put on rental bowling shoes and went for it. It had never occurred to me that you could just take your kids bowling on a Tuesday evening for no reason. We had them put the bumpers up so there were no discouraging gutter balls and played a wild game. I suck at bowling, but I was having fun, and the kids loved it. Justin had his own style, very dramatic, a lot of flourishes. I had to help Megan the first few times, but she got the hang of it. Put the ball down and push it. That seemed to be the best technique for her.

I'd never seen a ball roll so slowly. I was afraid it would just stop halfway down, but somehow, it never did. I laughed, and the kids laughed, and I didn't even mind the weird looks I was getting in my skirt. Not exactly the prescribed bowling outfit, but so what? I didn't need to impress anyone. After my day at the beach, I didn't need to look for a man to marry me and make me whole. I was already whole and married to myself, with all the freedom and confidence and permission that brought. Bowling. I thought it was a pretty good choice for a wedding after-party.

So now the kids were passed out, and I wasn't far behind, but I wanted to think about it all for a minute. The beautiful ring on my left hand caught my eye and made me smile. Strange to think I'd be just going back to my cube tomorrow as if nothing had happened. And maybe nothing did. I took a day off and went to the beach. I bought some new clothes. Dined and danced, wept and wed, but so what? Tomorrow was Wednesday, and I'd be right back at work.

But I felt that something in me had changed somehow. And I wanted to keep feeling it. I didn't want to write this whole thing off as some kind of weird anomaly. The day had been special, and I wanted it to mean something. I wanted it to be real—being married to myself—every bit as real as being married to Rick had been. Maybe even more so, since this time I had a lot better idea of what I was getting into. What made a marriage real anyway? When I was getting divorced, it seemed more like a matter of dissolving a business than anything remotely having to do with the emotional commitment of two living people. That seemed to be the real deal in America: who owned what. But what made for a marriage? How real had mine been if it had gone down the drain so easily? How could I be sure to honor this new vow I'd made? What would stop me from just walking out on myself?

It occurred to me that maybe I should write it down and sign it. That would make it a bit more official. After that, I felt I really should consider a honeymoon. Yeah, right. Okay, Grace, slow down. At this rate, I was going to start sending engraved announcements, contacting the newspapers. Why not throw a shower, register me and myself at Macy's? I could just see it. My sister would be horrified. They'd probably lock me up. Maybe I was getting carried away. Marrying myself. What a silly idea.

I looked at the beautiful ring. I supposed I could wear it on the other hand. I tried it. It simply didn't feel right. No matter how weird it all was, I couldn't quite talk myself out of it. Deep end or not, I was off. I wanted to see this through. I didn't know exactly what I was up to, but it felt right. I got out a piece of paper and wrote it down.

"I, Grace, take me, Grace, to be my..." No, that was too ridiculous. I tried again.

"Be it known that from this day forward, I, Grace, promise to love myself, to honor myself, and to cherish myself; for better or for worse, for richer and for poorer, in sickness and in health, for as long as I shall live, so help me God." I wasn't sure if the "so help me God" was from the wedding vow or the thing you said with your hand on the Bible in court. But I left it in because, given my history with myself, I was pretty sure I was going to need all the help I could get. I sat there looking at it.

As I read it again, out loud, I started to feel stupid—I mean, really stupid. More than just stupid, I felt naked and scared and stupid. It came out of nowhere and ambushed me. How pathetic was I? A grown woman sitting in her bed, alone, writing marriage vows to herself. Was it sour grapes because I didn't have a man? Or was it just some kind of New Age blah-blah: "You've got to love yourself before anyone else can love you..." I mean, everyone said that. It was all over *Oprah*. I think I'd even said it to a friend or two. "You've got to love yourself first." Duh. It wasn't like any of this was news. It shouldn't have been such a big deal. Why was I getting all carried away? It was embarrassingly obvious. Love yourself. Self-esteem. That was right up there with flossing.

Yeah, well, to tell you the truth, most of the time, I didn't floss either. I knew I was supposed to love myself. But a lot of the time, I didn't. Love was only for the deserving. It felt sinful to love myself when I didn't deserve it. That was what I'd always thought. I used it to make myself behave. If I did this, I'd be a good person. If not, whammo! Hate, punishment, rejection. Where on earth did "love yourself" fit into that? Loving myself unconditionally had always seemed like a recipe for complete moral collapse. Not to mention that it was patently impossible.

But something had shifted that afternoon. Or maybe it had been shifting since Bea started writing those letters. I read my vows again. For better or for worse, etc. To love myself, honor myself, and cherish myself no matter what I did? Or didn't do? No matter what I weighed? I wondered if I'd thought about what I was promising when I'd married Rick. I certainly treated him the same way I treated myself. I loved and cherished him when he behaved himself. And I didn't when he didn't. I sure didn't love, honor, and cherish him when he took up with Tiffany. I think what I really signed up for was to love and honor and cherish him as long as he didn't hurt my feelings. I hadn't signed up for the worse part, and neither had he. It was for better, for richer, and for health. Would I have ever married him if I'd really thought about what I was promising? Would anybody ever marry anyone? No wonder the divorce rate in California was near 80 percent.

It was bigger than I'd ever realized, this ideal of unconditional love. Love that was not tied to an outcome. Love that was there no matter what. All the books and magazines said we were supposed to have this for ourselves, but what was it? We mothers were supposed to have it for our children. It was considered natural. Did I have that? Of course I did. I would love Justin and Megan no matter what. I'm sure my mother would have sworn she loved me and my sister unconditionally. But did she? If she did, then where did I get the idea that she only loved me if I was skinny, if I kept clean and looked pretty in my dresses, if I was popular like my sister? What had happened? It seemed more like she used love as a bargaining chip. I could have it if I'd do this or that. Or if I didn't do the other. Then I could have her love, and maybe even a brownie. Love hadn't been unconditional at all in my home; love was a training tool. Behavior modification, like the voice you'd use with a puppy. Love was the reward. You got it if you behaved.

And now I used it to control myself—and my children. Of course I loved them. I would have died for them. In a heartbeat, no questions asked. But would they know that? What they saw was sweet mommy if they were good and mean mommy if they were bad. What were they supposed to think? What else would they think? That I loved them when they were good and didn't when they were bad? What a mess. But what was I supposed to do to teach my kids how to behave? What should I do when they'd pushed me to the end of my rope? I couldn't be sweet all the time, no matter what they did. Not if I didn't want them to become spoiled monsters. That wasn't really love. I saw parents like that. In restaurants or at the mall. I thought they must be on drugs: Valium, Prozac, lithium, martinis, whatever. Their kids were these horrible monsters, and they'd just smile and say how cute it all was.

Arrrrggghhh. I was spinning round again. I started with one thing, this idea of unconditional love, and somehow I got all wrapped up in this mess of parenting styles, and I suspected it didn't need to be that complicated at all. I mean, I didn't really have to work out all the details right that minute, did I? Thinking was just one of my sand traps, just a tried-and-true habit that kept me from having to feel anything. I'd just try to understand it mentally. I would rather spin circles in my head than deal with something directly. This was simple enough. It was about me, committing to love myself, starting immediately and never stopping. Just doing it as well as I could. I read the vows again. Out loud. "I promise to love, honor, and cherish myself, so help me God." I felt the same queasy, exposed feeling. I was fighting something big here, challenging a lifetime of being a certain way. If I loved myself no matter what, If I gave myself permission to love myself even if I messed up, even if I really, really messed up, I was sure "they" would never approve of me, "they" would abandon me, "they" wouldn't want me, "they"...

So what?

Huh? I stopped myself in my tracks with that one.

So what if they didn't, if they wouldn't, if they'd...whatever? I didn't have to abandon me. I could always start again if I needed to. And again and again if necessary. No one even needed to know. I could fall off the wagon and get back on. I could give myself permission to love myself, to not use love as a weapon or as a training tool. I could learn to be gentle with myself, like Bea always said. This love could become mine; it would be in my own hands, and no one could ever take it away from me. If I was married to my own self, I'd be the one in charge of whether or not I walked out on myself, if I cheated on myself, lied to myself, or any of it. The real problem had never been that Rick had lied to me; it was that I had started lying to myself. I came to believe that he was more important than I was, that he held all the cards, all the power to make my life mean something. And because I had given it all to him, he was able to take it all away. Except he hadn't really. I made that up.

So that was what Bea meant when she talked about reclaiming the cave and kicking out the robbers who'd taken over. "They" weren't someone else taking advantage of me. The robbers were just the cut-off parts of me. If I refused to abandon myself, I would never be so alone again. I could see it was pretty simple, if not always easy. I signed the paper. Signed my vows to myself. I gathered all of Bea's letters into a neat pile and put my signed vows right on top. I took a deep breath and fell into a peaceful sleep.

CHAPTER TWENTY-SEVEN

Africa

The airmail envelope was postmarked Tanzania. So she'd made it after all. I opened it carefully, afraid to tear the fragile paper.

Dear Grace,

You have embarked on a path few actually choose. Be advised that there will be resistance. You will meet skeptics and naysayers and the truly poisonous people, who claim to already know it all.

Do not allow them to rob you of your homecoming. Do not hide your glory for fear of their criticisms. You, full in yourself, loving and honoring and completely inhabiting your perfection in each moment, will thrill some and terrify others. Total strangers may try to discourage you. They may approach you in the market with horrible stories of this or that, stories designed to send you back under the rock of fear and hiding. They may look at you with undisguised disgust or with the dreaded disapproval, their silent attempt to get you back under control. The fearful ones cannot abide anyone's movement toward freedom.

You will come to learn who is and is not able to support you in your becoming. Your body will tell you. Pay heed to its subtle messages. It tells you this or that person is not to be trusted. They are not. Your body will know. You will feel the tightness starting deep within, feel yourself trying a bit too hard. In that very moment, as soon as you recognize it, stop.

Know that these people have chosen to play a difficult and essential role in your growth and you in theirs. They seem to be outside yourself, walking around in other bodies as they do, but they are only mirrors for the very parts of you that still resist and fear this new growth in you. You could not even see these "others" if you were not still wrestling yourself. They offer the opportunity to choose tenderness over your practiced reign of terror. What a tremendous sacrifice they are making to help you. For to be so frightened that one cannot abide freedom in another is its own particular hell, a prison itself. By your very *presence, you are causing them great pain. You are a crack in their reality, an opening into something they long for and fear greatly. For they also could not see you, if some part of them was not struggling to express itself in ways they are too frightened to allow. You and they are dancing a delicate dance. Sometimes they are the ones leading; sometimes you are.*

By noticing that no one is separate from you, you recognize that it is yourself who is withholding the love, you who disapproves. This will tell you just where you are rejecting and controlling yourself with punishment. You see where you withhold love from your fearful self. This is where you can choose to set the armor down and begin the healing embrace. This comes more and more easily.

Did you think you had bested your inner demons? Are you dismayed to discover them showing up all around you? Know that it is possible to soothe those voices so that you can continue to explore the tender territory outside the fixed world of damnation and domination. Recognize that you will be letting some habits go. They will fight to survive.

Begin, as always, with tenderness. Find a tenderness for the part of yourself that still so badly wants these others' approval, that needs their love, and an equal tenderness for the part of them that is too afraid to give it. Whether a from a stranger or a longtime friend, you can begin to shield yourself without refusing love. Know that you are full and they can neither give nor take anything you need. Allow them the space to be where they are and allow yourself to be safe from their hooks.

As difficult as it may be, it is time to let the old ideas about yourself slide away from you. Let them go from yourself and see what happens. Either the others will embrace a new sense of you, or you will part ways. As you let the ideas, and sometimes even the people, go, you must also become active in your quest for new ideas, new connections. Open your heart and eyes and mind to notice them. They may be old friends who suddenly reappear with much to share or strangers whose gaze seems to flicker with recognition, with a shared spark—open yourself to them, even for the brief instant of a genuine smile, a heartfelt word. We are all moving through the world hoping to find a home in each other's eyes. Become that welcoming home to those you feel safe to open to. In time, you will be able to be a safe home to anyone, without surrendering yourself, your truth. You will, one day, be able to greet the entire world with love, with compassion, no matter what it sends your way, but for now, I want you to begin to notice your allies.

It is time to find your tribe. You have gone this far alone, bravely battling the inner demons and clearing away the wreckage. Your path has taken you deep, and you have emerged whole. Now you must begin to build an outer world that supports the inner. Now you will seek and find strength and companionship. You are creating the structures of a new life, of new actions, new habits. Soon you will even find yourself supporting others, in the divine cycle of maiden, mother, queen, and crone. But for today, simply begin to open yourself to the possibilities, to the others who share your path. Be not discouraged at the challengers; they are only proof that you are indeed walking a high road, one many wish to take but are afraid to. You are a lovely and terrifying beacon to them, less frightening if they can cause you to stumble.

And if you do stumble, you know what to do. As ever, be gentle. Begin again.

Love,

—B

* * *

As I set the letter down, I marveled at how she seemed to know so much about inner freak-outs. I checked the postmark again, studied the gorgeous stamp. Africa. I didn't know how you could fake something like that. How did she do it? She was in Africa, of all places, writing this letter in her elegant, spidery handwriting on tissue-like airmail paper from... what, some grass hut? Some tent in the bush on safari, shooting elephants by day, magically spying on me by night? Do they even shoot elephants anymore? I hoped not. I was pretty sure they were endangered. Probably not shooting elephants, then. Though I could almost see her staring down a rifle at a charging herd. But seriously, what business did a little old lady have in Africa? It was almost Christmas. Shouldn't she have been home by the fire, knitting mittens somewhere? Maybe she really was some kind of voodoo priestess or something. You know what? I hoped so. I figured when I was her age, I'd sure rather be out sacrificing chickens than rotting away in some old folks' home.

To tell the truth, I was jealous. I was the young woman, and I should have been the one having the wild, adventurous life. Wasn't that the way it was supposed to work? Okay, maybe it wasn't. Perhaps you had to stay home first and raise your kids, and then you got to go off and have wonderful adventures. As long as I was going to get to have them eventually, I guessed it was okay. It just seemed weird.

But not as weird as what she'd written. How the heck did she know what kind of trouble I was having here on this side of the planet? Every day, it seemed I ran into someone who cut me down. Strangers would give me dirty looks if I smiled at them; the girls at work would just shake their heads as I walked by in one of my new outfits. And that grocery store thing. How did she know that? It was at the beach actually. I'd taken the kids there to run around in the sand after work. Even though it's the middle of winter and the days are so short, it's often warm enough, and ever since my wonderful day playing hooky, I just couldn't get enough of the beach. We'd bring a picnic supper, and I let the kids get wet if they wanted to.

So one evening, this old man had just come right up to me and started talking about all this horrible crap. Bacteria in the water. Kids getting kidnapped. Women getting raped. How I really should be home with the doors locked, that kind of stuff. But he said it as if he was really some kind of concerned father figure. It was so creepy. I kept being polite to him, but everything in me wanted to tell him just to get the heck away from us. Finally, I gathered up the kids and went home to get rid of him. He kept trying to give me his card, like I was going to want to go out with him or something. I took the card just to shut him up and tossed it before we even got to the car. Uggh. As if.

Quite a lot of men had been giving me their cards lately. Weird. I married myself, and suddenly, all these men wanted to go out with me. Didn't it just figure? But I was still pretty skittish after the whole Steve thing. I fell so hard for him, and afterward, I got all twisted up. I still worried about my body, sometimes thinking something was horribly wrong with it, that I was, if not totally deformed, certainly not attractive. It was getting better with time, but I just didn't think I could go there again. Not yet.

I admit it was kind of fun, though. I liked the attention. Justin teased me about it. If some guy flirted with me when he was there, he'd roll his eyes and make a face at me. It was kind of cute. I think he was jealous. But he didn't have anything to worry about. Not for a while at least. I looked at the shining ring on my left hand. I was still getting the hang of being married to myself. And I hadn't given up on the idea of a honeymoon. I mean, why not? Rick and I had never had a real honeymoon. I'd wanted to go to Paris; he'd wanted to go lie on a beach and drink mai tais, and we never managed to do either. We spent a week at his cousins' place in Florida. It had rained. Every day. I hated Florida. We had planned to take a real honeymoon on our first anniversary, but by then I was pregnant and puking, and somehow, we never got around to it. Maybe I should take myself to Paris. Bea was in Africa, after all.

Open With Love

I found myself staring at the framed poster on the wall. The Parisians rushing along under their umbrellas. The Eiffel Tower glistening behind. The letter sat forgotten on my lap. The kids were sleeping. I had the sliding door open, and a cool breeze was coming in. Paris. It seemed impossible. So far, so expensive. What about work? What about the kids? Paris. I really wanted to go to Paris. Alone? I'd never gone anywhere by myself.

I looked at Bea's letter again. Africa. Was she alone in Africa? She had been alone when I'd met her. Walking along the boardwalk with her head high, her feet tapping along, almost as if she was dancing, not walking. Yet she had seemed so much a part of that scene. As if it could not have existed without her. She didn't seem like a woman alone. On the contrary, she seemed to know everyone she passed. Even me. Not for one second had she hesitated when she'd invited me to join her. She looked me right in the eyes and asked me if I would like to join her. Actually, she had told me to join her. It seemed impossible that I would have refused. No, Bea was not alone in Africa, even if she had no one traveling with her. Bea was a part of her world, wherever her world happened to be that day. That's what the letter was about, wasn't it? Going to Paris, or anywhere in the world. But not by myself. With myself. Why not?

I was often afraid of people. People like that creepy old man; smelly, homeless people; angry gangbangers. Even, or maybe especially, the perfect people, the grown-up POGS. But what about Al and his buddies on the beach that day? The beautiful ponytailed man in the shop where I'd bought the ring? The girls with the piercings in the other shop? Could it be true that everybody I met was just acting out some part of myself? I didn't think so, not really. It seemed impossible. People were doing their own thing, having their own lives. Weren't they? I expected so. I mean, I was having my own life, wasn't I? It didn't have anything to do with anyone else, right?

But how could I be sure? It did seem awfully arrogant to think that people acted the way they did because of something I believed about myself. If that was true, then the opposite would have to be true as well: that I was doing what I did because of some idea in their minds. I didn't like it. I couldn't quite get my brain around it and wanted to dismiss the whole idea. But what if there was something to it?

If I thought about it, I could see it happening on the playground when I'd pick up Megan. There was this one little boy they all picked on, which seemed so terrible, right? But when I watched carefully, those times when I'd arrived but they hadn't noticed me yet, I could see how he inspired it. His hangdog posture, the way he tried too hard, cried too easily. He'd pick his nose and rub it on his pants and kept on doing it even though the other kids attacked him for it every time. It was like he was asking for it.

I was always very clear with Megan that she shouldn't be mean to this boy, and she was so kind-hearted that she really wasn't, not like some of the kids, but to tell the truth, I didn't exactly want her to be friends with him either. That was probably an extreme example, but what if we really did inspire the treatment we received? What if we simply got more sophisticated the older we got, more sensitive—like a radar system? What if the ideas we had about ourselves did stick on us like those boogers on his pants, and somehow people could feel them and respond? And vice versa? Why were the popular kids so popular? Maybe they were rubbing some kind of attractive energy—whatever the opposite of boogers would be—on their pants.

Ha. The World According to Grace. The all new super-scientific theory of psychic pants booger-detection and attractive, anti-booger popular juice. Sometimes, even I astounded myself with my brilliance, my keen analytic mind, my insight, my... okay, stop already.

It was getting late. I wanted to understand what Bea was asking of me. I was pretty sure it had nothing to do with boogers, psychic or otherwise. She wanted me to have compassion for people who were mean to me and recognize that they were my mirrors, that I was somehow attracting their energy, but also to stop associating with them and look instead for people who "sparked" with me. I thought that was it. I figured I could do that. I might invent bizarre theories to make sense of it all, but I could certainly be a little more careful about who I let into my life. And I could start looking for new friends. That was a pretty good idea. I could use some new friends.

I folded up her letter and looked again at the postmark, at the zebras running on the stamp. Africa. If she could go to Africa, maybe I could go to Paris. I went to bed and dreamed of my wild woman, swirling under a black umbrella, the Eiffel Tower looking sternly on.

CHAPTER TWENTY-EIGHT

Friendly Faces

I had to admit, it made a real difference. As the holidays came and went with their usual intensity and traffic and crowds, instead of fighting against all the madness, I just started looking for people to connect with. And softening myself toward people who didn't seem to want to connect. I just let them go by and stayed out of their way as much as I could. And I did notice that I seemed to upset them as much as the other way around. So many people looked like they were just "getting through" their lives. I sure understood about that. I felt as if I'd lived most of my life just getting through. But I was experimenting with being happy, with loving myself, with being in my body, rather than being miserable, hating myself, and being at war with my body. I was out looking for beauty, looking for pleasure, and yes, looking for friendly faces. I was finding them too. In the most unexpected places.

I went to get the mail one Saturday morning in early February (bills and ads only, nothing from Bea), and next to me was a woman who lived in my building. I'd seen her but never spoken to her. She was what I'd call an "older woman." Older than me, but not "old" like Bea. She seemed friendly, so I smiled at her. Really looked her in the eyes and smiled, not just a passing thing. The usual "How are you this morning?" turned into something entirely different. She began to tell me her story.

It turned out she was moving to Hawaii. She'd sold her condo and used the money to put a down payment on a decrepit avocado plantation on Maui. She and a friend were going to build a house there. In the middle of the avocado trees. She was leaving LA and going off to do this crazy thing with a friend. She was really doing it, getting the heck out of here. She was some kind of Web designer or something like that—I never understood that stuff, so I didn't pay too much attention—but whatever it was, she said she could do it from anywhere, and her friend was an architect and working on a book, and they were really going to up and do it. The condo was sold, and she was packing everything. It was going into a container and then by boat to Hawaii. No kidding. She invited me and the kids to stop in; there were some things she was getting rid of that she thought we might like to have. I assured her we would. The kids would love that.

I walked away from the mailbox in shock. I could barely imagine it, moving your whole life to an avocado plantation. I'd never even heard of one before, though I supposed avocados must come from somewhere. I told her I'd bring the kids up that afternoon. I wanted to hear more.

And that wasn't all. I said hello to a woman pumping gas across from me, and she told me she was just back from Antarctica. She'd been there for two weeks. I wondered what on earth you'd do for two weeks in Antarctica. I wondered what it was like. It must have been summer there. Was it like Alaska, where the sun never set? I didn't have time to ask her if she'd seen penguins. I bet she did. What would call someone to Antarctica? The entire world was opening up to me. I was meeting these kinds of people everywhere. Interesting people doing interesting things. Maybe Paris wasn't so impossible after all.

CHAPTER TWENTY-NINE

The Body

Dear Grace,

Have your been playing in your body? Discovering her beauty, her wisdom? Or have you been busy attending to other pieces of your puzzle, other deep mysteries? No matter, it all is there for you when you choose, when you are able. I return again and again to the body because she is your temple, the home you carry, and she must serve you all your days.

When you have spent many, many years in your temple, as I have, you will come to relish her delights and to respect her wisdom. I wish for you to revel in her now rather than looking back with longing or regret at what you took for granted. These bodies change as we go, and the changes may not be to our liking if we have been stingy with our pleasure, with our love.

When you have been deeply involved in the wonders of your body, the changes are met with curiosity and acceptance rather than resistance and rage. There is no greater gift I could wish for you than to greet your body each morning with the love and attention she deserves, to feed her with the lovely whole foods she craves, to caress her with the most tender touch, and to care for her with the utmost attention to detail. In time, you will find that no one will ever approach your body with anything less than reverence, because that is what your body has come to expect. When you choose to share yourself with a lover, he will reflect your own relationship with your lovely body. The lover's touch mirrors yours and will only ever show you how you love yourself. In the form of another, there is only what you yourself create.

You may think I harp too long on this, too often. Perhaps I do, but I know the body is both the portal and the stumbling block for so many women. The other journeys, even the inward journeys, must be supported, must become realized in the flesh. Your flesh. Your body, your beauty, your love, your power—as woman, these are one and the same. Do not believe, as the Christians would teach, that the body is sin, to be mortified, or as the Capitalists would have you believe, that the body is commerce, for the consumption of others. Do not even believe, as some yogis would teach, that the body must be trained and controlled with postures and poses, dominated. Your body is meant to move, to flow, to breathe, to dance, to be strong and free, and she may need something different in each moment. Ask your body, lovingly, and in each minute be quiet enough to hear the true answer. Some days, she may want strong action. By all means indulge. On some days, she may desire gentle, slow stretches. Give her that. On some days, a long walk, on others a dance class or yoga or the gym. And on some days, she may want to rest.

Your body will tell you if you truly listen. But if you ignore her quiet urgings, your body will have to try harder to get your attention. You must come to know her language. Her signals become clearer as you begin to notice. She will cause pain, stiffness, queasiness, a sense of anxiety when she has been ignored or mistreated. You can go to a doctor—indeed, if she has gone too long unheeded, you may need to—but why not start with the joy? Start with the delight? Notice what your body really loves, not what you would have her love. Start today.

Start by telling your body that from this point forth, you will listen to her. Write it down, now. Apologize to her for the years of mistreatment and for the mistakes you will continue to make. Then ask her to tell you what she wants. What she needs, what she loves. Be a patient and willing listener, a good and trustworthy steward of this most precious chariot. Release your preferences, your habits, your ego desires, and truly listen to your body.

Listen carefully, for your body will not always communicate in ways you understand. Notice the immediate response, the one before thought and training can interfere. Which music, what temperature, what tastes, which colors...your body has an immediate and perfect answer for you. A softening "yes" or a clenching "no." Listen quickly, before it is gone. And begin slowly to trust this wisdom. As you do, it will reveal itself more and more clearly. Follow pleasure. If it leads you in a direction which surprises you, so much the better. If it changes direction, accept its wisdom. And if you override it, notice the consequences. And remember, nothing is finished until you are. Everything can be begun again. Every cell of your body will renew itself. Every thought and feeling you have about yourself, your world, your body, can be changed in a heartbeat.

Allow your body to choose your thoughts. Which ones expand you and which contract? Which opportunities call to you, even through your habitual no, through your reactive fear? Let your body pull you forward; it knows. You know. Be quiet and listen. Follow pleasure; that is your body's yes.

—B

* * *

The letter was postmarked Albuquerque. I guess she made it home from Africa. Amazing, that woman.

CHAPTER THIRTY

Charlotte

I'd been spending a lot of time with my new friend from the mailbox, Charlotte. That was what she called herself. Her real name was something else. She did tell me what, but I forgot. Diane, I think. She changed it. I supposed you could just go and do that, though it had never occurred to me before. Movie stars, sure, they always changed their names. But regular people? Turns out anyone could. She changed it after her divorce. She wanted a fresh start, and never felt her old name was really her. She pronounced it with the accent on the last part: shar-LOT. I liked it, even if it was a little odd. She was a little odd, and that was part of what I liked about her. When the kids and I first visited her condo, I was blown away. Every possible spot held something. Framed photos of her travels, her kids (now grown, probably my age), artwork, collages, and natural things like tree branches, shells, and gourds. There were baskets of rocks and crystals, shelves with wonderful vases, all kinds of things. She had given me an entire tea set, four yellow cups and saucers with gold rims and delicate green flowers painted on them. She'd given the kids a great big box of art supplies: paper, crayons, paints, sparkly glues—enough to mess up our place for weeks.

She had whole walls of books, two big overstuffed chairs, an old wooden table serving as a desk, a candelabra, and tiny bottles everywhere she used as vases for dozens of little sprays of pink jasmine. Her life was everywhere. It was wonderful, so different from my place, even though it had exactly the same floor plan. Her bedroom was like a harem. Her bed was raised up very high, with drawers underneath, and she had enclosed it with royal blue silk curtains. With beads. She had her necklaces hanging from one wall. Another wall was books and art and flowers. Her closet was open; she'd taken off the horrible mirror doors that always fell off the tracks, and she'd hung colorful scarves across the opening. An enormous plant went all the way to the ceiling in one corner. It was amazing. She'd looked so normal when I'd first met her, and yet she slept in this temple.

But she was a bit overwhelmed at the reality of packing it all up. She had piles of boxes in the guest bedroom, and she also had a storage unit to contend with. So I'd been spending a lot of time helping her out. I liked doing it. It gave me something outside myself to focus on. The kids came over and watched her tiny TV or played with the boxes; it was fun for all of us to be somewhere else for a change. They even liked to help pack boxes of books (which I often repacked when they weren't looking). After the first couple of evenings, she handed me an envelope with a hundred-dollar bill in it. At first, I refused, but she insisted.

"What am I supposed to do with this?" I asked.

"Surely there's something you want for yourself." Her eyes twinkled. "Something really special?"

"Well, there's always my honeymoon in Paris," I said, like it was a joke. "It's high time I left the country."

"Paris, then," she said seriously. "Only promise you'll go."

So I took the envelope. I put it in my underwear drawer. I wrote "Paris" on it. Why not? Over the next few weeks, the envelope was joined by others.

Slowly, her wonderful home was stripped of character. All of her precious things were packed away in boxes to go into storage for a few months and then onto a container ship, to arrive once Charlotte and her friend (boyfriend, it turned out) had gotten their new house built. The whole project had been tricky, separating what she would need immediately, what she might need during the construction project, and what would go into long-term storage. The bedroom was last. It was time to pack her clothes and jewelry. I had assumed most of the jewelry I saw hanging and the scarves were for decoration only and would get packed away with the rest of her trinkets. But she stopped me. "I need these to dance," she said. "I have a class tonight, and I'll want them with me when I go."

"What class?" I was holding a heavy scarf, sewn all over with coins that jingled when it moved.

"Belly dance."

I must have looked shocked. Or worse. Horrified might have been more like it. I looked at Charlotte. She was a dumpy, pear-shaped, menopausal white woman. I mean, she was a really cool person, her decor was certainly interesting, and she was going off to build a house with a man in the middle of an avocado plantation in Hawaii and all, but *belly dance?* I tried to compose my face. She laughed.

"The dance of the sacred feminine," she continued. "You should come with me."

CHAPTER THIRTY-ONE

The Dance of the Sacred Feminine

So that's how I found myself in Charlotte's black velvet push-up bra, with her jingling scarf tied over my own turquoise skirt, barefoot in a room full of women of all shapes and sizes. It was a dance studio, so there were mirrors along one wall and a ballet barre in the back. The mirrors were intimidating, and the barre was a memory of torture. When I was ten, my mother had decided ballet might be a good way to make me lose weight and develop the "poise" she was so sure I lacked. I'd spent six months in a pink leotard and tights, trying to get my body to look and act like the bodies of the girls who'd been doing this since they were three. I couldn't even get my hair to stay in a bun; there was no way I could manage jettes and arabesques. The mirror alone made me want to turn and flee, but Charlotte was marching on ahead, introducing me to the teacher.

Aparecida was a black-haired goddess in flowing red and gold skirts, gold-coin bra top, and matching belt with beaded fringe. She was an illustration of sensual womanhood, moving so smoothly across the floor to greet me that she seemed to be floating. Her wavy, waist-length hair framed her as she came. What's that old nursery rhyme about rings on her fingers and bells on her toes? Aparecida tinkled softly as she walked; bangles, anklets, rings, every inch of her was adorned somehow. She even smelled exotic, in a musky, deep sort of way that was beyond cologne. It just seemed to well up from the essence of her. She had caramel skin, fiery dark eyes, and a big, open, slightly gap-toothed smile as she greeted me in her throaty Brazilian accent. Aparecida. I had never felt so white, so stiff, so boring, and so unfeminine in my life. I wanted to hide. I felt exposed in the silly bra and jingly belt, a poor imitation that had just encountered the real thing. I would gladly have hidden in the bathroom for the rest of the evening had I known where it was. But I didn't, and Charlotte was my ride, so I was staying till the end of the class. There was nothing to do but smile back at her and pretend I wasn't feeling like such a fake. Double fake.

I took a place near the back and tried to follow along. Hip circles, to the right and then left, okay, I could do that. Then figure eights and then in reverse, I was still doing okay. Then figure eights parallel to the wall, and I started to lose it. My hips just didn't want to move like that. I watched the teacher; she moved like a snake, moving just her hips up and then out to the side, around and up the other side. She was amazing. Me, not so much. I was anything but snake-like. My hips seemed more like rusty hinges that you'd be afraid would crack off if you forced them.

Five minutes into the class and I was breaking a sweat. More from concentrating so hard, I think, than anything. We went on to undulate our ribs, then our arms. I tried to do some hips-going-up-and-down things, and I really was sweating then. The moves were pretty subtle, and I wanted to get them right. It was hard going. I was glad to be in the back where no one could see me, except in the mirror. I caught a glimpse of Charlotte, watching me as her hips swiveled perfectly in time with the pulsing tribal music. She smiled. I smiled back, missed a downbeat, and got completely confused. Oh well.

Every time I almost got the hang of something, we went on to something more complicated. But I hung in there, because it was starting to feel pretty good. My hips were moving more smoothly; maybe they'd just needed to warm up. After all, I did just sit on my ass all day at work, so I supposed it made sense that I would be a little stiff. The stretching and reaching started to feel good too. I wondered if I would be sore tomorrow. I tried to do what I knew Bea would tell me to do: enjoy my body. To inhabit it. Breathe. Begin again. Bea would probably have loved this class. She'd plant herself right up front, with bells on. She'd probably look great in a velvet bra, eighty years old or not. It wouldn't even matter how she looked; she'd feel great, and that was the difference between us. But I was there, and I was doing a lot of those moves, and to tell you the truth, I didn't feel nearly as awkward as I thought I would.

After we'd been following along with the teacher for about forty minutes, she changed the music and told us just to dance however we wanted. She turned the lights down even further and the music up, and suddenly, everyone was just doing her own thing. That's when I got anxious. I couldn't do it. I didn't know those steps. The music was very strange to me, not like the pop music I could have danced to in a bar if I'd had to. Charlotte seemed to be off in her own world, eyes closed, swaying slowly, arms lifted as though in prayer. The younger girls were dancing together, laughing and kind of shimmying, making their belts jingle. A much older woman was shuffling her feet, making these butterfly movements with her hands and fingers. Others were doing some of the moves we'd been learning (well, I'd been learning; they already knew them and were practicing) but making them flow together, so it looked effortless. I really wanted to go hide in the bathroom. The black-haired goddess was watching me from behind the CD player. I didn't want to be a party pooper, so I started to move my hips around in a circle. But it felt really awkward.

"It's easier when you close your eyes," Charlotte said, passing by me. "Just close your eyes and feel your body. You don't have to do it right."

Well, at least if I closed my eyes, I didn't have to know who might be looking. So I shut them tight and tried to feel my body. What was it Bea was always saying? Where was my body in space? Notice it. What felt good? What hurt? Breathe into each part. Play. Explore. Follow pleasure. I wasn't sure what she'd meant when I read that, but I figured this was as good a place as any to try to find out. I relaxed the death grip of my eyelids and got curious. Find five things to love, remember that? Okay, I tried it. I loved…well, I liked…the music… when I let myself relax and listen deeply. It had an under beat of drums, and a woman's voice singing in some kind of Arabic over the top. It wasn't exactly something I'd want to listen to in the car on the way to work, but it did have this haunting quality.

Okay, what else? I liked the way my body felt, stretched out and loose. All the muscles seemed alive after the earlier work. My shoulders felt strong but tight. I experimented with stretching them out, up, all around. I tried moving them along with the rhythm, and that felt good. I just let the movement go from my shoulders into my rib cage, breathed into the tight, catchy spots, slowly down into my hips, until I was swaying my whole body. Keeping my eyes closed, I surrendered to the movement, explored my body, followed pleasure. It became very sensual. I could feel my breasts in the bra, brushing against my arms. I noticed how I could move my hips in a way that felt really good. I was actually getting a little aroused, which made me nervous. I sneaked a peak, but no one was paying any attention to me at all. I closed them again and went back inside.

Whenever Bea wrote those things about following pleasure, being in my body, whatever, it always made me a little uncomfortable. I always thought you were supposed to save that for the bedroom. That pleasure was something a man should give me, but only while he was also getting pleasure from me. Well, really, my pleasure was second to my making sure he was happy. But Bea had never once mentioned pleasing a man, even though her last letter had mentioned someday having a lover. But it was all about how he would treat me, not how I was supposed to treat him. And this was a belly dance class. Wasn't belly dance like right up there with stripping? It was all about pleasing a man, being sexy, right? I mean, look at the outfits.

I was holding my breath. I had totally stopped moving while I was thinking all this. Completely shut down. So much for following pleasure. I opened my eyes. There weren't any men here. And some of these women, actually most, were heavier and older than I was. Like Charlotte. I watched her face. She had her eyes closed and was twisting around like an eggbeater. But I could tell she was loving it. She was deep inside her body and loving it. Loving herself. No judgments, simply dancing. I could tell just from watching. It was pretty cool, I have to say.

The music changed and faded away. All the women became still. Then slowly, they moved to the mirror wall and sat down, facing the center of the room. I looked at Charlotte. Was the class over? I thought she said it was two hours. There was still a lot of time left. She smiled, a little mischievously, and gestured that I should sit next to her. So I did. I twirled my "wedding ring" nervously as Aparecida walked to the center of the room. She smiled directly at me.

"And now we will have our *witness dance*. It is spring, the time of new beginnings, the shedding of our winter skins. It is time to let go of what you no longer need and welcome in the new. We welcome you, Grace. You do not have to do it, but we invite you to take your turn dancing as we hold the space for you."

Witness dance? I looked at Charlotte. She avoided my gaze, but I could tell she was smiling. Shit. What was this about? I never would have come if I had thought for one second… of course, she must have known that…How dare she!…But it was too late. The music was starting, and one of the women had moved to the center of the floor. She closed her eyes and began to move slowly, almost as if she was in a trance. I watched with my mouth hanging open. This was certainly nothing I'd think of as belly dancing, nothing like what I'd seen in movies or once in a while at an Indian restaurant. The woman seemed to be drawing something up from deep inside herself, almost a prayer. And then she was moving faster as the music progressed, surrendering herself to the rhythm, and somehow, I could almost see her letting things go, things she had been carrying: pain, fear, sadness. She danced these things into the room, and she laid them down, spinning to release them and, as the music faded, turned to welcome the new day. I could hardly breathe when she finished. This regular-looking woman smiled shyly and returned to her seat. One by one, the others took their turns.

I watched with fascination and growing dread. Soon, it would be my turn. My heart was pounding. I thought I might be sick. No way I could just stand up there and dance in front of all these women. I tried to figure out how to get out of there without being seen. Charlotte grabbed my hand and held it tight. She looked at me steadily, breathing slowly and deeply, no trace of mischief in her eyes now. I felt a little better. I watched another woman dance. She was younger, thin, blond, very pretty. But she was stiffer than the others, disconnected somehow. She was doing some "moves," and I could tell she was trying to look good. Aparecida's voice from the shadows softly guided her

"Close your eyes, Amy, move less. In fact, don't move at all until your body has to. Let it come from inside you, and let it all the way out. Smoothen out the hips. Go very slowly... Yes, that's it. Go inside first..." The girl was barely moving now, and yet somehow, she was more compelling than when she had been doing all of that "dancing." She slipped to the floor and lay still for a second. Her face was tight, as if she was trying to hold something back. I was afraid she had hurt herself, but Charlotte held me tight, kept me from offering to help. I noticed the girl was moving her hand against the floor, as if she were pushing something away from her. The movement grew from her hand up through her arm, until she had pushed herself upright and was kneeling in front of us. She was making this sweeping movement against the floor, side to side, and her stomach was working as if she might be ill.

"That's right, Amy, let it come from deep...Let it finally go." The beautifully accented voice was soothing yet determined. Amy's movements became gathering ones; she was at once pushing something away and gathering it toward herself, and finally, she lifted the burden she was holding and, as the music faded, offered it to the sky. Tears were streaming down her face. Mine too.

As she made her way back to the line of watching women, those nearest her supported her and held her as she collapsed against the mirrored wall, stroking her hair and gently wiping her cheeks dry. I was torn between pity and envy—pity, because she must have been going through something terrible in her life, but envy at the freedom to express it, at the support of the other women, the love she was getting. I wiped my own cheeks and wondered if the pity I felt was really for myself, the outsider here and everywhere, locked up tight for so long.

Charlotte danced next. As she stood there gathering herself, waiting for the music, I found myself becoming nervous for her. Critical, in the way I am of myself. When Amy had begun dancing, I'd found myself envying her thin body and her beautiful hair and features. I compared myself to her and felt fat, ugly, invisible, and angry. And I was glad to notice that she was dancing like a puppet; it made the sting a little less. Or it seemed to, yet it also made the fear I felt about dancing so much worse. I wondered how I would be able to dance in front of these strangers, in this outfit, and allow them to see me—fat, ugly, and so clumsy. But after those few words from Aparecida, Amy had come into herself somehow, and as I became involved in her process, my judgment both of her and of myself fell away. It was almost as if I was dancing with her up there, helping her pull these things from deep within herself.

As my friend began her dance, I found myself wanting her to do it "right," to do a good job, whatever that meant in this very odd circumstance. I was on edge, nervous for her, and increasingly aware that soon I would be the only one who hadn't danced. I became more and more critical, dissecting her movements, analyzing them for technique, trying to decipher

her intentions from what I knew of her life, her story. I became so anxious I couldn't take it, so instead I watched the other women watching Charlotte. They didn't seem to be judging her at all. I could almost feel the love and tenderness radiating out from each woman toward my friend. It reminded me of Bea's constant admonitions to be gentle. The tenderness I saw in these women toward Charlotte was like mother to child, sister to sister; it was simple and pure, and so deeply feminine.

I simply couldn't imagine a man looking at another man with such deep love and tenderness. What had Charlotte called this? The dance of the sacred feminine. Maybe there was something to that. I looked back at my friend, her eyes closed; she was undulating slowly, and she did seem to be some ancient goddess, some primeval statue, come to life. I allowed myself to look at her body. To really look at it. It occurred to me that we are never given permission to look deeply and long at women's bodies. It's strange, since our bodies are used to sell everything from toothpaste to truck parts, that we actually aren't allowed to simply look at each other. It's considered rude, or worse. That must be why men go to strip clubs. Just so they can look at women's bodies without getting in trouble. But we women don't have that option. Not really.

Not that you'd find Charlotte dancing in a strip club. Or me, or even Amy, for that matter. We were all just ordinary women, with ordinary bodies; yet it was fascinating to watch her dance. Intoxicating. I allowed my eyes to linger on the curves. There were so many. Where her neck met her shoulder, the swell of her soft breasts, the fullness of her hips emerging from the small of her back, the rounded belly. I saw that exactly as she was, she was beautiful, and it was a gift she was giving, allowing us to really see her. She danced before us, completely present to her own body, her own beauty; nothing hidden away in shame. She was not holding her stomach in or trying to look good in any way. She was, as I said before, a pear-shaped, middle-aged white woman, and I was shocked to discover that she was not only beautiful, but in this moment, she was sexy. Not because she was trying to be. I think that would have perhaps been vaguely embarrassing. Pathetic, even. No, she was sexy because she was enjoying the movements of her body. She was following pleasure, like Bea always said.

Watching her dance was like remembering something from a dream. It was a hint of some vague thing I knew yet didn't quite know. An elusive understanding of something possible, something beautiful, long buried and long forgotten. Or stolen. Those thieves and robbers that Bea was always talking about, they must have stolen this too. Charlotte's dance was a window into sensuality, something earthy, basic. Utterly different from the adolescent prancing "sexiness" I saw everywhere around Los Angeles, not at all the plastic prettiness the POGS liked. This sensuality was not designed to attract or ensnare a man; it was emanating from the very depths of Charlotte's core being. It was her very self showing through; not an act, not a game or a show. I found myself wondering about her lover. Her friend with whom she was moving to Hawaii. Did he see her this way? Was she a goddess to him? Did he have any idea how lucky he was to have someone so free and so in touch with herself? Or did he wish she was younger, thinner? I always assumed the men I'd been with wished I was someone else. Did that come from me or the men? Would they able to recognize something as exquisite as the dance of Charlotte?

Bea said the world was starving for our womanly beauty. Finally, I had a sense of what she meant. This was what had been forgotten, this deep woman-ness, this profound sensuality. Maybe this is what men really wanted when they went to those strip clubs, when they catcalled, and when they whistled and stared. Maybe their souls were hungering as much as their bodies, and they didn't even know it. And if that beauty was there in Charlotte, it must be there in all of us, somehow. Even, maybe, in me.

As the music faded and she came back to her seat, there was a pause, a question in the air. I knew it was the moment of truth. Was I going to get up there and dance? Aparecida's black eyes were watching me, her jeweled fingers ready to begin the music. Everyone seemed to be holding her breath. Well, okay, it was me. I was holding my breath. I'd never been so scared and so eager at the same time. Well, not, at least, for many years. Charlotte just looked at me curiously, tenderly. It was another example of that thing I'd realized on the beach, what Bea always said, that whether I walked this path or not was only up to me. I could choose not to dance, forget the window I'd just peeked into, go back to the world's plastic facsimile of beauty, and never look back. No one would know or care. Or I could begin right in that moment to allow myself to be seen, to allow what was inside to well up to the surface and move on. I could let go of the self-pity, the envy, and the shame and judgment; I could stop hiding and follow pleasure. I could begin in this place, in this moment, with these women. Or not. The choice was mine. Slowly, I stood up and walked to the center of the room. I closed my eyes and began to move with the music.

I knew that Aparecida would encourage me to go deep, to move slowly, to allow the movements to come from inside. I knew Bea would say be willing to begin, to be tender with myself, to explore, to begin with the breath. I started there. I just took a minute to feel my breath, feel my body in space, my feet on the floor. I knew Bea would want me to tell the truth of this moment with my body, just as so many months ago, she had encouraged me to tell the truth on paper. The truth in that moment was that I was terrified. I was afraid of doing badly, of being laughed at, of being shamed. Okay, where did that live in my body? That fear? It was in my stomach, my chest, my heart. I breathed there and moved gently, timidly, tenderly. I remembered the way these women had looked at Charlotte, the way they had held Amy. Tears came to my eyes as I realized that no one in this room would shame me the way I shamed myself. That the only one who kept me outside of myself, ever, was me.

I tried to be tender, but a great rage welled up in me. Shed my winter skin? How about a lifetime of skins? How about an entire life of hiding out, of holding back, of trying to be what everyone else wanted with absolutely nothing saved for me? I found that my fists were clenched in front of my body, that I wanted to pound the ground, the air, myself...Those movements were indeed coming out of my body. I found my feet pounding into the ground, my muscles tight, fists pushing away from me, and then my shoulders convulsing and bringing them back to my heart. I wanted to rip my skin off, to throw away from me everything that felt so tight. The music was louder and faster now. I allowed its pounding rhythm to carry me into a spin, around and around. I was dizzy and had lost track of where the mirror was, where the other women were. I fell to my knees and felt the room spinning wildly. My hands dropped to the floor, and I arched my back, rolling my head around and around as my spine bucked, trying to escape the years of holding, hiding. I felt as if I might retch, might fly apart into a thousand uncontrollable pieces, as if I might spin right out of myself and never come back.

And then I felt it begin to go. To drain out of my body dripping into the floor, pouring out from me at first like a great brown sludge and then more softly, lightly, easily, like raindrops dripping from my fingertips, the ends of my hair, my toes. The music was softer now, and I felt weak, soft, and heavy like a sleeping cat. I gave in to it and slid onto the floor, feeling the cool boards smooth against my skin, feeling my heart pounding and ribs heaving with the breath that became more and more still. I lay there as the music faded, as I became aware of the women watching, of the spinning room slowing to a standstill. I raised my head and smiled tentatively. Charlotte had tears running down her face, and she held out her arms to me. As I made my way to her, I thought I heard Bea's voice in my ears. "It is good. It is the beginning. Welcome home."

CHAPTER THIRTY-TWO

A Gift

It was, finally, the day for Charlotte to go to Hawaii. We had taped up the last box to be shipped, hauled the last load to the trash, and packed her lone suitcase for the flight. Leaving the echoing emptiness of her condo, we sat together on my lanai, sipping cups of sweetened tea until it was time for the cab to take her to the airport. I had offered to drive her, but she'd refused, saying that she preferred to leave the headache of LAX to the professionals. I couldn't argue. That place was a zoo.

We'd never spoken of the dance class. We'd both been quiet on the drive home, but it had been a comfortable, easy silence, not an awkward one. I'd felt a tangible sense of peace, a deep and profound ease in my body and my heart. Words hadn't seemed appropriate then, and in the following days, we'd been on overdrive, preparing for Charlotte's departure. I was sad to lose my new friend so soon, and there were a million things I wanted to ask her. About the amazing sensuality I'd glimpsed in her dance; the power and release I'd felt in mine. I wanted to know everything about what had led her to this place in herself, how she had learned to dance like that, where she got the courage to uproot herself and move into the middle of the Pacific Ocean. I'd seen her in a whole new light, and I wanted to know more about her. I longed to tell her about the letters from Bea, about the mysterious journey I found myself taking. But words wouldn't come in the car, they hadn't come in the midst of these last-minute preparations, and they were failing me still. And soon, she'd be gone.

I was wishing I knew how to bring any or all of this up when she set down her teacup and started rummaging around in her purse.

"I have something for you, Grace," she said, pulling out an envelope. I felt awkward. She had been so adamant that she didn't want a going-away present, that my help had been gift enough, and that she had no room for anything at all where she was going. This was all probably true, since the house wasn't even built yet.

"You shouldn't...I mean...I don't..." I fumbled, and she ignored me, holding out the envelope. I took it cautiously.

"Oh, c'mon, open it up," she said roughly. "It won't bite you." Inside was a handwritten gift certificate for a month's worth of classes with Aparecida, and a small stack of hundred-dollar bills. Five in all.

"You know I can't take the money, Charlotte. You've already paid me for helping you. I can't…"

"You can, and you will. For Paris. You simply must see Paris. Soon. The classes are a gift from Aparecida—a scholarship, if you will. Dance and fly away. Someday, you will give another woman a chance to spread her wings, and you will think of me when you do it. For now, accept this. You've worked hard for it, and you deserve it. Send a postcard. Next year, come visit and show me your pictures."

She took my hand and looked into my eyes. "You must see Paris." I nodded. It was a promise. To her, to myself. I was going to Paris. Somehow. Then we both heard it; the insistent horn of the taxi in the street. It was time. In a whirlwind of tears and hugs and gathering of bags and kisses for the children, my friend was gone.

CHAPTER THIRTY-THREE

A Choice

Dear Grace,

Is there a single moment of your life which is not sacred? Yes? Think again. What is not a sacrament? Washing the dishes? Time stuck in traffic? Waiting in line? Every second is the razor's edge of life and death; each breath occurs only once, and then it is gone, never to return. There is not a single breath of your life that does not deserve to be precious. The choice is yours alone. If you treat your life, your breath, your heartbeats as expendable, predictable, meaningless—then that is the quality your life will have.

Your death is certain, and you are in control of nothing but how you greet this breath. Because once you have chosen, it is gone. And you have the chance to choose again. Happily ever after occurs one breath at a time, one choice at a time. And though each *choice is freely made, a pattern emerges. Each choice becomes a piece of the story you tell of your life and what it is worth.*

Not to choose is a choice. When you neglect to choose, you are squandering a precious opportunity. Do so at your peril. Do not "get through" another day. There is no need. You have everything you need to choose wisely and well. You have come far and gone deep. You have found the keys to your deepest cavern. You have met your fears, met your longings, met your deep, unfettered self—there is nothing at all to prevent you from claiming this moment, no matter what it may seem to contain.

Claim it as holy and endow it with the quality of ritual. It can be a holy ritual to drive an automobile, merging into the ceaseless need of humans to be someplace other than where they are. It can be a divine honor to prepare a meal, a sacrament to enjoy it, and a reverent act to return the kitchen to order after it is consumed. Standing in line is an opportunity to notice the breath, the body in space and time, the beauty of the people around you. Claim your life. Each breath is your playground. Each space you pass through is your home. Own it. Everything is a creative possibility, every page a chance to draw, every step a chance to dance, every breath an opportunity to sing. You are leaving your mark upon this place.

Revel in it.

Or not.

The choice is yours.

And can be—indeed must be—made again and again.

Even the most holy of rituals becomes profane when it slips into habit. The remembering is part of the fabric of the sacred. The exquisite and unpredictable dance of falling into the fiery pit and rising from the ashes, the birth and death cycles of this place are what make up the fullness of experience. Without the fall and the resurrection, there would be no point to any of it. There is no perfected, sacred place to "get to." There is only the endless arriving and leave-taking. The welcome made sweeter by the bitter farewell. The deeper and deeper appreciation for life as it is actually occurring. This breath, this place, this step, this pain, this laugh, this joy, this agony. This is the only breath you will ever have any control over.

Now this one.

Now this.

Choose.

—*B*

* * *

I carried this letter with me everywhere. It seemed to contain the essence of the lesson. Somehow, I felt calmer when I read it again and again. It was like a reminder of something I'd always known, and at the same time, a key to a possible world I'd never known existed. A world in which everything mattered, in which I was powerful, choosing how each moment would unfold rather than being at the mercy of life happening. It made me the queen in a very real way. The moments could be rotten, pain-in-the-ass headaches, or they could be filled with such beauty I almost couldn't stand it, and it didn't matter when I simply remembered that as soon as each moment arrived, it was also gone. I lost my attachment to both the beauty and the hassle. And sometimes—rarely, I admit, but it did happen—I would notice, just for an instant, that the moment was full of both the pain-in-the-ass headache *and* the unbearable beauty. It took my breath away.

CHAPTER THIRTY-FOUR

Begin Again

The days were getting longer, but racing by more quickly than ever. I was dancing every Wednesday. My sister watched the kids for me so I could go. I'd been back to that clothing store on the beach for a few more skirts, some stretchy tops, and a jingly belt of my own. I'd started making friends with a few of the women in class, and my body was becoming less awkward, my movements more fluid. I felt graceful. At least some of the time.

And I was fixing up my bedroom at last. It might never become the exotic temple that Charlotte's had been, but it was coming along. I'd decided I would have nothing in there that I didn't love. I wanted to go to sleep and wake up surrounded by things I thought were beautiful, colors I delighted in. It was a trial-and-error process, but I loved doing it. I was even beginning to keep it tidy. I'd hang my clothes up before I crawled into bed, that sort of thing. Would wonders never cease?

Work was still the gray, boring cubicle hell that it had always been, but I'd been slowly making changes there too. I'd been decorating my cube a bit, claiming it as my mini-temple. I figured if I was going to spend a third of my life there, it might as well be part of that sacred…*whatever*…that Bea wrote about. I brought my lunch most days to avoid the cafeteria food or the fast food from across the street. I took it up on the roof and made a little picnic for myself. It was special time for me. I volunteered for the early lunch shift, before it got too hot up there. I also figured I was less likely to run into any of the smokers who were always sneaking up there now that smoking was illegal in the whole building. I'd never actually seen the smokers, but there was a coffee can full of butts, and I could tell they had been there.

I loved to spread out a beautiful cloth I'd gotten at the beach and set up my space. I could look out over the whole city while I ate and breathed the outside air. It was still Los Angeles, so it wasn't exactly fresh air, but it was better than the recycled air in the building. Sometimes, I'd even find myself stretching, moving, dancing around the roof all by myself. It made the day go faster; that's for sure.

I was just settling in, opening my Tupperware salad bowl one day, when I heard the door open. I froze. Even though I didn't really think I'd get fired for being up there, it still made me nervous to break the rules. My heart was pounding. I told myself it was just one of the smokers, that I should relax, but I stood up anyway. It wasn't like there was anywhere to run, but still. I saw a man come out of the door and pause. The sun was behind him, so I couldn't make him out clearly.

"Hey, Grace, is that you?" It was Joe, the meter reader who'd introduced me to the place so long ago.

"Hey, Joe." What was he doing here? The readers should have been out in the field hours ago. He started to come toward me, and I noticed he was limping badly. "What happened to your leg?" I asked when he got close enough not to have to yell.

"Dog bite. Got infected. They've got me doing paperwork for a week or two until the doctor says I can get back out there." He smiled at me. "So I'm grounded. Thought I'd come up here to get a break from it. I don't know how you can stand being indoors all day. Yuck."

"I can't." I motioned to my little setup. "I come up here and eat, at least. It helps. Wanna sit down?"

"Yeah." He eased himself down next to my scarf, as if he was afraid of messing it up. "Thanks."

I could see the edges of a bandage where his pants rode up at the ankle.

"That looks pretty bad. You okay?"

"Yeah, sure. Just stupid. I was reading a meter over a fence to avoid a yappy little rat dog and didn't even notice the pit with pups in the yard I was standing in. Oops, duh."

"Pit?" I wasn't sure what he meant.

"Sorry. Pit, short for pit bull. Terrier. You know, the kind…"

I knew about them. The ones that were always in the news. I just thought maybe he'd meant a pit, like the kind you fall in. "Yeah, those dogs are really bad, aren't they?" I couldn't imagine having a job where I might get attacked by a dog. I was a little afraid of dogs.

"Nah, they're fine. They're really good dogs mostly. It's the owners who are awful. Well, and the ones protecting their pups." He smiled sheepishly.

"I don't know how you do it. Aren't you scared when you're out there?"

"Only sometimes. Dogs are really pretty easy to read, as long as you know they're there. Like I said, it's the owners you've gotta watch out for." There was a silence. He was looking at me intently. "You look different," he said. "Did you change your hair?" I shook my head. "Well, something's different about you. You look…" He kept looking at me and finally shrugged. "I don't know. But it's good."

I blushed. I knew what he meant. I'd seen it too. That brittleness was gone from my mouth, and my eyes had come out of hiding. I'd changed nothing, and yet everything was different. Inside. It was nice to know he could tell. We both looked away, out at the skyline, at the yellow-brown smog to the northeast, obscuring the mountains.

"I've wanted to thank you," I began, not looking at him, "for showing me this place. It's really helped."

"Yeah. No problem. I wondered what ever happened to you," he said, also not looking at me. "I thought you didn't…" He trailed off.

"I was not in a good place," I said. "I'm sorry." I took a deep breath and turned toward him.

"And now?" His eyes were so blue. I smiled.

"Better," I said. "Much better now."

And so for the next week, while his leg healed, we met every day for lunch on the roof.

We talked about all kinds of things. My kids, his dreams. He was going to night school, studying anatomy, kinesiology, other pre-med stuff. He wanted to be a chiropractor. He had it all mapped out. It made me think about my dreams, or my lack of them. That day on the beach, it had occurred to me just how big the world actually was, just how much was possible. But I'd never stopped to figure out what else I might like to do, let alone how to do it. But here was Joe, working his job and still moving toward his dream. I guess some part of me was just waiting till the kids were grown, then I thought I would consider what I might like to do with my life. What was left of it. Maybe it was possible to begin right away. Why did I have to wait? I could come up with an idea and make baby steps toward it. The only dream I currently had was Paris. And I had that envelope burning a hole in my underwear drawer. Nine hundred dollars. Money from Charlotte.

"Hey, where'd you go?" Joe was looking at me. I must have been lost in thought. I hadn't heard what he'd been saying.

"Oh, nothing," I said. "I'm sorry."

"Am I boring you, Grace?" I looked at him; he didn't seem to be joking. "I do talk a lot about myself."

"No, it's not that." I reached for his hand to reassure him. "I just started thinking. Your plans are so…so real. It made me think of Paris."

"Paris?" He looked bewildered. I guess he had a right to be. It did kind of come out of nowhere.

"Nothing." I laughed. "Long story." I went to pull my hand away, but he wrapped his hand around it and held tight. His fingers traced the shape of my ring, the turquoise, on my left hand. He looked at me.

"I don't want to, um, step on any toes here," he said slowly. "I mean, this doesn't look like a wedding ring, but are you? I mean, I know you were, but I thought…" He trailed off.

I don't know why I hadn't seen it coming. I guess I'd been so caught up in the changes I'd been making in my own life. Something really had shifted in me that day I bought the ring and vowed to love and honor myself. As absurd as it sounded, I really had married myself. I just hadn't been searching for a man like I always had been before. Maybe that's why I'd been so comfortable around Joe, why I hadn't been the awkward old Grace trying to impress him, trying to make myself into someone I thought he'd want me to be.

Even thinking about him like that, for that split second, I could feel that familiar tug. The feelings racing between hope and shame; the wishing I'd worn makeup, fixed my hair, worrying that…For crying out loud, there it all was rushing in through the tiniest crack, still there. And there was Joe, right in front of me, just waiting for me to say something, looking like maybe he was sorry he'd opened his mouth in the first place.

I took a deep breath and tried to shut up all the thoughts. Just answer his question, I told myself. But I found I didn't know how.

"I'm not married to someone," I began slowly.

"But you're seeing someone," he finished for me, taking his hand away, looking truly dejected. "I knew it. You seem so different than last year, so confident and relaxed. I guess I was just hoping…" He looked out at the skyline.

"Joe." I reached for his hand again. "I'm not seeing anyone either. It's not like that. It's something, but it's not what you think. I, well, I…" He was looking at me curiously. What was I supposed to say? I met this crazy old lady and one thing led to another, and then I married myself…And I was still learning so much about beauty and life, and I was afraid of getting off the track and going back to the miserable life I'd always had where I thought I was nothing without a man, and…It was dizzying. And it was true. But did I need to be afraid of this man who had become my friend? Did I need to jump off the deep end and surrender to the POG notion of who I was supposed to be? I liked who I was becoming, and apparently, Joe liked her too. I guess this was part of "begin again." I could try to do it differently.

"It's a long story, and I don't know how it turns out," I said to him, holding his hand. "I'm in a committed relationship…" He looked down as I went on. "…with myself." He looked up at me, a question in his eyes, a tiny smile at the corner of his mouth. "I know it sounds weird, and I'm still learning how it works." Okay, I'd said it, and I hadn't died of embarrassment. Maybe it wasn't so bad. I took a breath and kept going.

"I have promised myself that I will not abandon myself for anyone, that I will always take care of myself first. I don't know how that might work out with seeing you." I smiled at him. "I couldn't do it if it meant cheating on myself." I couldn't believe I was feeling so light, almost playful. At first, the words had come out in a rush; I was nervous, afraid of what he might think, but then I felt the relief of saying the truth, of being willing to say it, of knowing that I was in charge of myself, and that I would be fine, no matter what he thought of me. It was wonderful.

The hint of a smile turned into a full grin. "Well, ma'am," he said, "I would never want to come between the two of you. But what if I could interest you ladies in a threesome?"

I laughed out loud. "I know it sounds silly…" I started. He pulled my hand to his heart and looked deep into my eyes.

"No, Grace, it's not silly at all. It's the best and most important relationship you'll ever have. And I would never want to see you compromise yourself. But I would like to see you. Really." My heart was pounding. "We could take it very slowly. I want to get to know you. The new and improved you."

I looked at him. I wasn't sure how I felt about him, where it might lead. I knew I didn't want to go back to my old habits, and somehow, I knew I probably would mess up at least a few times. But Bea's advice had been clear. Be tender with myself. Know that I was safe. Know that I could begin again, that each breath was a new chance to choose. I had the tools to handle it, even if I made a mistake. Each moment was precious, and this one had just become extremely precious. "Okay," I whispered, "but just so you understand that I have to take care of myself first."

"I wouldn't want it any other way." He looked at me for a long moment. I thought he might try to kiss me. I wasn't sure I wanted him to, but I wasn't entirely sure I didn't. It felt kind of nice, the question.

"So," he finally said, dropping my hand and taking a drink from his water bottle, "you have a ring. Did you go on a honeymoon with yourself?" I scanned his face, trying to tell if he was being sarcastic. His eyes were still smiling. He seemed playful.

"Not yet," I replied seriously. "There hasn't been time. But I'm going to."

"Let me guess." He put the bottle down and stood, offering his hand to help me up. "Paris."

"Of course." I brushed off my skirt. "Where else?"

CHAPTER THIRTY-FIVE

Something Unimaginable

"Ladies and gentlemen, please make sure your seat backs and tray tables are in their upright and locked position. Any carry-on items you may have taken out during the flight must be stowed securely for landing. We are about to begin our final descent into Charles de Gaulle International Airport."

Rain lashed the window of the 747. When I was married and we'd flown together to visit Rick's mother, I'd clutched his hand during the landings, especially rough ones. He complained that I was breaking his fingers, but he always let me do it. I'd never flown without him—until now. The large plane was lurching toward the earth like a child's toy. My fingers were digging holes into the armrests, and I was breathing slowly and deeply to calm my roiling stomach. But I wasn't afraid. I was flying into Paris, and it was raining. I stared intently out the window, though I could see nothing but gray and streaks of water beading off the window. It didn't matter. Three Paris guidebooks and Bea's last letter peeked out from the seat pocket in front of me. They were all the comfort I needed. The lights dimmed. I felt the landing gear lock into position. I braced myself for what promised to be a bumpy touchdown. It was. At last, we were on the ground. And I was in Paris. Me. On my honeymoon—not by myself, but with myself. And it was raining, which might have upset a normal girl on a normal honeymoon, but for me, it was perfect. The first thing I would do was buy an enormous black umbrella.

As the plane bobbled to a stop in front of the gate, I said a silent thank-you to my sister for taking the kids for a whole week. To Charlotte for her generous gift that made it real. To Aparecida, for guiding my dance. To Joe, for being so supportive as I started and stopped and fumbled and began again and again from scratch to love him without abandoning myself. I even said a prayer of thanks to Rick, for leaving me, for I saw that I'd never have been on this plane if he'd stayed. But most of all, I thanked Bea. For everything. For this amazing gift of myself. It was so funny. I'd simply started following this wonderful old woman down the boardwalk, thinking she could give me a few pointers on how to be more like her. Instead, she'd done something unimaginable. She'd introduced me to myself.

A Last Letter

Dear Grace,

Is yours to be a sacred life? The choice is yours to make and make again each time you remember to ask the question. For the real secret is this: there is no rest from becoming. But there is deep peace in knowing who you are all the way through. In knowing there is no blackness inside yourself or anyone that you cannot look upon with tenderness and no light too bright to bear. It is simply more richness to be plowed into the soil that shall bring forth your next lovely blossom. There is nothing to resist.

Do you wonder why you were chosen to receive this initiation? Do you think it was something particular about you? Yes, and also no. You are a divine, particular being, as we all are. You happened to be ready, hungry for something not to be found or purchased outside yourself. All of that is true. But above all else, you are woman, constantly giving birth. Everything issues from you. Life itself and also death, beauty, hope, and love. Choose to birth beauty and love, and notice the world falling to *its knees in wonder and gratitude. Meet the world on these precious terms. For no reason except joy. For no reason except that it is possible to live thus. This is your precious moment. You are Grace in the world. Grace-like-that. Thank you for accepting my invitation. Welcome to the beautiful forest of yourself.*

Love beyond measure,

—B

* * *

End.

Acknowledgments

While this is a fictional story, at least one of the characters is deliciously real. Aparecida, the beautiful Brazilian goddess, taught me the dance of the Sacred Feminine and mentored me for many years, for which I am eternally grateful. One of my best friends, Dina, did indeed move away to Sacramento, and I have been blessed to be able to share this book with her as it developed. Lora, thank you for being my ever-present cheerleader; Tom, thank you for believing in me more than I did. And thank you, of course, to my mother, for telling me I could do anything I wanted—and meaning it. There are so many more people without whom this never could have been written: teachers, friends, lovers…I hope you all know who you are and how much I am indebted to each and every one of you. As Bea says, I am made up of all of you. Thank you all. But above all else, the person most responsible for this book is my daughter, Frances Raye, who inspires me every single day to be a better person, to live a life that gives her permission to live her own life to the fullest. Thank you, Frances, for being.

Made in the
USA
Middletown, DE